The Future for Higher Education

Proceedings of the
19th Annual Conference
of the Society for Research
into Higher Education 1983

Edited by
David Jaques and
John T.E. Richardson

The Society for Research into Higher Education
& NFER-NELSON

Published by SRHE & NFER-NELSON
At the University, Guildford, Surrey GU2 5XH

First published 1985
© The Society for Research into Higher Education, 1985

ISBN 1-85059-000-1
Code 8935 02 1

Direct 18300 (5.0)/9.95 4.85

Typeset and Artwork by FD Graphics, Fleet, Hampshire.

Contents

The Society for Research into Higher Education

The Society exists to encourage research and development in all aspects of higher education: highlighting both the importance of this and the needs of the research community. Its corporate members are universities, polytechnics, institutes of higher education, research institutions and professional and governmental bodies. Its individual members are teachers and researchers, administrators and students. Membership is worldwide, and the Society regards its international work as amongst its most important activities.

The Society discusses and comments on policy, organizes conferences and sponsors research. Under the imprint SRHE & NFER-NELSON it is a specialist publisher of research, with over thirty titles currently in print. It also publishes Studies in Higher Education (SHE) *(twice a year),* Research into Higher Education Abstracts *(three times a year),* Evaluation Newsletter (EN) *(twice a year),* International Newsletter (IN) *(twice a year) and a* Bulletin *(six times a year).*

The Society's committees, groups and local branches are run by members with limited help from a small secretariat and provide a forum for discussion and a platform for ideas. Some of the groups, at present the Teacher Education Study Group and the Staff Development Group, have their own subscriptions and organization, as do some local branches. The Governing Council, elected by members, comments on current issues and discusses policies with leading figures in politics and education. The Society organizes seminars on current research for officials of the DES and other ministries, and is in constant touch with officials of bodies such as the CNAA, NAB, CVCP, CDP, UGC and the British Council. The Society's annual conferences take up central themes, viz. Education for the Professions (1984, with the help and support of DTI, UNESCO and many professional bodies), Continuing Education (1985, organized in collaboration with Goldsmiths' College, the Open University and the University of Surrey, with advice from the DES and the CBI) and Standards (1986). Special studies are being commissioned. Joint conferences are held, viz. Cognitive Processes (1985, with the Cognitive Psychology Section of the British Psychological Society). Members receive free of charge the Society's Abstracts, SHE *(corporate members only), annual conference proceedings,* Bulletin *and* IN, *and may buy SRHE & NFER-NELSON books at discount. They may also obtain* EN *(published jointly with CRITE),* SHE *and certain other journals at discount.*

Further information from the Society for Research into Higher Education, At the University, Guildford GU2 5XH, UK.

SRHE 1983 Conference Organizing Committee

Ronald Barnett	Council for National Academic Awards
John Calvert	Loughborough University of Technology
David Jaques	Hatfield Polytechnic
Haydn Mathias	University of Southampton
John T.E. Richardson (Chairman)	Brunel University
Michael Shattock	University of Warwick
Graham Stodd	West Sussex Institute of Higher Education
David Warren Piper	University of London

The SRHE 1983 Annual Conference Organizing Committee is grateful for the generous financial assistance of the British Council, for grants from the CNAA and from the Longman Group of Companies towards the costs of persons who would otherwise have been unable to attend, and for the interest in the conference taken by the British Government's Department of Education and Science.

Contributors

Christopher Ball, Chairman, National Advisory Body for Local Authority Higher Education

Donald Bligh, Director, Exeter University Teaching Services

Derek Bosworth, Department of Economics, Loughborough University of Technology

Ernest L. Boyer, President, Carnegie Foundation for the Advancement of Teaching

Peter Brooke MP, Parliamentary Under Secretary of State for Higher Education at the Department of Education and Science

Clifford Butler, Vice-Chancellor, Loughborough University of Technology

Stroud Cornock, School of Fine Art, Leicester Polytechnic

John Darling, Department of Education, King's College, Aberdeen

William Fleming, Educational Services Unit, University of Birmingham

Colin Flood Page

Nigel Grant, Department of Education, University of Glasgow

Margaret L. Haughey, Faculty of Education, University of Victoria, British Columbia

David Jaques, Centre for Educational Development, Hatfield Polytechnic

Peter Knight, Deputy Director, Lancashire Polytechnic

Maurice Kogan, Department of Government, Brunel University

John Maddox, Editor, *Nature*

Haydn Mathias, Department of Teaching Media, University of Southampton

Peter J. Murphy, Faculty of Education, University of Victoria, British Columbia

Guy Neave, Maître de Recherche, European Institute of Education and Social Policy

Richard Pearson, Institute of Manpower Studies, University of Sussex

Robert M. Pike, Department of Sociology, Queen's University, Ontario

Paul Ramsden, Educational Development Services, Newcastle-upon-Tyne Polytechnic

John T.E. Richardson, Department of Psychology, Brunel University

Desmond Rutherford, Advisory Service on Teaching Methods, University of Birmingham

Peter Scott, Editor, *The Times Higher Education Supplement*

Graham Stodd, Bishop Otter College, West Sussex Institute of Higher Education

William Taylor, Principal, University of London

David Warren Piper, Head of the Centre for Staff Development in Higher Education, Institute of Education, University of London

Gareth Williams, Director, Institute for Research and Development in Post-Compulsory Education, University of Lancaster

Alan Woodley, Institute of Educational Technology, The Open University

Foreword

In all its history, the Society for Research into Higher Education (SRHE) has never been more active than it is at present. Nor has it had a stronger or more influential membership. SRHE membership crosses the binary line between the university and the local authority sector of higher education, and gathers together under one umbrella all the various groups engaged in the study of higher education – the entrepreneurial professors, the mainstream academic researchers, the senior administrators in national agencies, and the enlightened representatives of special interest. This strength and diversity is reflected not only in the membership of the Society's Governing Council and its working committees, but also in those individuals who were gathered for the Society's 1983 Annual Conference.

The mission of the Society is to promote research and development in higher education. It seeks to achieve this in a number of ways. It provides a forum for research workers through its conferences, through the journal *Studies in Higher Education,* through *Research into Higher Education Abstracts,* and through the *Bulletin,* the *International Newsletter,* and various interest groups. A new interest group on women in higher education was indeed proposed at the 1983 Annual Conference. In addition, the Society helps researchers by talking to funding bodies, espousing the need for research into higher education. It persistently and publicly advocates that public policy concerning higher education should be informed by research. There has never been a greater need for sustained and sophisticated policy on post-secondary education and particularly on higher education. It is a matter of disgrace that the United Kingdom's only chair in the study of higher education is unfilled. To reverse that, and perhaps to establish other chairs, is just one of the causes championed by the Society.

During the last few years, the Society has successfully moved towards the position of being an effective pressure group for the needs of higher education. Not only has the SRHE Leverhulme programme of study brought together researchers, politicians, civil servants, journalists, industrialists and other interested parties, but the Society's Governing Council has itself begun a series of meetings with politicians and administrators at the national level. This movement is both correct and necessary. But we are at base a Society of commentators upon, analysts of, and researchers into higher education. It is our job to probe, to measure, and to describe.

It is also our job to provide analytic models for policy makers and managers. We can, for instance, produce models which distinguish and relate the various purposes of an education system. In working under an administration which sees education as a social service open to all, it is legitimate for a learned society to point out the conflicting functions of the education system – those of producing highly qualified specialists and of passing on aspects of our intellectual culture and heritage from one generation to the next. Equally, under an administration which advocates the discouragement of people from entering non-vocational courses, it is legitimate for a learned society to inquire just how vocational professional courses actually are. (This is one of the topics which will be central to the Society's 1984 Annual Conference on the theme of professional education.)

It is also legitimate to seek to demonstrate that higher education contributes to prosperity not by bread alone. Education makes a direct contribution to the satisfactoriness of life, a contribution which is not mediated by money. Richness of life is not guaranteed by a booming economy alone. The assertion that vocational training is to be equated with educational productiveness is one which needs to be met; and the way for a learned society to meet it is with an intellectual critique putting that assertion into a theoretical context which shows it up as the simplistic populism that it is. Moreover, a learned society can produce evidence undermining the certitude with which such an assertion is typically made.

Over the breadth of its work, it is necessary for the Society to keep a proper balance between the study of policy concerning higher education and the study of the processes of higher education. The Society's 1983 Annual Conference highlighted matters of policy and purpose, but it is important that in the long run these 'sexy' topics should not eclipse the study of the educational process itself. We shall find we have an empty vessel if, for instance, we focus our attention on matters of access to higher education yet neglect to study the nature of the experience to which people are seeking and gaining access. Policy studies taken in isolation will lead us into a cul-de-sac, albeit a long one.

Let us, therefore, wholeheartedly support the establishment of a centre for the study of higher education policy, and let us continue to press for its public financing. But let us equally strive for properly established centres for the study of human cognition, adult learning, and adolescent and adult development. Let us not neglect problems of educational measurement, of institutional evaluation, and of the management of people — the learners and the learned — in our colleges, polytechnics, and universities.

David Warren Piper
Chairman, Society for Research into Higher Education, 1981-1983

Introduction

David Jaques and John T.E. Richardson

Higher education is currently undergoing a period of crisis and change. Individual teachers and institutions, and entire systems of higher education are being evaluated in new ways; they are having to address themselves to changing objectives and priorities. The ivory tower image is being shattered by fiscal policies and by searching questions that challenge many of the basic assumptions of academic life. It cannot be easy for colleagues to give attention to the rethinking demanded by such policies when so much time is taken up by the process of making difficult, and sometimes embarrassing, economies. What then are the prospects for institutions and systems of higher education in such a climate, and what research is needed to facilitate decision-making and policy-making at individual, institutional, and national levels?

The Society for Research into Higher Education (SRHE) has made a distinctive contribution to the discussion of these issues with its recent programme of study into the Future of Higher Education, known informally, from the generous support given it by the Leverhulme Trust, as the Leverhulme programme. The programme has involved a wide cross-section of the academic community, as well as politicians and industrialists, in an appraisal of the higher education system in the United Kingdom. Its central activity was a series of specialist seminars whose findings were published by the Society as a set of ten monographs (see Appendix C). The findings in turn led to a final report, *Excellence in Diversity*, published in May 1983.

It was thus in following up the SRHE Leverhulme programme that the Society chose as the theme for its 1983 Annual Conference, 'The Future of Higher Education'. The conference was held at Loughborough University of Technology on 14-16 December 1983, and attracted representatives of most of the institutions of higher education in the United Kingdom, as well as participants from twelve overseas countries ranging from Sweden and the Netherlands to China and

Papua New Guinea. The conference programme comprised a set of invited papers on key issues related to the Leverhulme conclusions, contributed papers and workshops on matters arising from the Leverhulme programme, and a session in which discussion groups proposed research initiatives to inform future policy-making.[1] This book, *The Future for Higher Education*, includes most of the keynote addresses presented by the guest speakers, together with most of the papers submitted by members of the Society. In addition, the proposed research initiatives are reported in Appendix A.

The book begins with a series of statements of current perspectives, each from a different position both within and outside the United Kingdom. Sir Clifford Butler describes the situation from the point of view of a British vice-chancellor, while Christopher Ball speaks from his position as Chairman of the National Advisory Body for Local Authority Higher Education, with its responsibility in England and Wales for allocating resources to institutions in the public sector. For comparison, Ernest Boyer, Guy Neave, and Nigel Grant describe the contemporary scene in the United States, Western Europe, and the Soviet Union, respectively.

The second section contains papers on the processes for change involved in implementing the recommendations of the SRHE Leverhulme programme. Gareth Williams, programme director, gives his proposals for survival in a harsh climate, while Peter Scott draws out four main themes from the final report. From his position as minister with responsibility for higher education in the Thatcher Government, the Rt. Hon. Peter Brooke MP gives a timely reminder of the financial constraints which will determine future developments. Papers by Haydn Mathias, William Fleming and Desmond Rutherford consider the involvement of academic staff in these developments, and put up some reasons why they might show resistance to some of the formal programmes for professional development designed to help them contribute to change.

The third section includes various accounts of the expectations and perceptions of the consumers and providers of higher education. A major study in this area was completed in 1983, under the direction of Maurice Kogan. Here he reviews its main findings concerning the assumptions of academic institutions and the preferences of employers in selecting graduates from higher education. William Taylor comments on this research, and draws out its main implications. Paul Ramsden summarizes his own research on the experiences of students in the university and public sectors of higher education in the United Kingdom, research which tends very much to contradict the stereotypes expressed by both teachers and employers in Maurice Kogan's survey. Finally, John Darling gives a fictitious though none the less salutary

reminder of the possible fate awaiting the universities that are insufficiently responsive to the changing demands of contemporary society.

The fourth section contains papers which point out the issues to be
faced in terms of changes in the structure of higher education, either in
single institutions or in the entire system. It also addresses the policy
issues raised by current developments. Peter Knight gives an impas-
sioned criticism of the current relationship between the Council for
National Academic Awards, which has responsibility for validating
courses and awarding degrees in the public sector of higher education,
and the National Advisory Body. Graham Stodd describes an imaginary
but sensible experiment in institutional collaboration which bridges the
two sectors of higher education in the United Kingdom. Derek Bosworth
considers the prospective student's evaluation of the various types of
courses now being considered as alternatives to the traditional three-year
Honours degree. Alan Woodley analyses the academic performance of
mature students in higher education, and suggests that institutions have
much to gain and little to lose by recruiting such students in the future.
Finally, Stroud Cornock describes the special problems involved in
courses in the area of art and design, whose strength lies more in the
visual and practical than in the verbal and theoretical genre of
mainstream academic culture.

The fifth and last section of the book considers strategic responses to
current problems, paying particular attention to the implementation of
new educational technology in institutions of higher education. John
Maddox discusses the role of the research enterprise in such institutions
and Donald Bligh contrasts his conclusions with those of other speakers
at the conference. Richard Pearson argues that the use of new
technology will help institutions of higher education to respond more
readily to future manpower needs, while Peter Murphy and Margaret
Haughey point out that such technology can also be brought to bear
upon the problems involved in distance learning, thus substantially
broadening the total constituency of higher education. Nevertheless,
there may be a price to pay, and Robert Pike points out the social,
economic, and political dangers inherent in new educational technology.

As Graham Stodd reminds us in his contribution, 1983 saw the
publication of three other major documents on the future of higher
education in the United Kingdom. The National Advisory Body and the
Council for National Academic Awards both produced consultative
papers on future strategies in the public sector of higher education,
while the chairman of the University Grants Committee sent a list of
questions to each of the vice-chancellors in the United Kingdom (see
Appendix B). The latter 'examination paper' is discussed in detail by
Clifford Butler in his contribution to this volume, though the other two
documents were perhaps temporarily eclipsed by the row over the use by

the National Advisory Body of quality advice from the Council for National Academic Awards, which is recounted by Peter Knight. Given that serious political, organizational, and institutional issues had been raised by all three documents, we offered the Society's 1983 conference as a forum for discussion of these too.

Towards the end of 1983 people had begun to talk of 'the great debate' on the future of higher education. Nevertheless, it has to be acknowledged that the impact of the debate upon the day-to-day life of academics and administrators and upon the community at large was fairly minimal. Those who had followed the Leverhulme programme and who had a special interest in policy issues were of course aware that serious questions were being posed, but it is not at all clear that there had been any raising of consciousness about the state or the future of higher education outside this rather limited circle. Seven weeks after the conference, the following comments were made in an editorial in *The Times Higher Education Supplement:*

> The truth is that no one is eager to engage in such a debate. The very idea is unfamiliar and uncongenial. Disciplinary and professional specialization has decisively shifted the territory of the modern university away from the broader education and intellectual considerations that must be an important ingredient in any debate about its future which tries to be both wide-ranging and fundamental.... Higher education policy itself has become entirely divorced from public culture. Instead it has become a closed world littered with impenetrable acronyms, ruled by managerial values, and inhabited by academic bureaucrats. (3 February 1984, p.32)

Admittedly, the editorial related specifically to the response of the universities to the famous 28 questions posed by the University Grants Committee, but we are not convinced that the picture is any less gloomy in the public sector of higher education.

Perhaps it is true, as a subsequent editorial in the same paper suggested, that there is both a 'tactical disunity' between the various sectors of higher education in the United Kingdom and a 'fundamental disagreement about values and priorities' which makes for easy acceptance of cuts when they are applied to rival or lowly regarded institutions or disciplines (2 March). Yet it is equally probable, as a letter to *The Guardian* suggested (17 February 1984, p.12), that the muted response to current questions and threats is a measure of the amount of time which many academics have been spending in emergency meetings to cope with cuts and to discuss petty economies, the closing down of departments or courses, early retirement schemes, and impractical mergers. If we also take account of the fact that staff/student ratios have considerably worsened since 1981, it is not difficult to see why there has been little open debate of the real issues. But, as Peter Scott argues in this volume, if academics fail to engage fully in the very debates that affect the future of their institutions and, by implication, of their professions, then others will do so, possibly with 'less scruple or sensitivity'.

There is little doubt that the chronic uncertainty resulting from the various cuts and checks has led to some loss of enthusiasm for long-term planning, while it has also caused some institutions to take 'calculated risks and push ahead in the hope that the resources will follow' (*The Times Higher Education Supplement* 9 March 1984, p.32). Neither policy is necessarily a recipe for success as the nature of the 'game' has not yet been revealed to the players, the referee, or the linesmen. The likelihood of demographic changes is another factor to be taken into account. Can they be predicted with sufficient accuracy to determine student demand ten years hence? Or is it possible that higher education could stimulate demand in such a way as to confound demographic predictions, perhaps by the development of shorter courses and recurrent education?

Finally, it is also apparent that the health and survival of higher education in the United Kingdom is not a serious enough issue to arouse political passions at a national level. None of the major political parties has spoken out in opposition to the financial cuts which have been imposed over the last few years, and none identifies higher education as a major issue on its agenda for the future. John Darling's contribution to this volume contains a chilling reminder of what may be in store if this situation persists.

This book of conference proceedings is presented not merely as a record of what occurred at the SRHE 1983 Annual Conference. We hope very much that the papers which it contains will reach a wider audience, and thus help to inspire more interest in, and awareness of, the dilemmas facing higher education, both in the United Kingdom and in other countries. For publication, the order in which the papers were given has been restructured so as to present a coherent sequence of ideas, albeit one which covers issues raised at widely varying levels of analysis. Our colleague, Colin Flood Page, has kindly provided a personal assessment of the main points, especially as they relate to the future of research into higher education. And we would like ourselves to point out some recurring themes in the various contributions to conference and book.

Institutions of higher education have two main tasks: to teach academic disciplines as they are presently constituted; and to revise and develop those disciplines by means of scholarship and research, partly in relation to the changing interests and demands of their social, industrial, and, more latterly, political environment. The question of the relationship between these two functions of teaching and research is perennial in discussions on the nature of higher education, and it is not surprising that it is given prominence by Clifford Butler, Guy Neave,

John Maddox, and Donald Bligh. John Maddox suggests that 'we could think it entirely permissible within the United Kingdom for some of our universities, some of our institutions of higher education, to be places whose chief social contribution is undergraduate teaching, and whose contribution to research is negligible.' He goes on to suggest that certain universities in this country function essentially as liberal arts colleges in this manner, but one might also comment that his suggestion will have come as no surprise at all to those conference participants who were from institutions in the public sector of higher education. Moreover, they would doubtless be aware of the implicit hierarchy that operates throughout higher education, one which accords high esteem to research and scholarship rather than teaching, and to 'pure' rather than to 'applied' study. The emphasis upon teaching in the polytechnics and colleges of higher education is one of the reasons for the low status of these institutions as documented by Maurice Kogan, though Paul Ramsden's research indicates that it is also responsible for a superior quality of learning in those institutions. It is perhaps a measure of the communication gap between higher education and the general public that much misinformation about the nature and relative merits of different elements in the higher education system still exists.

Several contributors consider the possibility that the allocation of funds for research should be selective either between institutions or within institutions. What they perhaps leave implicit is the point that if there is to be selectivity of funding then there must be a serious attempt to evaluate both the teaching function and the research function. In terms of the latter, as Clifford Butler points out, 'the peer review system ... is probably the best instrument available', but John Maddox suggests that peer review, at least as practised by the research councils in the United Kingdom, may actually inhibit creative innovation in science. Indeed, it is not clear that the same instrument would be appropriate to evaluate research across all disciplines. As Stroud Cornock's paper indicates, in some areas it is not even obvious what is supposed to count as 'research'.

Conversely, if certain institutions are to be devoted mainly or solely to teaching, and if funding is to be selective, then there must be many more serious attempts to develop techniques for evaluating teaching. At institutional level, universities in the United Kingdom rely upon the system of external examiners, the subject of a preliminary research report presented at the conference by David Warren Piper. The public sector enjoys a much more sophisticated system of evaluation through the Council for National Academic Awards. This essentially extends the principles of peer review to the evaluation of teaching, and has recently been developed to include representatives of the institutions being evaluated in a system of 'partnership in validation'. However, many observers, including our contributor Peter Knight, consider that the whole edifice created by the Council for National Academic Awards has been endangered by its decision to use evidence collected for the purposes of threshold validation in offering quality judgements to the National Advisory Body.

There would be few who would disagree that a lack of coherence exists in the various policies and pressures being applied to higher education in the United Kingdom today. Perhaps the time has come, as Peter Scott suggests, for a national commission to be established that would overlap both the National Advisory Body and the University Grants Committee, with a remit to produce a 'public and sophisticated plan for all higher education'. It is certainly the case that there has never been a stronger need for informed discussion and debate on the nature and future of higher education. We would stress the word 'informed' as indicating the particular need for scholarship and analysis in the field. Of course, as Peter Knight pointed out in the concluding discussion at the conference, policy decisions have to be made too quickly in some cases and cannot wait for the appropriate research to be completed; and it is arguable anyway whether the academic community takes much notice of research recommendations in respect of its own activities. Nevertheless, at least for political purposes, there is a pressing need for further research and for close collaboration among researchers. The Society for Research into Higher Education provides the only national forum for fulfilling this need, and *The Future for Higher Education* constitutes one attempt to open that forum to the whole community of higher education in the United Kingdom and elsewhere.

Note

1 A comprehensive evaluation of the 1983 Annual Conference was carried out by Anne Castling of the Newcastle-upon-Tyne College of Arts and Technology and by Ed Conduit of the Central School of Speech and Drama. Copies are available from the Administrator, the Society for Research into Higher Education, at a cost of 50p.

Part 1
Current Developments

1 Universities in the United Kingdom

Clifford Butler

I very much welcome the publication of the reports of the SRHE Leverhulme programme of studies (see Appendix C, p.239). They will have a substantial influence on all branches of higher education and on national and local government during the present round of discussions on future policy.

I have been asked to say something about the attitude of the Committee of Vice-Chancellors and Principals (CVCP) to the recommendations of the SRHE Leverhulme reports. Undoubtedly, initial reaction to them tended to be critical; nevertheless I am confident that several will prove to be of value in universities during the preparation of replies to the 'examination paper' which was recently set by the Chairman of the University Grants Committee (UGC)(See Appendix B). Already the CVCP has set up two important study groups:

   i   To review academic standards and in particular to study the operation of the external examiner systems.

   ii To consider how universities might decrease their dependence on the UGC block grant and home student fees.

The SRHE Leverhulme discussions make a good starting point for this important work.

Here I wish to concentrate on school curricula, degree studies, and their relationship with research. The views I express are my own; they have not been endorsed by the CVCP or by Loughborough University of Technology.

The School Curriculum

Following acceptance of the Lockwood Report by the government the Schools Council for the Curriculum and Examinations was established in 1964. Effectively the Council became the government's main advisory body in its subject for England and Wales. I attended the meetings of the new Council from the beginning, as a member nominated by the CVCP. Very early on it became clear that there was a general desire to find ways of broadening the pattern of sixth-form studies, which was predominantly a combination of three academic subjects taken at the Advanced level ('A' level) of the General Certificate of Education.

Geoffrey Templeman (then vice-chancellor of Kent) and I soon realized that the universities as a whole would have to be consulted. In 1965 the CVCP agreed to establish a Standing Conference on University Entrance (SCUE), with Sir Robert Aitken as its first chairman. Before long the Council for National Academic Awards (CNAA) was invited to be represented at SCUE meetings. From the beginning many members of SCUE were sympathetic to the objective of broadening the sixth-form curriculum, but all members were aware of the restraints imposed by the short Honours degree system, which were particularly strong for science-based degree courses of the sort taken by about half the university undergraduates.

Early work in the Schools Council was initiated by the Council's own staff. They tended to favour a pattern of major and minor subjects following the tradition of the old Higher School Certificate, and the European qualifications such as the German *Abitur*. By 1969 the then Headmasters' Association and the Headmasters' Conference were recommending maintaining 'A' levels but introducing new Intermediate levels which were not necessarily a step to 'A' level but could be. The possibility that the 'I' level should be a two-year programme with about half the content of an 'A' level was also envisaged.

The university voice in the Schools Council was not very strong, and after consultations the chairman of the Council and the chairman of SCUE established a joint working party drawn equally from the two parent bodies to try to formulate a broader but nevertheless acceptable sixth-form curriculum. The Q and F scheme was published in 1969 and the N and F five-subject pattern followed in 1973 after the rejection of the Q and F. In designing the N and F pattern the working party was expressly instructed to produce a scheme compatible with the current three-year degree system. I personally believe the 'N' level (content about 60 per cent of an 'A' level) and the 'F' level (content about 75 per cent of an 'A' level) with a flexible arrangement of 3N + 2F or 2N + 3F for the majority of university entrants was a reasonable scheme. However opinion in schools and universities was divided, and despite much further work no real progress towards a widely agreed scheme was made.

In 1979 the new Conservative Government announced their intention of continuing 'A' level. Sadly, I believe this was a wise decision considering the lack of agreement on N and F. Perhaps not surprisingly some educationalists, particularly in independent schools, went back to the concept of 'I' level (content about 50 per cent of an 'A' level). In 1980 the Department of Education and Science published a green paper which sought opinion on the 'I' level. Support was quickly forthcoming from SCUE and the CVCP. The Royal Society also endorsed the recommendations and I believe that support was also forthcoming from many school teachers.

Undoubtedly an A + I pattern of possibly four subjects (2A + 2I) poses difficulties for schools. It may well be difficult to find adequate teaching resources in small sixth forms and it may not be easy to obtain reasonably fair arrangements for admission to degree courses. I am glad to be able to report that the latter issue was considered at a recent SCUE meeting at which many universities maintained their support for the introduction of 'I' levels provided that entrants direct from school or college completed at least two 'A' levels. I believe it would be possible for such a system of As and Is to grow slowly and indeed I express the hope that the government will soon give their approval and that 'I' levels will be introduced within the next few years.

Why are we in England and Wales so keen on maintaining specialized studies in the sixth form? Firstly there is a strong commitment to 'A' level by school teachers and many pupils who wish to concentrate their interests after 'O' levels. There is undoubtedly substantial continuity between school and degree work for at least half of all university students. For science-based university courses a sound basic training in science and mathematics is needed, and 'A' levels are currently found to be adequate. The relatively short university and CNAA degrees which we operate certainly maintain the need for advanced studies in the sixth form.

I cannot accept the view expressed in the SRHE Leverhulme reports that the universities have imposed unwarranted specialization on schools. There is still, I believe, substantial support for 'A' levels in schools and for this reason a radical broadening of the school curriculum is unlikely to be agreed. It certainly would be impossible without the introduction of longer science-based degree programmes, and that seems unlikely in the near future.

Questions 24 and 25 of the UGC examination paper (see Appendix B, p.229) appear under the heading 'The Leverhulme Proposals'. My answer to Question 24 is 'Yes – but only to a limited extent'. Question 25 asks if a radically broadened curriculum could be adopted by some pupils as an alternative to the present 'A' level pattern. Sadly, I don't think alternative systems can co-exist and provide absolutely fair treatment to applicants for places on degree courses.

Degree Courses

Both the Robbins Report and the SRHE Leverhulme studies concluded that we place too much emphasis on single subject Honours degrees. It is easy to paint a picture of the single subject degree as narrow, primarily intended to maintain a particular academic discipline through the career structure of Honours degree, research for a PhD, and teaching appointment. Although this can happen I do not believe it is the reason why the single subject system survives and indeed flourishes. The study in depth of a single subject is demanding and attractive to young people who are basically willing to devote a great deal of time and effort to what they are good at and what they enjoy. Furthermore many subjects are not narrow. My own subject of physics cannot in any conceivable way be described as narrow. An Honours degree in physics is a splendid initial qualification for work in industry and is a valuable stage towards a professional career in applied physics or engineering. Of course we need variety in degree programmes and I would have thought this is just what we have in universities, polytechnics and colleges. A wide variety of vocational courses, which are often interdisciplinary in character, has been introduced in recent years. Joint Honours degrees continue to flourish alongside the traditional single discipline degrees. For Honours they almost all are three-year programmes, although sandwich courses are one year longer and some professional courses (mainly medical) are longer still.

The SRHE Leverhulme recommendations fall into three parts:

i   A broad school curriculum
ii A broadly based two-year pass degree for all
iii Specialist and professional education built on to (ii)

I have already argued that (i) seems unlikely to be implemented in the foreseeable future and since recommendation (ii) depends to a great extent on (i) it too seems unlikely to be adopted. Even if (i) were a realistic possibility I doubt if adequate support for (ii) would be forthcoming from academics. Recommendation (iii) was not worked out in detail in the reports. Adequate specialist and professional education would take two or more years based on the general education envisaged in (i) and (ii). Perhaps there were too few participants in the programme of studies from science and the professions to present this point of view.

The extent to which undergraduate courses might be shortened in overall duration by increasing the number of teaching weeks in the year needs more discussion. Students need adequate time to mature and to undertake vacation work such as industrial training, field work, etc. Indeed the present arrangements are themselves intensive, particularly for vocationally orientated courses, so I do not believe three-year Honours courses can be squeezed down to two years.

There may well be good arguments in favour of some two-year Pass degrees based on a reasonable ('A' + 'I') level entry. Indeed I have two first degrees from Reading − a three-subject general Honours degree taken at the end of two normal years, and, because three years' residence was required for a degree, I had to stay (not unwillingly!) and I took a second degree, a special degree in physics. This arrangement is not unlike Parts I and II of the Cambridge Tripos in natural sciences, but there the Part I does not provide a degree qualification. Certainly I believe that some two-year degrees could be offered and some successful students might take jobs right away and possibly upgrade their degrees by part-time or even full-time studies later in their careers.

I certainly welcome the SRHE Leverhulme view that universities and the CNAA should consider awarding Pass degrees on two-year programmes. Some of these courses might be vocational in character: for example they might provide the first phase of training for technician engineers. Of course my support for the two-year Pass degree is conditional upon a reasonable entry standard being adopted. They would have to co-exist with the existing three-year and longer Honours degrees.

In his contribution to the SRHE 1983 Annual Conference, Mr. Peter Brooke, the Minister for Higher Education, rejected the concept of two-year degrees for all, but lent strong support to two-year diplomas. I am sure the government is right in their first decision but I wonder if they would reconsider the two-year diplomas. If entrants to such courses have reasonable initial 'A' level qualifications then I believe the pass degree after two years should be the goal. If the initial qualifications are poor then an extra 'conversion' year somewhere would be needed. A degree has a status value which the DipHE lacks and might well be popular in its two-year version. I doubt, however, if the two-year diploma will grow significantly, except possibly in a limited number of institutions.

Universities and polytechnics currently demand and obtain high standards from their 18-year-old entrants. There are, however, alternative routes which need to be fostered. There may well be a growth in the number of mature students. Should we contemplate widening access further, particularly to compensate for the demographic fall in the number of degree course aspirants which is expected in the 1990s? Presumably this would mean lowering entry standards somewhat. I can only reply from a personal knowledge of science-based degree courses. For these I do not believe we should contemplate widening access without lengthening the courses. Maybe something akin to the old 'Intermediate' needs to be introduced, possibly in colleges of further education, to provide a special introductory course for those who, for various reasons, do not measure up to the normal degree course requirements.

Question 26 in the UGC examination paper refers to two-year modules. While not rejecting such a scheme totally I do not believe it could easily become universal. Question 27 refers to the degree pattern in Scotland. I feel that the Scots have been fortunate to maintain substantial numbers of three-year Pass degrees and their four-year Honours pattern following the Scottish Higher Certificate, particularly given the growth of the school-based Certificate of Sixth Year Studies.

Credit Transfer

The educational system in Britain is complicated and there is a considerable variety of pathways through the maze. When interviewing candidates for senior appointments I am usually impressed by the numbers of those who have 'come up the hard way'. It can be done, but there is no doubt that more thought needs to be given to creating new and more clearly signposted pathways. I am glad that the new Engineering Council is anxious to provide ladders and bridges between the various streams of engineering education and development.

It would certainly help people who are anxious to develop their careers in unusual ways if information were more readily available on what is possible. For some years now the DES have funded a study project in this area and I have been involved in the steering committee. The hard work is approaching fruition and a pilot information service will be starting up early in 1984 in the South West of England. This new service is called the Educational Counselling and Credit Transfer Information Service (ECCTIS). It will, I hope, go some way towards easing the path of people entering higher education with unusual initial qualifications and provide some help to those who wish to upgrade their qualifications.

Research and Degree Studies

In universities there has long been a view that undergraduate teaching benefits substantially from the research activity of the teachers. The SRHE Leverhulme discussions challenge this view and argue that there is really very little connection. This is a very important issue which needs further research.

My own view stems from a specialist interest in science and engineering. Over a period of thirty years I taught physics at Reading and Manchester Universities and at Imperial College. In my day physics research was very small in scale at Reading, it was large-scale at Manchester and very large-scale at Imperial College. In all three institutions research had a profound effect on the undergraduate teaching, particularly on the experimental work at third-year level and on the elective or optional courses offered. Physics is a broad subject and, in a three-year Honours degree, students can study a wide range of fundamental concepts and be encouraged to reach almost to the frontiers of knowledge in one or two limited or highly specialized areas. The particular research interests of the staff provide essential material for these brief but valuable visits to the frontiers. That this is a good way to proceed is widely agreed in what might be described as orthodox scientific circles.

The sceptics are unlikely to be persuaded by my opinion. I respond, however, by asking them: where is the physics department which attracts very good undergraduates, has nationally recognized first degree standards and graduates in great demand but which has no research at all? I know of no such department. The essential minimum requirement for good teaching is a dedicated staff with sufficient time to keep up-to-date, attend conferences, keep in contact with relevant work in industry and government laboratories, etc. Some postgraduate research experience early in his or her career will serve such a teacher in good stead for some years. You need some research experience to gain real familiarity with some part of the frontiers of physics. With hard work but no actual day-by-day experience one can then, as I know from experience, keep reasonably well informed about what is going on. Second-hand experience, however, is a poor substitute for the real thing. Undoubtedly some degree course teachers have to be content with this kind of approach but I still contend that within a physics department at least some research must be in progress if high quality first degree teaching is to be maintained over many years. I certainly don't contend that every physics department of high repute must have research projects covering the whole range of important topics within physics. This would be quite impossible for the smaller departments which already have to develop their expertise in strictly limited areas.

I believe these considerations probably apply to most science-based disciplines and maybe to many others. Some people claim experience overseas is different. It is sometimes said that the Grandes Écoles in France attract exceptionally able students, though they are not usually noted for research and development work. My personal experience is limited, but for many years from the late 1940s onwards I was closely involved in a research collaboration with physicists at the famous Ecole Polytechnique in Paris. Without doubt it was hard to keep up with their superb research in high-energy physics. In the USA there are a small number of distinguished colleges with good first degree records but no research. I suspect that their teaching staff live on their past research experience. Perhaps the turnover of staff is sufficient to maintain lively teaching. Nevertheless the universities, both private and state institutions, which are able to attract active researchers and have a long tradition of research usually have undergraduate programmes which are very attractive to bright students as well.

So far I have spoken about the influence of research on undergraduate studies. If we turn now to taught Masters programmes then I would argue that in science-based disciplines both research and applications experience is essential for worthwhile postgraduate teaching. The word research is being used here in its widest sense, stretching from basic studies through strategic research to short-term applied studies of day-by-day concern to industry. Although I cannot claim expert knowledge I tend to believe my conclusions apply to a considerable extent in many arts-based disciplines as well.

Separate Funding for Research and Teaching?

The SRHE Leverhulme reports, and several recent ones by the Advisory Board for the Research Councils and the Advisory Council for Applied Research and Development (ABRC and ACARD), recommend separate funding for teaching and research. The initial reactions of the CVCP are strongly against such a move. My view is that more discussion and detailed feasibility studies are needed before a decision can be taken.

In universities we have a system in which teaching and research are almost inextricably interlocked. Academic time is not fixed in extent each week and it is not a straightforward task to classify time under teaching and research headings. Laboratories and equipment are often used for both kinds of activity at different times of the year. Similarly, support staff, secretaries, computer programmers, technicians, etc. often have duties which span teaching and research in different ways in different weeks. Recurrent expenditure for travel, consumables and other miscellaneous items may sometimes but not always be directly attributed either to teaching or to research. Altogether this is a complex scene which would require a considerable additional bureaucracy to classify all the expenditure under teaching and research heads, and even then considerable ambiguities would remain.

If the present university income from home student fees and the UGC block grant were somehow separated into teaching and research components, could either activity exist without the other? I suggest they could not. Perhaps we should begin with the first priority. I envisage that most universities would put teaching as the first priority. If so we should set out to cost the existing teaching activities in a few 'typical' institutions, assuming they were to be free standing on their own. Provisionally I have the opinion that costing undergraduate and postgraduate course teaching reasonably, allowing all the teaching staff adequate time for scholarship, keeping up-to-date, attending conferences, industrial and commercial visits etc., would, in many universities, take up most of the present budgets. This is my personal perception of the situation at Loughborough University of Technology. The UGC block grant and home student fees give us low unit costs relative to many provincial English universities, nevertheless we are able to carry out a considerable volume of applied research. The value of all our current research grants and contracts at 31 July 1983 was £8.5 million. Undoubtedly this research effort could not survive without the infrastructure required for teaching.

This is not an argument for maintaining the status quo. It might well be worth the UGC considering splitting their grant notionally between teaching and research: ie indicating how they felt the money might be spent in broad brush terms but not going as far as requiring separate audited accounts for the two activities. Maybe such a split in the basic grant would prove to be a helpful guide for universities. Another possibility which I believe might be acceptable to many academics would be the earmarking of part of the UGC recurrent and capital equipment grants for some technicians, some consumable supplies and some capital equipment solely for research. Academic time would not be split between teaching and research. Although a restricted division of this kind would produce some extra administrative costs, it would be relatively free from guesswork. I repeat that I do not believe decisions should be taken until the methodology has been worked out and the feasibility of what is proposed properly assessed.

Selective Funding for Research

The advocates of indicated or earmarked funds from the UGC have also proposed both that there should be selectivity between institutions and that the institutions themselves should concentrate their own research funds into successful areas. Now we already have considerable selectivity in the award of basic grants to universities. At least it seems like that here at Loughborough with our low unit costs. Nationally, however, it does appear that the available research funds from the research councils are insufficient to support all projects approved by the peer review system. Reluctantly I believe that this must mean increased selectivity for basic scientific research. The development of science research over my working career has been phenomenal. Thanks to that and to the increasing sophistication of modern experimental techniques, very substantial resources now have to be deployed in many areas of science if the frontiers of knowledge are to be rolled back. It would be sad if in Britain a reasonable number of well-supported research groups could not participate in all aspects of this international effort. I believe we need more discussion on the very scale of our national effort in basic science. The SRHE Leverhulme reports are right to point out that research effort should not necessarily be related linearly to the number of undergraduate and postgraduate course students, which was basically the hope of the post-Robbins period. How best to decide how to concentrate basic scientific effort is another matter. The peer review system, inadequate as it undoubtedly is, is probably the best instrument available.

Basic statistical data such as the number of research students and the amount of external earnings, from research and consultancy, etc., per staff member may be useful. At national and international levels citation analysis may also be helpful when comparing similar disciplines in a large number of institutions. However, new ideas will not necessarily be born in favoured institutions. Ways must be found to start up new research groups in the less favoured institutions in order to promote long-term flexibility.

Turning now to applied research and the wide variety of consultancy work, initial surveys and related activities pertaining to the needs of industry, commerce and public sector activities such as education and the social services, I do not believe that for these activities there needs to be planned selectivity. A wide diversity of agencies, research councils, government departments and the private sector already provide considerable support for applied research and development. Research at Loughborough is predominantly applied in character and we would wish to make an increased contribution in the future. Applied research needs the latest equipment, which is also needed for the teaching programmes. Many problems, of modest extent, crop up regularly that are suitable for student projects. Many arts-based disciplines can also concern themselves with immediate social or educational problems which in like manner can be investigated effectively in a technological university. In broad brush terms these are the reasons why I do not believe that research overall should be severely concentrated in the future.

There remains the difficult issue of selectivity within individual institutions. It is attractive to argue that this approach may be more important than selectivity between institutions. A number of recent reports have urged universities to accept the responsibilities that autonomy brings and make highly selective distributions of resources. This is often done already, in a modest way. The reason why I am sceptical about a marked shift to internal selectivity in research support is the lack of an acceptable methodology for doing so. The criteria used to guide decisions must be widely accepted by the academic community as reasonable and fair. Once again the possibility that valuable new ideas will in practice arise from the less favoured academic areas must be taken into account. This is another area in which more discussion on methodology is urgently needed before decisions are taken.

2 The Role of the National Advisory Body in the United Kingdom

Christopher Ball

The future of higher education sometimes appears to offer little more than a fierce and unequal struggle between government and defenders of higher education for adequate resources, though I personally believe that its future will be more complicated, more interesting and more purposeful than that.

In starting a discussion of the future of higher education I would like to begin by reviewing the work of the National Advisory Body for Local Authority Higher Education in England and Wales (NAB) in its first two years, describing the tasks that we have undertaken to complete in our third and perhaps final year, and the challenges that will face us if we survive after the end of January 1985.

The most significant task which NAB has undertaken in its first two years has been the so-called 'short term plan'. Reviewing the exercise, I am keenly aware of the almost insuperable difficulties that we faced − many of which remain to challenge us or our successors in the future:

1   The inadequacy of the database
2   The over-short time-scale for the exercise
3   The lack of experience and knowledge in conducting such a national planning exercise
4   The need to maintain and strengthen (at every point) the fragile consensus of interests that is represented on NAB's Board and Committee
5   The conflicting imperatives of access and the unit of resource, of student demand and employment needs, of quality and cost-effectiveness (though in the best managed institutions these last two can and should be reconciled)
6   The need to offer a dispersed provision (for the sake especially of the part-time student) and the equal need to protect and strengthen the major institutions
8   The enormous problem posed by the roll-forward of the expanded 1982 intakes (and possibly also of a similar expanded intake in 1983).

This is not a complete list and problems which I have outlined will in many cases persist into the future. There are three lessons however which we in NAB learned from the short-term planning exercise and which we must and will try to apply in future.

Firstly, any future system-wide planning exercise must be conducted over a longer period of time. It is intended that our next major exercise will start in the autumn of 1984 and that we will issue advice to the Secretary of State some eighteen months to two years later, in 1986. Secondly, we recognize that next time we must be in a position to conduct the exercise on the basis of an agreed and approved and clearly understood strategic framework. I hope that this will be achieved by building on the responses to NAB's discussion document on longer-term strategy for the system, and by offering to the Secretary of State, in parallel with the University Grants Committee, strategic advice which will underpin the next planning exercise. Thirdly, we cannot afford in this country to plan again for one half of higher education in ignorance of — or without taking full and proper account of — the other half. The need for integrated planning of higher education in the future is evident. At present we lack a forum where this sort of planning can take place.

Perhaps the most important lesson which can be drawn from our first planning exercise is simply that it can be done. Many people predicted that the task which NAB had set itself was impossible. This was not the case and I take heart from the experience and believe that a firm sense of purpose, resolution and careful thought can, in the long run, be successful.

Looking forward to the tasks to be undertaken during 1984, in conjunction with the development of the longer-term strategic advice to which I have already drawn attention, the Committee and the Board of NAB have determined *inter alia* to:

1   Review the provision of art and design courses (especially higher DATEC courses — of the Design and Art Panel of the Technician Education Council)
2   Review colleges engaged or recently engaged in teacher education (including their diversified provision)
3   Carry forward work on the development of a research policy for local authority higher education
4   Consider the possible establishment of formal NAB visitations to institutions
5   Re-consider the categorization or classification of institutions.

All this work will be undertaken by employing a selective approach, paying particular attention to the dual principles of quality and cost-effectiveness.

What of the longer term? What are the longer-term problems? I would instance the real and inevitable uncertainty about:

1   The resources available for higher education
2   The desirable and appropriate limits to access to higher education
3   The pattern of student demand for higher education courses
4   The needs of industry and the world of employment.

Together with these problems it must be recognized that higher education has long lead times and can only tolerate a relatively slow rate of change without disruption of quality and, significantly, of morale. Planners and government should not forget this point.

However, higher education is in some ways less than true to itself in its attachment to traditional forms and methods, and in its apparent suspicion of innovation and new ideas. Tradition can be a fruitful ground for inspiration and renewal, an anchor, a force for unity and continuity, but it can also be a moribund force. Suspicion and defensiveness will inevitably be counter productive. We are entering an era of considerable change in British higher education and it will surely be better for the nation if the changes are largely created and carried through by the initiative of institutions and teachers rather than by fiat of government or planning bodies. How can a national planning body liberate initiative, encourage responsibilities and develop confidence at the institutional level and within institutions? This is no idle rhetorical question but a central one which we must seek to answer in the next few years.

In considering the next decade it might be fruitful to look at two possible and contrasting models for British higher education – the 'doomsday' and the 'responsive' models. Briefly, the 'doomsday' model assumes that there will be no serious attempt on the part of central and local planners to extend access to higher education by meeting the needs of adult and continuing education or of non-traditional entrants. It assumes the maintenance of a high threshold of entry defined in terms of, traditionally, 'A' level scores and the continuation of specialized three-year degree courses as the norm. It also assumes a 20 per cent reduction in the level of qualified and willing 18-year-old entrants to higher education, together with a reduction in the unit of resource for the whole system in the order of, let us say, a further 10 per cent. Within this model there may be perhaps 100 major institutions (50 university institutions and 50 polytechnic and major colleges) and an even-handed reduction on both sides of the binary line. But will there be an even-handed approach, an even-handed reduction of resources on either side of the binary line? Anything other than even-handedness will surely create an insoluble management problem for the 'disadvantaged' sector, be it the universities or the public sector. The case for integrated planning, to meet the longer-term needs of our society, is surely self-evident.

On the other hand, the so called 'responsive' model assumes (in line with the SRHE Leverhulme reports) a serious and early attempt by all sectors of higher education to explore the new markets within the adult and continuing education field and among the non-traditional entrants to higher education. Hand in hand with this, there must be a willingness to consider the evidence of stagnation in participation in the 1970s, and a willingness to redesign courses and entrance requirements, to review course lengths, to consider cost effectiveness at the points in the system which affect student support and research funding, and to develop a working partnership with government and industry to offer a service to the nation that can be shown to be effective. Access to higher education must no longer be defined in terms of the Robbins principle: it is an inadequate formulation for the future. We must explore the limits of participation which will be useful and profitable to society and rewarding for the individual. I do not believe that we are yet near the margins. This model assumes that if access is as flexible as policy makers and institutions can allow, so too will be the funding for higher education. It is my firm belief that resources usually follow coherent and well-argued purpose. I see this as the major challenge for the system over the next ten years: to create the 'responsive' or the 'doomsday' model. It is as much the choice of we who are working within the higher education system as it is of government.

Higher education is responsible for its own future. I hope that local authority institutions and voluntary colleges will join together with NAB to realize something like the responsive model. If this is to be done, it will be by defining and defending the distinctive contribution of the public sector of higher education and by adhering to the principle of adapting institutions where necessary to achieve 'fitness for purpose'. I expect NAB to continue to emphasize the importance of part-time students (and of adult and continuing education in general) and of non-degree work, and to plan for a system of dispersed access to higher education built around a range of major institutions of proven quality without neglect to the needs of full-time students and of degree-level work. I believe this will be achieved by the use of a selective approach incorporating the twin criteria of quality and economy. I do not believe that the nation will willingly or lightly dismantle and throw away a system of higher education that can and has proved itself to be cost effective, and of quality, which is striving to meet the needs of employers, and is offering opportunities to a wide range of students including the non-traditional groups, the unemployed, the late developers and other mature students, adults requiring professional updating or retraining, and those who live far away from the nearest university.

Disraeli, who believed that 'upon the education of the people of this country the fate of this country depends' also said that 'change is inevitable: in a progressive country change is constant.' British higher education must learn not just to resist change, not just to permit it, but to volunteer and create change; I believe that the system is quite capable of taking the initiative, in order to confront the difficult years ahead, and I hope that it will do so creatively and with purpose.

3 Trends in the United States

Ernest L. Boyer

I have been following with great interest the SRHE Leverhulme seminars and I have read the excellent summary report *Excellence in Diversity* (see Appendix C, p.239). I am greatly impressed by the thoroughness and thoughtfulness of the debate about the future of higher education in Great Britain, and I should like to comment on several themes in the report that relate especially to conditions in the United States. As an introduction to the topics of access, content and academic quality, I should say that in every instance we are moving from a traditional to a non-traditional model, from a more restrictive arrangement to one that is more flexible and more open.

Access

Consider the key issue of access to higher education. The SRHE Leverhulme Report declares that one central aim of the plan is: 'To provide opportunities for all who are able to benefit from some form of higher education and to encourage access from a broader social spectrum than at present' (*Excellence in Diversity* p.4). The report goes on to talk about the low participation of some ethnic minorities and there is a call for 'renewed efforts' to overcome the problem. This goal has, of course, been our aim in the United States as well. Since World War II educational opportunities have expanded for all groups in the USA, but discrepancies remain and they may indeed be getting worse:

- In 1945, 45 per cent of all 17-year-olds in the United States completed secondary education. Today, it is 73 per cent. I should note, however, that the current rate is slightly less than the peak of approximately 76 per cent that was reached in 1970.
- Since 1946, degree-credit enrolment at post-secondary institutions grew by 495 per cent – from 2 million students to more than 12 million in 1982.

There are, however, shifts in the demographic pattern in the United States that will have dramatic impact on enrolment patterns in secondary and higher education. Because of declining birthrates, the number of 18 to 24-year-olds in the United States will drop 23 per cent by 1997. Further, the ethnic and racial composition of young America is changing. While the population as a whole is ageing, the youth population among black and Hispanic Americans remains large and will proportionately increase:

- Today, slightly more than one-quarter of white Americans are under 18 years of age, but nearly one-half of all Hispanics and over one-third of all blacks fall into this youth category.

Of special concern is the fact that black and Hispanic young people are precisely those with whom most of our nation's colleges and schools have been least successful:

- In 1979, 80 per cent of white 19-year-olds in the US were high school graduates.
- However, that same year, 64 per cent of black and 60 per cent of Hispanic 19-year-olds held high school diplomas.

If minority students continue to leave school at the current rate, 150,000 additional young people – the equivalent of eleven entering freshman classes at the giant Ohio State University – will lose their opportunity for further education by 1990. Further, minority students also have a disproportionately high drop-out rate:

- In 1979, 21 per cent of all white students who had completed one year of college the preceding year did not return.
- For blacks the drop-out rate was 24 per cent and for Hispanics, 29 per cent.

In short, the face of young America is changing and will have significant impact on college access and retention in the days ahead – unless we become more successful than we have been in serving children from black and Hispanic families.

A second trend of consequence is the ageing of white Americans. And this too is affecting the demography of higher education:

- In 1972, 9 per cent of all college students were 35 years and older. By 1980, 12 per cent of the college population were in this age group.
- Overall, the median age of college students rose from 20.6 years in 1968, to 21.6 years in 1973, and to 22.4 by 1981.

Further, there has been a shift among the types of institutions students now attend – related, in part, to the changes in age and racial and ethnic composition:

- Between 1946 and 1970 two-year institutions attracted less than 20 per cent of all enrolments.
- Today these institutions have become increasingly popular –

especially among Hispanic students – and today two-year college enrolments have a 38 per cent share of total enrolment.

Another trend of consequence is the shift from full-time to part-time attendance in higher education.

- In 1970 there were 1.2 million part-time undergraduate students in the United States – 20 per cent of undergraduate students.
- By 1975 the part-time population had increased to 26 per cent and by 1982 it was up to 34 per cent.

This trend is expected to continue. Part-time students are projected to reach 4.6 million in number by 1985 – or 44 per cent of total undergraduate enrolment. By 2000 almost 47 per cent of the projected undergraduate population is estimated to attend college part-time.

Here then is the picture. Between now and the beginning of the twenty-first century, American colleges and universities face a transformation. The nation is growing older and an ageing, majority population is returning part-time for lifelong learning. Black and Hispanic America continues to be under-represented. And minorities who do continue formal learning are increasingly choosing a two-year option – with a two-year terminal certificate or associate degree.

Indeed, one of the most remarkable shifts in American higher education is the growth of the two-year college – and the move of these institutions away from the 'traditional' transfer role. The emphasis of the community college increasingly is on *community*, not *college.* Transfer rates of community college students into the universities vary widely from state to state. In 1979, they ranged from 4 per cent in California to 30 per cent in Minnesota. Still, the transfer trend is down. There is, in fact, something called the 'reverse transfer' phenomenon, where students previously attending four-year institutions transfer to two-year colleges:

- In 1979 approximately 15 per cent (3500) of all students in Illinois who transferred that year left four-year universities in Illinois to matriculate at Illinois community colleges.
- Also in 1979, more students transferred from the University of California to California community colleges than left these community colleges to relocate within the University of California system.

Content of the Curriculum

Next I would like to comment on the curriculum as discussed in Section V of the SRHE Leverhulme Report. The report struggles with the tension between general and specific education, suggesting that 'a wide-ranging debate is needed about the content of undergraduate courses in the light of contemporary needs.'

In America we are in the throes of a debate on this very point. One side argues that the traditional college curriculum − with its emphasis on general education − is doomed. Careerism and professional specialization, they say, have pressed further and further into the colleges and schools, and there is no turning back. And the evidence is impressive.

Such fields as English, history, the fine arts, and education − which were at one time strongholds for degree candidates − have been displaced by such fields as chemical and electrical engineering, computer science, business management, or a technical programme in building and mechanical trades. Meanwhile, the proportion of freshmen who reported either fine arts or history as a probable major has declined by 71 and 65 per cent since 1973. During the same period, freshmen who had selected engineering as a major field increased by 84 per cent.

Other majors which have become in vogue are computer sciences, data processing, and technical degree programmes. Since 1978 the proportion of freshmen intending to major in computer science and data processing has increased by 206 and 139 per cent respectively, to nearly one in every five students. Technical degree programmes during the same period have increased in popularity by 39 per cent from 7 per cent of all major fields of study to nearly 10 per cent today.

Fields of study which have lost student interest are education and English. Since 1973 the percentage of all freshmen planning to major in these disciplines has declined by 54 and 40 per cent respectively.

But there is another movement in America − one supportive of Lord Robbins' denunciation of the 'iniquitous habit of ultra specialization at tender ages ...' (Robbins 1963, p.5). Frankly, I liked his staying power when he added, 'As regards specialization in the later stages of schooling, we are completely out of step with the rest of free societies...and run the acute danger of turning out a race of citizens virtually uncomprehending each other as regards the broader topics of civilized talk....Extreme specialization suitable for research scholarship or professional training should be reserved for the graduate schools' (p.6).

While I do not share Lord Robbins's confidence, based on my American experience, that 'specialization in the later stages of schooling' will put Britain 'out of step with the rest of free societies,' I can report that there is a growing 'anti-specialization' movement in the United States − a noticeable yearning for coherence − a move away from early specialization.

At the pre-collegiate level, the National Commission on Excellence in Education has led to a tightening of 'general' requirements for all students. In our own report, called *High School*, we recommend that the secondary school core requirements be increased from one-half to three-quarters of the total time and include more time in languages, mathematics, civics, history and the arts. State after state is stiffening core requirements.

Further, the debate about undergraduate education is more vigorous than at any time since publication in 1945 of the so-called Harvard 'Redbook' and, later, David Bell's *The Reforming of General Education*. In 1981, at the Carnegie Foundation, we wrote a little book entitled *Quest for Common Learning*. We summarized the history of general education in American higher education and outlined a suggested common core. We asserted that general education should concern itself with those shared experiences without which human relationships are diminished, common bonds are weakened, and the quality of life is reduced. It should focus on areas of human interdependence, where members of the human family and of a specific society link with individual needs and interests. In short, general education should concentrate 'on those experiences that knit isolated individuals into a community.'

We sketch in *Quest* six broad themes that are, we believe, the proper concern of general education:

Shared use of symbols
Membership in groups and institutions
Producing and consuming
Relationship with nature
Sense of time
Values and beliefs

Seeing 'the connectedness of things' is, we conclude, the goal of common learning.

The concern about undue specialization has moved to graduate education, too. In December 1983, at a National Colloquium on Graduate Education in Princeton, Jaroslav Pelikan, Sterling Professor of History at Yale, called for cross-disciplinary majors in undergraduate colleges that would link better with the cross-disciplinary programmes of study. In biochemistry and elsewhere in the natural and physical sciences there are examples of such cross-fertilization. Interdisciplinary connections will become more common in graduate and professional education, Pelikan predicts. This being the case, what we need, he says, is a 'plan for a divisional admission to graduate school, together with its counterpart, a divisional major in the college.' This is heady talk in a 'hi-tech' world where generalists seem out of place.

Here then is the picture. While the curriculum in higher education has become more sprawling, more 'market-driven', there is at least a modest counter-movement, a desire to shape a curriculum that focuses on the more traditional themes of liberal education.

Academic Quality and Institutional Integrity

I would now like to comment on what in the SRHE Leverhulme Report is called quality and integrity in higher education. This is perhaps the issue of gravest concern to us in the United States.

In 1981-82, the Carnegie Foundation carried out an extensive examination of the governance of higher education. Our central concern was this: How can colleges and universities that are increasingly in the nation's service sustain their traditions of self-control while being accountable to the various constituencies they serve? We conclude that maintaining the integrity of higher education is absolutely crucial. This means permitting the academy to continue to have − without outside interference − the freedom to determine:
  − Who may teach
  − What may be taught
  − How it shall be taught
  − Who may be admitted to study
These conclusions were in fact reached by Justices Frankfurter and Harlan in a celebrated Supreme Court Case, Sweezy v. New Hampshire, in 1957.

We also conclude that demands for accountability by government agencies threaten to erode the integrity of the campus. There has been what we call a 'cumulative impact' − one regulation added to another, neither one of which alone is too intrusive. But many regulations, added together, have become a serious problem; they have quite literally begun to smother institutions.

It is generally felt among academics that, under the pressure of accountability, state agencies have become too deeply involved, not just in the fiscal affairs of the institution, but in educational matters, too − including the evaluation of academic programmes. As it turns out, in a survey of several hundred colleges and universities, we found that most key functions are still under the control of the institution − although 'outside' agencies are actively involved in setting campus missions and admission standards, and approving new graduate and undergraduate programmes.

What we are searching for, of course, is an appropriate balance between integrity and accountability. And the pressure for such a balance is growing more intense now that many institutions confront cutbacks and retrenchment.

The squeeze is particularly acute at the large public institutions that expanded after World War II:
  − The state of Wisconsin, for example, has frozen salaries at the University of Wisconsin.
  − The University of Michigan is engaged in a $20 million re-location plan.
  − The University of Minnesota has raised tuition 15 per cent this year and has cut back several programmes.
Indeed, one of the most consequential shifts in public higher education in the United States is the shift away from low-cost education.

Largely in response to the budget squeeze, there is a growing trend to raise fees and then to provide scholarships for those who truly need them. Here is how David Berg, the Budget Director at the University of Minnesota, states the case:

> If you adopt a philosophy of high tuition (fees) and high aid you get a much more efficient use of state dollars because you spend your limited financial aid funds on those who need it and not on those who can afford the higher tuition. (Wisconsin Report, 18 October 1983, Vol.2.)

That is pretty obvious, of course, but what Berg does not say is that this current high tuition push is a dramatic move away from a low-cost public policy that has been at the heart of the public institutions in America since they began. It is, of course, not at all clear how this shift will affect access, the point where we begin, but there is evidence that there will not be scholarship money available to serve all legitimate needs.

One further point. We are having a tug of war in the United States over how the quality of the nation's colleges and universities should be assessed. Traditionally, we have had accreditation controlled by the colleges themselves. Colleges go from campus to campus evaluating one another. Many now feel this formal system is not working very well. Only the very weakest institutions are not accredited and there is a fear that it is often a procedure in which academics scratch each others backs. A counter movement is beginning to emerge. Student grades are being published by independent organizations – *The New York Times,* for example – while informal 'college ratings' are reported in the press. Simply stated, quality control is moving from traditional to more non-traditional arrangements.

The Academic Profession and Leadership

One final point: just a word about the matter of the academic profession discussed in Section VIII of the SRHE Leverhulme Report. In America, faculty members increased from 266,000 in 1955 to 873,000 in 1983, up 228 per cent. Impressive, yes. But we have paid a price for rapid growth. Recent surveys indicate that perhaps three-quarters of all current faculty members with a PhD or the equivalent have not published more than one peer-review article in a respected journal or leading magazine in their academic lives. Put another way, only a quarter of today's more than half-million professors can be considered scholars in the historical sense of the word.

Indeed, by the mid-1970s, the extraordinary postwar boom in higher education had begun to fizzle. And many observers in America believe today the professoriate is in disarray – demoralized by retrenchment, feeling insecure and unappreciated, devoid of incentives – inclined to hunker down and pray that this too shall pass.

Dr Burton Clark of the University of California has a massive study now underway – commissioned by the Carnegie Foundation – on the condition of the professoriate in America. We should know much more, in a year or two, about whether the conditions I have just mentioned are true. For now, I must report that my experience suggests that most of these criticisms seem to be justified.

Even among administrators there is a paucity of leadership now. Clark Kerr and David Riesman are currently looking at college presidential leadership. One of their preliminary findings is disquieting. It is that while the need now is for leadership in American society that welcomes new ideas, promotes persons of courage and audacity, what we find on campuses are leaders who are efficient managers, time and motion experts, or therapists and hail-fellows-well-met.

Unfortunately, too many higher education leaders, from presidents on down, feel almost overwhelmed by the demands of a bureaucracy that call for accountability but provide few rewards, and give campus leaders little freedom to make their own decisions. Even trustees feel pressured and confused, their own governance function almost hopelessly constricted within a complicated bureaucratic grid.

The ever-increasing role of outside agencies in campus matters is gradually wearing down internal governance structures. As leadership is diminished, power and initiative flow even more rapidly to bureaucracies outside. Under such circumstances, administration too often means simply responding to an impersonal system, flowing along on a ceaseless tide of forms, reports, and computer printouts. As Harold Enarson, former president of Ohio State University, once put it in a moment of exasperation: 'I could once say decisively, "the buck stops here." Now it never stops.'

This destructive cycle must be ended. What is most required is no less than a rebirth of leadership in higher education. Quite obviously, the steps towards such a renewal of leadership cannot be spelled out in a series of recommendations. Yet some of its characteristics can be suggested. It must be a leadership that will take the initiative in prodding colleges and universities to define their own academic standards and social obligations rather than waiting passively for such standards to be imposed by others. It must be a leadership that can redefine, in contemporary terms, the fragile tradition of academic freedom. It must be leadership that will forcibly remind those within the academy that independence and self-governance can survive only if they are willing to shoulder the burden of making it not merely a matter of pious rhetoric, but a living, working reality. It must, in short, be leadership of vision and creativity sufficient to define and defend the spirit of the academic enterprise.

If such a new spirit of confidence were to emerge in American higher education, we are convinced that many of the current frustrations would dramatically shrink in importance. They would not vanish, but they would cease to be stiflingly oppressive, as the academy once again began to define its own purposes and consider larger questions that relate to access, content, quality and integrity — issues that are of common concern and are the true point for this splendid conference. Whether such a rebirth of leadership is possible may well be the central question facing American higher education in the year ahead.

Reference

Robbins, L. (1963) *Report of the Committee on Higher Education* Cmnd.2154. London : HMSO

4 The University and the State in Western Europe

Guy Neave

There are few arts more hazardous than prediction, and predicting what will be the state of the university in ten to fifteen years time, no less so. Nor is it by any means sure that those timid trends emerging from certain higher education systems in Western Europe will, inevitably, take the same direction in Britain. Though all countries in Western Europe, with the possible exception of Ireland, are facing the prospect of a dramatic drop in the size of the age cohorts entering higher education, and though all are faced with economic difficulties, the way governments respond to this is very different. Much depends on what one might call the ideological constellation which underlines government thinking and the way in which higher education is perceived.

It is, I think, very important to underline this sea change in the intellectual climate. There are several reasons for this. In the first place, the rise in certain countries of Economic Libertarianism or the theories of the Chicago school, has brought about a totally different concept of the role and place of the university in society. Second, the advent of the new utilitarianism represents not just a break up of the consensus that underlay higher education's development from the early sixties. It represents the break up of an international consensus as well. Thus, most Western European policies towards higher education in the sixties and seventies were broadly similar both in their strategic purpose and in the way they emerged. With hindsight, this period may be seen as harnessing higher education to the broad purpose of the welfare state to advance equality of opportunity, to remove the structural and financial obstacles to access to higher education, and, in certain instances, to provide second chance education for those who had missed out in their earlier careers. There are, to be sure, still countries that adhere to this neo-Keynesian consensus: France is one (though for how long is a different matter), Sweden is another, and Greece, with the current reforms of higher education, may constitute a third. At the other extreme of this same dimension stands the United Kingdom where the social model contained in supply side economics is very rapidly being applied in the determination of higher education development. In between these two extremes, one can locate the majority of European countries, their policies having in common the need to reduce expenditure, to place limits on student numbers in certain fields. But generally speaking these cuts are pragmatic rather than being a wider attempt to operate a major shift in social values.

It is, not unnaturally, difficult to foresee just how far those countries such as the Netherlands or the Federal Republic of Germany might not move over to a more hard-nosed approach. This said, how the university will evolve in future depends, to a high degree, on the place that the conflicting ideologies assign to it as a prime instrument of social and economic change − which is the Keynesian thesis − or as an ancillary vehicle acting in support of the broader goal of stimulating private enterprise, individual initiative and the nation's industrial performance. In short, we stand at a very crucial period in the history as well as the development of higher education. The role of higher education is changing from being an instrument for broad range collectivist and interventionist strategies for social change based on the concept of social justice and instead, it appears to be moving, in certain countries at least, towards being a supplementary institution whose actions are based on what may be termed the individualist, competitive ethic.[1]

The future of the university is governed by the coincidence of three crises: the demographic downturn, reduction in public expenditure and the ideological redefinition of its role in the nation. And, if the latter may appear somewhat far fetched, one has only to remember how far expansion twenty years ago was affected by what today is known as the neo-Keynesian consensus.

This said, there are four areas which, if current developments in Europe are the shape of things to come, will be profoundly affected and, perhaps for that reason, profoundly different in the university system of ten to twenty years ahead. These are: the structure of studies and the student clientele; the status of academic staff; the research relationship; and university funding patterns. If one were to resume these four themes under a single heading, what they all point towards is an increasing and more detailed intervention by the state to regulate, fine tune or profile areas which, hitherto, have either been in the hands of academia or subject to joint negotiation between academia and the relevant state administration. In short, the shift in the balance of power between the university, higher education and the state will most firmly be in favour of the latter.

In many ways this shift has already begun. Over the past ten years there has scarcely been any of these four fields that has not been subject to increasing scrutiny and legislative enactment, whether this takes the form of the Hochschulrahmengesetz of 1976 in Western Germany, the Loi d'Orientation of 1968 and its successor currently under debate in France or the 1977 Higher Education Reform Act in Sweden.

Let us take these by turn.

Structure of Studies and Student Clientele

Between 1983 and the end of the decade, most European systems of higher education will have had to cope with the arrival of the demographic hump of the largest age cohort born in the sixties. From the end of the 1980s on to the turn of the century the size of the age groups will diminish radically.[2]

In terms of sheer volume, disregarding such factors as age qualification rates and age participation rates, the decrease from the hump to the bottom of the trough will be in the order of 45 per cent for the Federal Republic of Germany, 39 per cent in the case of Italy and Denmark, and 35 per cent for Austria, Switzerland and the United Kingdom.

If we look at the situation in five countries for which projections about student numbers are available – Austria, the Federal Republic of Germany, Denmark, the Netherlands and the United Kingdom – the peak as far as numbers qualified to enter higher education is reached in 1985 for the Federal Republic, Denmark and the United Kingdom, and in 1990 for Austria and the Netherlands. To some extent, the fall in the overall size of the age cohorts may be offset by an increase in the age qualification rate, details of which are set out in Table 4.1 for those countries having made projections in this area. Against this is the fact that, in a large number of Western European states, the proportion of those qualifying and taking up places in higher education is steadily falling.

The prospect of spare capacity during the last decade of this century has led many observers to suggest that one solution is to diversify the

Table 4.1   Projections in the Age Qualification Rate for Certain Western European Countries: expressed as percentages

	1985	1990	1995	2000
Austria		26.4	27.1	26.9
Finland		40.0	39.6	39.7
Federal Republic of Germany	30.0	33.0	38.0	
Denmark		40.0	40.0	
Netherlands		14.7	14.9	14.9
United Kingdom		16.7	17.9	17.8

Source See Note 2.

student clientele, to place added emphasis upon adult students, to expand short courses and to expand the permanent education function as a makeweight.[3]

This, of course, is not a novel solution. Rather it is a continuation of a trend which was already emerging in the course of the seventies and most visible with the reforms undertaken in Sweden in 1977. Recently, for instance, the Dutch universities have begun to turn their attention to this potential.[4]

However, it has to be said that if diversification is rational from the standpoint of higher education, much depends here on whether governments are prepared to underwrite a latter-day edition of the biblical instruction 'Go ye forth into the highways and byways and compel them to come in that My house may be full.' It is an option entertainable so long as governments do not see the demographic downturn as an opportunity further to reduce higher education's budget in line with falling demand. In short, the decision to increase the number of part-time, adult students is not an inevitable development. It is, in effect, a decision that does not depend on the internal development of the institution of higher education so much as on the role ascribed to higher education by government policy.

Far more significant, from a long-term point of view, is the tendency for governments increasingly to intervene, either to restructure the length of undergraduate courses, to change what may be called the curricular pathways and subject combinations in them, and thus to win a closer oversight of such matters as the subject profile and balance. Restructuring of studies has, broadly speaking, assumed two forms — the first negative, the second positive. The negative form of intervention is familiar to all in higher education, though not necessarily seen from this particular angle. It is the drastic reduction in the number of places in the field of teacher training, the closure of certain institutes specializing in this area in the United Kingdom, the Netherlands, the Federal Republic of Germany and Denmark.[5]

Similar measures are taken in other fields, for example the decision to cut back the number of medical students in France in 1972 — a measure currently under discussion in the Netherlands and also in Denmark.[6,7]

The positive form of intervention is best seen in the Swedish University Reform of 1977, and, more recently, in the proposals contained in the French higher education Guideline Bill. These are remarkably similar to one another. They involve replacing the traditional discipline structure of undergraduate courses with a series of tracks, broadly corresponding to particular sectors of the national labour market. In the case of the Swedes, these were:

— The technical sector
— The administrative, economic and social welfare sector

- The medical and paramedical sector
- The teaching sector
- The cultural and information sector

For some, the importance of these developments lies in the explicit linkage of a curricular nature between the university and the labour market. For others, for whom the university may primarily stand as a scholarly community, they are examples of intolerable interference in the university's fundamental task, that of the free acquisition and transmission of knowledge. A third group may take another view on the matter and see in these examples a redefinition of the university's task towards the 'professionalization' of higher education: in short, a shift in the type of knowledge held necessary for a post-industrial society.

It is of course a historical anachronism to see anything particularly newfangled in the notion of professionalization. Medicine, law and theology, the heart of the medieval university, corresponded to well defined parts of the medieval equivalent of 'high level manpower' in the occupational structure of that time. Far more important is the change this represents in terms of what may be called the vehicular disciplines, through which the eternally important qualities of creativity, originality, capacity to synthesize, to draw relevant conclusions and to maintain a critical frame of mind, are fostered and perpetuated. The basic issue beneath the contemporary debate over 'professionalization' higher education studies is two-fold: on the one hand, to have a greater part assigned to those disciplines held to reflect the culture of industrial society – the sciences of organization, administration, human comportment, the organization, distribution and creation of wealth; and on the other a move beyond those historical vehicular disciplines which, in the past, formed what Montaigne called 'L'honnête homme'. Essentially, as all know, these were the study of the classics and the humanities.

Attempts to redefine and recombine the 'vehicular disciplines' are many. Indeed the French 1968 Guideline law placed particular importance on 'interdisciplinarity'. But it was a discretionary principle and fell on stony ground. No more than four per cent of students followed formally interdisciplinary courses in 1972.[7] The major difference between the rise of this notion in the early seventies and the gathering drive to consolidate it today lies in the fact that governments are less prepared to leave the redefinition in the hands of academia. Intervention by public authorities to 'profile' the disciplines in higher education, to place greater weight on some and less on others is a tendency that is gathering force. There are, of course, various stages in this development, ranging from the specific intervention designed to accelerate the development of those disciplines associated with 'high technology' – biology, computing and those disciplines associated with information technology – measures which can be seen at undergraduate level in

Denmark and France, among others, in informatics and technical subjects, and in the Netherlands in the proposal to boost agronomic and administrative sciences.[8] And, at the other end of the spectrum, there is the wholesale intervention and re-profiling at systems level which may be seen in Sweden and in France and in the current reforms being introduced in the Greek system of higher education.

The Status of Academic Staff

Personally, I believe this trend will be strengthened in the coming years as a result of the continued pressure to contain public expenditure on the one hand and on the other the relatively poor bargaining position higher education will face once the demographic downturn begins to bite. This has equally far ranging implications for academic personnel, their career structure and the relative standing of teaching personnel as compared to those acting as the professional intermediaries between institution and public authorities – namely the administrative estate.

Over the past decade, the academic constituency grew considerably: by around a third in the Federal Republic of Germany, by some 83 per cent in Spain, by some 75 per cent between 1965 and 1975 in the Netherlands, and in France more than doubled between 1966 and 1978 from 20,373 to 41,987.[9] This growth was accompanied by wide-ranging shifts in power inside academia, principally in the diminution in professorial power, the recognition of the right of middle and junior staff levels to take part in decision-making. Irrespective of the particular country involved, academia, in contrast to the situation ten years ago when expansion was, in Europe at least, largely born on the backs of growing numbers of young, part-time auxiliary staff, is now an ageing profession. Promotions are blocked and the difficulties that are likely to result from this, in terms of the research capacity of higher education, are a source of constant worry to most governments.[10]

Whether the academic profession is becoming more precarious in the security afforded to its members is largely a matter of the constitutional, legal and administrative status afforded to its members. In certain countries, such as France, Italy and the Federal Republic of Germany, the status of civil servant is a considerable protection – the equivalent of tenure, though with far more weighty guarantees in constitutional and administrative law than is the case in Britain. This means, in effect, that direct government intervention to accelerate departures can only operate at two particular levels: at the upper level by reducing the age of retirement from 70 to 65, for instance, or at the bottom level by dismissing, or by non-renewal of contract for, part-timers without civil servant status.

Looked at from a general European perspective, the most important factors that will bear down upon the academic profession over the next ten to fifteen years are two: first the effects in terms of advancement and funding that will flow from the trend towards 're-profiling' the disciplinary line-up; second, the shift in the balance of power towards university administration, seen less as the handmaiden to academia than the secular arm of financial accountability for central or local administration.

As regards the first, the consequence of assigning greater priority to some fields of study is the inevitable withdrawal of recognition from others. If pushed to the extreme, it may well be that the combined effects of 're-profiling' with the drive to harness higher education's research capacity to the perceived requirements of national competitiveness will create a highly stratified profession – stratified perhaps between research-oriented high technology fields and policy-oriented areas of the administrative sciences on the one hand and on the other hand the teaching areas revolving primarily around the humanities and some of the more esoteric of the social sciences.[11]

As regards the second, the press for financial accountability plus the growing trend to have outsiders, representatives of national or regional interests, whether political, commercial or industrial, on the various decision-making organs of the university (a development particularly evident in Sweden, Norway, and currently under hot debate in France and Greece) could well increase the power of university administration as the main co-ordinating instance between the institution and its increasingly complex ties with the outside world.[12]

How drastic this shift may be is difficult to determine, for if there is one thing that governments – whether reforming or merely pragmatic – have found to their cost, it is the power of the academic profession to resist change. But, taken together, these two developments suggest that the area over which the collegium will be able to operate in future may well be considerably more restricted than it is now. Whether this will lead to a strengthening of the managerial approach inside academia as an extension of its increasing role outside strictly academic affairs, is again difficult to foresee.

The Research Relationship

Despite the ideological differences that colour the place higher education is assigned in the social fabric, it is clear that all governments, whether left or right, have, over the past few years, paid closer attention to the role of research and the capacity of the university to contribute to the national effort in this area. Some countries, for instance France and Sweden, see university research as a way of priming the industrial pump, as a crucial part in accelerating economic recovery.[13]

Some of the administrative changes that have taken place in order to
'lock' higher education in with government research priorities have been
remarkable. In 1981, shortly after the French Socialists had come to
power, responsibility for the national research strategy was moved from
the Ministry of Education to the then Ministry of Technology and
Research. Similarly, the Social Democrat administration in Sweden took
further measures to strengthen the dialogue between researchers and
government. The deputy premier was placed at the head of a secretariat
for co-ordinating research policy whilst a new forum for discussion
between government and the universities was created, with the prime
minister chairing.

These are perhaps extreme examples of a more general trend towards
harnessing research to national priorities. Greater control over research
priorities springs from several considerations. First, the need to optimize
and at the same time to rationalize investment at a time when public
expenditure is being strictly limited. Second, the need to operate within
the research area a similar strategy to the 're-profiling' done at the level
of undergraduate study. Third, the necessity to make sure that sufficient
able students are attracted into research. And, finally, to counter the
possible decline in research capacity as a result of the ageing of
academia.

Amongst efforts to strengthen the graduate research base one can, of
course, point to the increased powers assigned to the Italian National
Research Council[14] and the marked shift in new posts away from the arts
and social sciences, with a concomitant reinforcement of science
appointments.[15] In West Germany, the use of Heissenberg Fellowships
– awarded for six years to post-doctoral students to continue high level
research – was recently strengthened by increasing the amount of
financial support for fundamental research and affording more 'favour'
financing for students destined for research in fields deemed of national
significance.[16]

These particular examples can be interpreted in a variety of ways.
However, whatever the interpretation, they are pointers to the fact that
'driven' or 'sectoral' research – inquiry specifically undertaken in
response to the demands of outside bodies, whether government
agencies or private enterprise (the customer/contractor principle) –
would appear to be on the increase. If this situation might be satisfactory
insofar as it brings into academia the competitive instinct – that
pygmy-killer dynamism which some feel is the driving force of business
– there are other concomitants that follow the rise of such research.
First, there is the fact that it also entails a change in the balance of power
away from the universities and towards those funding or commissioning
bodies from whence manna and half-roasted quails do flow. Driven or
sectoral research is less the result of granting public funds to free inquiry

than of applying a specifically tailored remit, with the power to determine what shall be investigated and what shall not lying in the hands of research councils, ministries, industry. Second, the incentives to move over to this contract research are considerable – additional posts, growth of consultancies and, for those countries where tenure remains unprotected by constitutional or administrative fiat, a lesser degree of insecurity.

But it also follows from this that the more links are laid down with outside agencies, the greater the possibility of further fragmentation within the academic profession. Such fragmentation might emerge in four strata:

- Those involved in fundamental, long-term research in priority areas backed by government.
- Those involved in short/medium-term contract research backed by the private sector.
- Those involved in research related to teaching on small personal grants.
- Those involved in teaching alone.

Some will point out that this is nothing new. And that the academic profession can always be divided between the research-oriented and the teaching-oriented. But, taken in combination with the rise of sectoral research on the one hand and the demographic decline on the other, the penalties of being in those fields which do not easily lend themselves to activities falling into the first two categories are likely to be rather unenviable. Disparities in terms of the type of resources, internal as well as external, research as well as consultancy, between the different academic fields are likely to grow.

There are many other possibilities which could affect the development of the research relationship over the next fifteen years. One is for increasing institutional stratification and the emergence of a particular category of 'research universities' on the American model, centres of excellence in regular receipt of earmarked research funding. Since the status hierarchy between institutes of higher education in many Western European countries tends to be less pronounced than it is in Britain or the United States – if, indeed it exists at all – this particular development poses rather a more radical change than it may in Britain. The second possibility is for research on a contract basis to move out of university and, increasingly, to be located in specialized institutes half way between academia and government. This pattern of research institute already occupies a considerable place in France[17], whilst the pattern of specialized research agencies closely associated with, but not directly part of, university life has long been a characteristic in Germany.[18]

There are several reasons for thinking this pattern might develop further elsewhere. First, the halt in recruitment to the academic profession has left a large number of highly qualified young people with the relevant skills but often without the opportunity to employ them. Second, the development of a para-academic diaspora may gain considerable impetus from the potential derived from the so called 'new information technologies'. Third, such institutes, seen from the standpoint of prospective commissioning bodies, whether government or private sector, may appear to be more responsive because less engaged in the multifarious other responsibilities of academia.

University Funding Patterns

The more specific point about the way research is funded raises the fourth and final topic which, I feel, will assume greater significance in the current range of issues that will affect the future of the university. If I were to hazard a guess, the university of the 1990s and the year 2000 will depend far more on multi-source funding than it does at present. It is, of course, a matter of record that the expansion of higher education in Western Europe was born on the coffers of central government. And it is equally apparent when one comes to look at recent developments and proposals in the domain of higher education financing which have been rather more gentle in Europe than they have been, for instance, in Britain.

The first question is whether university financing in the future will be directly related to student numbers. In 1977 the French authorities moved away from this criterion, and replaced it by a formula of such complexity that it can only have been devised by a polytechnician and thus understood only by others of that ilk.[19]

The abandonment of this yardstick has certain advantages, particularly if a country's higher education policy is to rise on the crest of the demographic wave rather than dive through it. The second question is whether, in the event of per capita funding being maintained, central government will not step in to fix an annual quota of places available in the *whole of the higher education system*. If this strategy seems somewhat unusual in the British context, there are nevertheless certain countries, amongst which Sweden and Denmark, where this is current practice. In the case of the former, the number of places is set by the Ministry of Education and in the case of the latter, it is set by parliamentary vote along with the higher education budget.

As for the matter of diversifying funding sources, here two trends appear to be developing at present. The first is to diminish the amount of financial support from central government and instead to increase the contribution from local or regional authorities. To be sure, the change in the source is not a shift from the principle of funding from the public purse. But it does mean that in certain areas higher education is more beholden to its immediate geographical region. This innovation was one of the main features of the 1977 reform of the Swedish university, partly to ensure that regional and local interests were possessed of financial teeth, partly too, as a means of giving substance to the policy of regional devolution and participation.[20] In France, a similar consideration emerged in the Freville Report on university finance.[21] Strangely, this issue, first broached during the dying days of the Giscardien regime, was taken up and given a new lease of life by the government of M. Mitterrand. And, though first conceived as a way of giving universities that lean and hungry look that apparently inspires initiative and entrepreneurship, the same proposal is now launched forth as part of a wider exercise to strengthen the regional tier of administration and to reduce that of Paris.

The second trend in funding patterns is to place greater reliance on private industry, either in the form of research contracts or by setting up short courses for retraining personnel at mid-career. The rise of contract research has been discussed in the previous section. And, though it has always been present, the development of 'science parks', whether in the Netherlands, in Belgium around Louvain la Neuve or in France at Grenoble, shows that the linkage between university and industry is becoming increasingly institutionalized and of growing significance. Contract training courses are seen as a major part of the current higher education reform in France, both as a means of diversifying funding, and as helping mid-level and senior management acquire those skills required by the development of high level technology.

Conclusion

If current trends in the Western European university *are* the shape of things to come, then the university of the future will be under even greater pressure for financial, political and performance accountability. Not only will those instances to which it will have to give account be more complex and greater in number. They will also be largely external to the higher education system. This means, essentially, that whatever the criteria used to denote, define and measure 'efficiency', they will tend to an increasing extent not to be those of the university itself. How far academia will be capable of resolving at best, or reconciling at worst, the potential conflict between internal academic values and those imposed from outside is largely a matter of guess work. Academia's power of accommodation to change from outside is, of course, considerable. Even so, it has been the burden of this paper to suggest that those areas over which academia has power, appear themselves to be shrinking. External control over student numbers, growing intervention, either through the differential allocation of posts and resources between those fields of academic activity deemed vital to the national interest, or through the outright reduction of others, all point to the very real possibility that those matters over which academia is seen as having legitimate predominance are becoming increasingly limited to the act of teaching, student evaluation and the appointment or advancement of colleagues within confines strictly determined by the state.

Over the past few years, the number of external bodies representing public interests, whether at local or regional level, has increased in number. And their voice inside academia has increased as well. In the area of the public funding of research, commissioning agencies, whether research councils or ministries, appear to be less the funding arms of academia than instruments of government policy. Indeed, the rise of the subfield of science policy and research policy within economics in some countries, higher education studies in others,[22] may be seen as a reflection of this alteration and a recognition of its importance for academia.

Some may care to see in these possibilities a very real threat to academic autonomy. Others may argue that by transforming higher education into the symbol of a competitive society, the system of higher education itself is becoming more closely linked to the political ideologies of the hour. And more subject to them. It may well be so. But even assuming that autonomy is conceived as the same thing from one country to another, which often it is not, it is no less obvious that the reality of such autonomy is that it is a changing concept, dependent on whether the state or representatives of the public are prepared to uphold a self-denying ordinance of non-intervention in those areas they recognize as essential to *Lehr- und Lernfreiheit.*[23]

Just how this will be agreed upon depends to a high degree on the policies governments will adopt to meet the forthcoming fall in student numbers, to meet the shift of public expenditure away from the dwindling numbers of young people in the population and towards the growing numbers of the old. It also depends on which ideological construct is placed on the role of higher education in society. The future of the university, no less than the nature and the extent of the autonomy accorded to academia, hang upon these three factors. No soothsayer worth his salt would dare to make any utterance as to their outcome!

Acknowledgement

This paper was prepared using material gathered by EURYDICE, the Education Information Network of the European Communities. I acknowledge here the help of all EURYDICE Central Unit staff.

Notes

1   Neave, Guy (1982a) On the edge of the abyss *European Journal of Education* 17 (2) 124 - 126.
2   *Child and Family: Demographic Developments in the OECD Countries* (1979) Paris: Organisation for Economic Cooperation and Development. Neave, Guy (1983a) Demographic trends and higher education: or, is fewer really better *Memorandum to the Standing Conference of Presidents, Rectors and Vice-Chancellors of the European Universities* Bruxelles, November 1983 (typewritten) Table II.
3   See Cerych, Ladislav (1983) in *Response to Adversity* Guildford: Society for Research into Higher Education.
4   Open universiteit mengt zich in slag om studenten *NRC Handelsblad* 3 March 1983.
5   *The Impact of Demographic Change upon the Education Systems of the European Community* (1981) Bruxelles: EURYDICE.
   Measures taken by Member states in response to the demographic crisis *Note to the Members of the Education Committee, Document V/1713/83-EN (123/en)* (1983) Bruxelles: Commission of the European Communities.
   Berlingske Tidende 17 - 18 February 1983.
6   Neave, Guy (1978) Foreign student mobility in France. In Burn, Barbara B. (Editor) *Higher Education Reform: implications for foreign students* New York: International Institute for Educational Exchange.
7   Stop bepleit op toeloop geneeskunde *NRC Handelsblad* 19 March 1983.
   Berlingske Tidende op. cit.
8   *Faits Nouveaux 2/83* Strasbourg: Council of Europe.
9   Neave, Guy (1983b) The changing face of the academic profession in Western Europe *European Journal of Education* 18 (3) (forthcoming).
10 Skoie, Hans, (1976) *Ageing University Staff* Oslo: Institute for Studies in Research and Higher Education.
   Teichler, Ulrich (1982) Recent developments in the Federal Republic of Germany *European Journal of Education* 17 (2) 167
   SOU 1981:29 *Forskningens Framtid* Stockholm: The Report of the Andren Committee on the Future of Research
   Neave, Guy (1982b) Mobility is the key to France's future *Times Higher Education Supplement* 29 January 1982.
11 Role and function of universities *Discussion Paper (83) 8* (1983) Paris: Organisation for Economic Cooperation and Development.
12 *Projet de Loi: Loi d'orientation de l'enseignement superieur* (1983) Paris: Ministere de l'Education Nationale (xerox).
   For Greece see *On the Structure and Function of Higher Education*

Institutes. Law No 1268/82, 1982 Athens: Ministry of Education and Religious Affairs (xerox) (English translation).

Neave, Guy (1983c) The regional dimension: some considerations from a European perspective. In Shattock, Michael (Editor) *The Structure and Governance of Higher Education* Guildford: Society for Research into Higher Education.

13   Interview with Dr Hans Landberg, Director General, Swedish Council for the Coordination of Research, Stockholm, 2 November 1982.

Neave (1982b) *op. cit.*

14   *Times Higher Education Supplement* 21 January 1983.

15   *Corriere della Serra* 9 July 1983.

16   Federal Republic of Germany: educational policy of the new government *Council of Europe Newsletter 5/82* (1982) p.19.

Teichler (1982) *op. cit.*

17   Machin, Howard (1982) *The CNRS and Social Science Research in France* London: London School of Economics (xerox) p.13.

18   ben David, Joseph (1979) *Centres of Learning: Britain, France, Germany and the USA* New York.

19   Goldberg, Lucien (1979) University financing in France. In Lyman, J. Glenny (Editor) *Funding Higher Education: A Six Nation Analysis* New York: Praeger.

20   Neave (1983c) *op. cit.*

21   *La Réforme du Financement des Universités (1981) Paris: La Documentation Française.*

22   Neave, Guy and Jenkinson, Sally (1983) *Research on Higher Education in Sweden. An Analysis and an Evaluation* Stockholm: Almqvist Wiksell International.

23   Neave, Guy (1982c) La notion de limites comme modèle des liens existant entre l'université et l'Etat *CRE Bulletin* 58.

5 Higher Education in the Soviet Union

Nigel Grant

With higher education in the USA having being examined earlier in this volume (chapter 3), the easiest and most obvious way of dealing with the USSR would be to point up the differences, which of course are real and substantial. It might be useful, however, to remind ourselves of some of the similarities as well, for some of these are just as important. Both countries share a social perspective, an almost religious conviction that, whatever the benefits to the economy and manpower planning, education is in a more general sense a good thing for the individual and society. In both countries economic considerations have led to increasing emphasis on the *instrumental* benefits of education, but underlying this are assumptions about its *intrinsic* value as well, usually in the form of personal and social development in the USA, general culture and socio-political values in the USSR. Manpower planning and the training of skilled specialists for the economy may loom large in both systems, but in neither is this the whole story.

Again, both are mass systems, though to differing degrees and in different ways. At the level of higher education, this is more obvious in the USA, with nearly half of the age cohort going on to university or college of some kind. The USSR has never been rich enough to operate on this scale; all the same, with over 5 million students in higher education and 4½ million in secondary specialized schools (which at least overlap the higher sector, as we shall see later), it is still sizeable. More to the point, it is still expanding.

The Soviet system also shares with the American a substantial ethnic question (as does our own, though it seems not to realize this fully yet), especially concerning the inequality of participation by some of the ethnic groups in the country. The Russians (now only 52 per cent of the population, and still falling proportionally) do better than most in this regard, but they are not at the top of the league table; Jews (who count as a Soviet nationality), Georgians, and sometimes Armenians are ahead.

41

By contrast, most of the Central Asian nationalities, and some others like the Moldavians on the Romanian border, lag behind proportionally in access to higher education. This is a potentially explosive matter; the Central Asian peoples have a much higher birthrate than the Russians and other Europeans, and may also be open to Muslim revivalist influence from the south. Apart from any other considerations, the persistence of this inequality could therefore be politically dangerous. The authorities are clearly aware of this, and appear to have been using both positive and negative discrimination in an attempt to redress the balance. The cut-back of Jewish admissions to higher education has attracted much attention in the West, but it is not unique; admissions of Georgians (another formerly favoured group) have also been reduced (though less drastically) in absolute numbers, and others have dwindled proportionally. At the same time, the numbers from the disadvantaged groups have improved, though less markedly. The difficulty here is that negative discrimination, administratively at least, is relatively straightforward; but simply raising the quotas for Kirgiz, Tadzhiks or Bashkirs solves little. If they are to be able to take advantage of it, they need a general improvement in their basic schooling as well, and this is inevitably a longer-term process. It is being done, and the gap is closing; but while the effect of cut-backs is immediate, compensatory policies take longer to show results.[1]

There are, naturally, many differences of structure, organization and content, and particularly of administration and control, to which we shall come presently. Two of these, however, are fundamental in terms of overall strategy. Firstly, the Soviet higher educational system is centrally planned. All institutions are state controlled, come under the Ministry of Higher Education of the USSR and the appropriate Republican Ministries, and have their enrolments and specialisms calculated to meet the targets of Gosplan, the state economic planning agency. In practice, this approach is riddled with problems. Drop-out, for example, can be as high as 20 per cent, which can play havoc with manpower projections. The problems of quality control are almost exactly the opposite of those in the USA. As we shall see presently, curricula and examinations are prescribed in some detail at ministerial level, often to an extent that proves unrealistic. The controlling mechanisms are not only detailed but, given the size of the country and the cumbersome nature of Soviet administration, clumsy and often unreliable.

Secondly, the Soviet higher educational system is still growing (although at a slower rate than hitherto), at a time when numbers in the general schools have been falling, a reflection of the lower birthrate. But the numbers of aspiring entrants have been growing even faster, largely as a result of the successful implementation of universal secondary schooling, and the failure (so far) to divert school-leavers in other directions in sufficient numbers. The chances of admission to higher education are currently about one in five, which puts great pressure on admission procedures. All selection devices, of course, have their margins of error; but the greater the gap between the numbers of applicants and places, the greater are the opportunities for mistakes. In the Soviet Union, one of the results of this is the awkwardly high drop-out rate; another is the large number of disgruntled young people who have failed to get in.[2]

One long-standing device to ease the pressure has been the use of part-time courses, either through evening classes or by correspondence (with paid leave for tutorials and consultations.) These are also both cheaper to run and less of a drain on the labour force – shortage of skilled manpower, rather than of jobs, is still one of the many problems of the Soviet economy. This was particularly obvious in the 1960s, when part-time students were in a majority. In 1965-66, for example, only 41 per cent of the students were full-time, while 15 per cent were taking evening classes and 44 per cent were studying by correspondence. This method of study was not only approved as a way of taking pressure off places, however, nor only to alleviate manpower problems; it was also an attempt to keep as many students as possible in touch with the realities of working life, for socio-political as well as economic reasons. On similar grounds, preference was given to applicants who had done a *stazh* or two-year minimum period of practical work. In Khrushchev's time, these accounted for about 80 per cent of all admissions.[3]

The problem was that *stazhniki* and part-timers alike were particularly vulnerable to drop-out. In 1965-66, for example, full-time students accounted for only 44 per cent of all entrants; but five years later (the actual length of most courses)[4], for 53 per cent of the graduates. Correspondence students seemed to be particularly vulnerable – 41 per cent of entrants in 1965, but only 34 per cent of graduates five years later. This led to various measures, including attempts to relate part-time courses more closely to the students' work, improving distance-teaching methods – and reducing the proportion of part-time students. In 1975, 60 per cent of all entrants were full-time, as were 63 per cent of graduates five years later; the figures for correspondence students were 27 per cent and 26 per cent respectively. Some discrepancies remain, but the gap has certainly been narrowed (see Table 5.1).

In another sense, Soviet and American higher education stand at opposite poles, with the United Kingdom somewhere in the middle. This is in the classification of institutions by function and discipline. The so-called 'binary system' of the UK, the functional division between vocationally-oriented public sector institutions and allegedly non-vocational independent universities, is only one way of structuring the system, and one that never had much of a rationale behind it anyway –

Table 5.1   Students, Entrants and Graduates 1940-1982; by Type of Study (Thousands; Percentages of Year Total)

		1940-41	1965-66	1970-71	1975-76	1980-81	1981-82
STUDENTS	Total	817 (100%)	3,861 (100%)	4,581 (100%)	4,854 (100%)	5,235 (100%)	5,284 (100%)
	Full-time	558 (69%)	1,584 (41%)	2,241 (49%)	2,628 (54%)	2,978 (57%)	3,011 (57%)
	Evening	27 (3%)	569 (15%)	658 (14%)	644 (13%)	649 (12%)	648 (12%)
	Correspondence	227 (28%)	1,708 (44%)	1,682 (37%)	1,582 (33%)	1,608 (31%)	1,625 (31%)
ENTRANTS	Total	263.4 (100%)	853.7 (100%)	911.5 (100%)	993.8 (100%)	1,051.9 (100%)	1,062.4 (100%)
	Full-time	154.9 (59%)	378.4 (44%)	500.5 (55%)	593.9 (60%)	639.9 (61%)	644.0 (61%)
	Evening	6.6 (3%)	125.2 (15%)	127.4 (14%)	129.7 (13%)	134.3 (13%)	135.4 (13%)
	Correspondence	101.9 (37%)	350.1 (41%)	283.6 (31%)	270.2 (26%)	277.7 (26%)	283.0 (27%)
GRADUATES	Total	126.1 (100%)	403.9 (100%)	630.8 (100%)	713.4 (100%)	817.3 (100%)	831.2 (100%)
	Full-time	97.8 (78%)	224.8 (56%)	334.8 (53%)	433.3 (61%)	518.0 (63%)	527.5 (63%)
	Evening	4.4 (4%)	43.5 (11%)	82.1 (13%)	79.7 (11%)	85.3 (10%)	85.8 (10%)
	Correspondence	23.9 (19%)	135.6 (34%)	213.9 (34%)	200.4 (28%)	214.0 (26%)	217.9 (26%)

Note Percentages have been rounded to nearest whole number.

Source Narodnoe Khozyaistvo SSSR v 1981 godu : statisticheskii yezhegodnik
(Moskva, 1982) adapted

except, just possibly, at one time, convenience. (The numbers of students pursuing non-vocational courses at polytechnics and central institutions, and of those taking medicine, law or engineering at universities, exemplify the absurdity of the vocational-general dichotomy; and recent governmental exercises in control through the tugging of the purse-strings has left university independence looking rather threadbare.) In the USA there is a distinction between private and state institutions, but this has nothing to do with any functional division — nor, if the full range is examined, with status or quality either. Most of the professionally-oriented colleges have long ago either diversified and become universities in their own right, or have merged with other universities. Whatever the divisions that exist in American higher education, that between universities and the rest is not one of them; as a category, the universities have practically absorbed the whole senior college system.

Table 5.2   Students and Graduates 1981: by Category of Institution (Absolute Numbers to nearest 100; Percentage of Year Total)

Type of institution	Students		Graduates	
Technology	2,148,300	(40.6%)	313,100	(37.6%)
Agriculture	463,500	(8.7%)	67,000	(8.1%)
Transport	177,300	(3.3%)	23,300	(2.8%)
Economics	646,400	(12.0%)	109,500	(13.2%)
Law	102,700	(1.9%)	16,700	(2.0%)
Medicine	384,500	(7.2%)	60,100	(7.2%)
Education	934,400	(17.6%)	169,600	(20.4%)
Art	43,600	(0.8%)	7,700	(0.9%)
Universities	384,500	(7.2%)	64,200	(7.7%)
TOTAL	5,284,500	(100%)	831,200	(100%)

Note   Some of the categories have been conflated from more complex entries in the original, or simplified. Thus, 'Technology' in the table is a summation for entries for energetics, metallurgy, machine construction, radiotechnics and communications, construction, hydrology, etc. This summation is in accordance with the usage for summary statistics used elsewhere. 'Agriculture' includes forestry, 'Medicine' is given as 'health care and physical culture' and 'education' as 'specialisms of pedagogical institutes and institutes of culture'.

Source   Narodnoe khozyaistvo SSSR v 1981 godu : statisticheskii yezhegodnik
(Moskva, 1982) adapted

In the USSR, however, it is just the reverse, for the institutional structure is specialized along largely professional lines — a system of monotechnics, as it were. Nearly all the higher professional training which is carried out by universities in Britain (to say nothing of polytechnics and central institutions) is undertaken in the Soviet Union in specific institutes – technical, legal economic, artistic, agricultural, pedagogical and so forth. In one sense, therefore, the universities have a residual role — non-specific, non-vocational, with responsibility for the pure sciences and the humanities. With 384,500 students, they account for just 7.2 per cent of the total (see Table 5.2). In practice, however, they are not completely devoid of vocational application; a majority of the graduates enter secondary school teaching (though the great majority of teachers are still trained in the pedagogical institutes); these tend to be the ones who have not managed to find a job in research, and, although more advanced in their specialist disciplines than their *pedvuz* counterparts, are widely regarded as less committed. In addition to the compulsory elements common to all higher education curricula — foreign language, physical education and political education — their courses include an element of teaching method, educational theory, psychology and teaching practice (though less than in the *pedvuzy*) in case they do find themselves in teaching.[5]

Legally, there is no difference between the universities and the other *VUZy* (*vysshie uchebnye zavedeniya* or higher educational institutions). They all have the same kind of faculty structure, award the same first degrees, conduct research and are, of course, under ministerial control; neither the substantive nor trivial (but perhaps psychologically important) matters that used to loom so large in the UK exist in the USSR. In practice, however, it is not quite as simple as that. The law may make no distinctions, but public opinion does, and the universities as a category do enjoy greater esteem than most other types of institution; and this is reflected in the numbers and calibre of students seeking places and staff seeking posts. In the very nature of things this is impossible to quantify, but there are a few pointers. For example, all institutions award the first degree (*diplom*), and all can prepare postgraduate students in research, but none can award the higher degrees (*kandidat nauk* and *doktor nauk*, literally candidate and doctor of sciences,[6] roughly equivalent to the PhD and higher doctorates in the UK respectively); this is the prerogative of the VAK (*vysshaya attestatsionnaya kommissiya*, the Ministry's higher qualifications commission), and applies to work done in any kind of *VUZ*, as well as in the various specialist research institutes. Universities, however, produce consistently more higher degree candidates, and conduct more research, than their share of the total number of students would lead one to expect. Even at first degree level their performance is better than most; with 7.2 per cent of the student body, they account for 7.7 per cent of the graduates — not a dramatic difference, but possibly indicative.

But this difference in prestige is by no means uniform. There are many other *VUZy*, like the Moscow Power Institute, the Dnepropetrovsk Mining Institute, the Gorki Language Institute and the Moscow Pedagogical Institute of Foreign Languages (to name but a few), which enjoy higher status and produce a higher standard of work than many universities. Moscow and Leningrad State Universities may stand on the unofficial pinnacle,[7] and there is no doubt that universities as a group are ranked higher than, say, pedagogical institutes. But, again, this does not always apply: the Herzen Pedagogical Institute in Leningrad or the Lenin Pedagogical Institute in Moscow, for example, would outrank the universities of Alma-Ata or Dushambe. Of the institutions given the right by the Ministry to construct their own syllabuses (*individual'nye plany* or individual curricula) instead of the prescribed ones, a disproportionate number are universities, but a great many are not. Generally, then, while recognizing that the universities tend to have, unofficially, a special position, we have to be careful about pushing this generalization too far; it is certainly not reflected in the organizational machinery of the system.

While not subject to the wild variations in standard that can be found in other mass systems of higher education, the Soviet system has problems enough. The clumsiness of the controlling mechanism has already been referred to. It is quite common, internationally, to find higher education under detailed ministerial control, but in the USSR this is complicated by the structure of Soviet government, the size of the country, the role of the Communist Party as virtually a parallel governmental structure at all levels, and sometimes by bureaucratic inefficiency. Notionally, the chain of command is straightforward. The outlines of educational policy are decided by the Central Committee of the Communist Party and the Council of Ministers, translated into detailed policy by the USSR Ministries of Education and of Higher Education, and passed down the line through the Ministries of the constituent Republics to the *VUZy* themselves. Actually, even at USSR level the responsibility of the ministries is less clear-cut. Most teacher-training institutions come under the Ministry of Education rather than Higher Education, and other Ministries are involved as well − Health, Culture, the Industrial Ministries, and so forth. There is also some ambiguity at Republic level, as some republics are readier than others to make their own voices heard. One effect of this is detailed and sometimes confusing prescription right down to the number of hours per week per subject per semester, number of tests, examinations, projects, even the distribution of teaching between lectures and seminars. Apart from institutions with their own *individual'nye plany* − and if they are *too* individual the right to have them may be withdrawn − the institutions sometimes find that their work is unduly constrained, and may have to resort to evasion to get anything done.[8]

Among other problems, that of drop-out, especially of part-timers and *stazhniki*, has also been mentioned, as has the partial solution of reducing the proportion of these categories − drastically in the latter case. But this is only a limited solution, since one reason for favouring these groups was social − an attempt to make admission more open, to lessen the gap between academic and working life, and to inhibit the growth of an academic and professional élite. This is one example of a clash between short-term imperatives of efficiency and longer-term social objectives; in this case, for the time being, the pragmatic solution has been preferred. In the case of another disadvantaged group, it has not. Students from rural areas have greater difficulty in getting into higher education than their urban counterparts, and those who do succeed are more vulnerable to drop-out during their courses. (For reasons too complex to go into here, there is still a gap between school standards in urban and rural areas.)[9] One solution would have been to take in fewer rural students, but this would have been politically and socially unacceptable. Accordingly, many institutions have since the 1960s been operating one-year preliminary courses to prepare for higher education proper those students deemed to be in need of additional training; overwhelmingly, these come from the countryside. Precise data are hard to obtain, but this device seems to have been moderately successful.

The greatest problem, however, remains the pressure on places; for all the attempts to shift the direction of school work during the early 1960s and again since the early 1970s, the schools continue to produce far more would-be students than the institutions could admit or the economy could sustain. Admission is based mainly on performance in entrance examinations, but other factors are taken into account as well. Some of these are political – a good Party or Komsomol[10] reference is a help – and others are social, points and quotas being manipulated to obtain a more acceptable balance of social classes, nationalities and area backgrounds than could be achieved by applying strictly scholastic criteria. This is likely to be a problem as long as demand for places so greatly outstrips supply; and although the system continues to expand slightly, there is no prospect of expansion on the scale needed to meet the demand. Nor have the Soviet authorities any intention of attempting this. It is not only that they could not afford it; what they are seeking to do is to encourage more young people to go into training for skilled vocations instead, and pursue their further education along that route.[11]

At this point, it is necessary to set Soviet higher education within the context of the whole educational system. Briefly, all children attend the general school for eight years, from age 7 to 15. A majority stay on for a further two years to complete what is usually referred to as the ten-year school. This is the main route to higher education, the final certificate being a necessary precondition of admission; it is not, however, a guarantee – the factors mentioned above come into play, and the entrance examination (unlike in the UK) has to be taken as well. (The school certificate is assessed at the level of the schools themselves, and is therefore liable to fluctuation in standards, whereas the entrance examinations are set at ministerial level, and are therefore thought to be more reliable.)

Alternatively, the pupils may go to one of two main types of vocationally-oriented school. The vocational-technical school (*professional'no-tekhnicheskoe uchilishche* or *PTU*) provides training in a skilled trade, very roughly analogous to an apprenticeship, but with formal instruction, examinations and, in its earlier form at least, a relatively minor element of general education (about 20 per cent of curricular time). Courses last as a rule from one and a half to three years, depending on the trade. The secondary specialized schools (*srednie spetsial'nye uchebnye zavedeniya*)[12] are of various types. One kind, known as an *uchilishche*,[12] deals with non-technical vocations such as nursing, music, clerical work and until relatively recently primary teaching, while a *tekhnikum* provides courses in technological fields, but at a higher level

than a *PTU* − engineering, agricultural machinery, electronics, computers, optics, etc. *Tekhnikumy* and *uchilishcha* alike provide both professional training and the general educational equivalent of the last two classes
of the ten-year school, and thus prepare students not only for jobs but
also for the possibility of entering higher education. Courses entered
from the eighth class (age 15) last normally for four years. It is possible,
however, to enter a secondary specialized school after completion of the
general school, in which case the course is of two years' duration, the
general educational element having been covered already. Thus, the *tekhnikumy* and *uchilishcha* overlap the secondary and tertiary sectors; they
are not quite in the same category as the short-cycle post-secondary
courses already familiar in some other countries (such as the American
community colleges, the university diplomas in France and the 'semi-
higher' institutes in Bulgaria or their equivalents in Yugoslavia.)[13] These
are unambiguously post-secondary, and in any case are entered a year or
two later. But they have some aspects of this function; it is not without
significance that they come within the province not of the USSR Ministry
of Education, but of the USSR Ministry of Higher and Secondary
Specialized Education (to give it its full title.)

   But the *PTU* are also available as post-secondary courses; furthermore, for some years most of them have been transforming into
secondary *PTU*, with a much greater element of general and
polytechnic education and courses extending to three or four years.
Recently, it has been announced that all *PTU* are to be raised to this
category.[14] The logic behind this lies in the changing nature of work, the
increase in both complexity and sophistication, and the faster pace of
change; it is expected that skilled workers with a stronger general
educational base will be better able to cope with changing and more
complex techniques, and will be more responsive to retraining. There is
already some evidence to support this, and already various forms of
further education and job retraining constitute the second largest
educational category in the Soviet Union − nearly 45 million at the
present time (see Table 5.3).

   Present policy, clearly, is to raise the status of the secondary specialized
schools and the *PTU* (especially the latter), thus making every type of
post-15 schooling a possible avenue to higher education. At the same
time, it is clear that more young people are to be encouraged to take
these routes instead of seeking higher education, and proceed from then
directly into work. As has been observed, this is partly to take pressure
off higher education; but there is more to it than that. One of the
weaknesses of the Soviet economy is at the supporting level of expertise,
that of the technician rather than the engineer − or, as one official put it,
'Too many chiefs and not enough braves.' To do his job properly, it has
been reckoned, one technologist needs the supporting services of about

Table 5.3   Pupils and Students 1940-1982: by Level of Schooling (Thousands)

	1940-41	1965-66	1970-71	1975-76	1980-81	1981-82
General educational schools						
Full-time	34,784	43,410	45,448	42,611	39,546	39,656
Part-time	768	4,845	3,745	4,983	4,729	4,600
Total	35,552	48,255	49,193	47,594	44,275	44,256
Vocational-technical schools (PTU)	717	1,701	2,591	3,381	3,971	3,998
Secondary specialized schools	975	3,659	4,383	4,525	4,612	4,557
Higher education	812	3,861	4,581	4,854	5,235	5,284
Retraining and further training	9,491	14,381	18,881	32,251	42,108	44,727

Source Narodnoe khozyaistvo SSSR v 1981 godu : statisticheskii yezhegodnik
     (Moskva, 1982) adapted

ten technicians, each of whom in turn needs the support of ten skilled workers.[15] This may be an exaggeration, but it is true nonetheless that the support level is essential, and that this has been relatively weak. Present policies are an attempt to correct this, and also to improve work skills and work sophistication, and to reinforce the work ethic by which the USSR sets so much store. It is not going to be easy; higher education carries high prestige in Soviet society, and although the financial rewards in certain skilled trades can be higher than in (say) teaching and medicine, the attraction of status remains strong.

Soviet higher education, then, has to be looked at in relation to developments in the educational system in general, and at the moment, especially, in the areas of professional and vocational training, since what happens at that level will profoundly affect the work of the higher institutions themselves. It will be of particular interest to watch developments over the next few years, since the relationship between the various types of higher education, between these and other sectors of the system, and between general and vocational education, is perplexing many other educational systems – including, conspicuously, our own.

Notes and References

1   For a fuller discussion, see Kravetz, N. (1980) Education of ethnic and national minorities in the USSR: a report on current developments *Comparative Education* 16 (1) 13-24; Halevy, Z. and Halevy, E. Etsioni (1974) The 'religious factor' and achievement in education *Comparative Education* 10 (3) 193-200; Grant, N. (1983) Linguistic and ethnic minorities in the USSR: Educational policies and developments. In Tomiak, J.J. (Ed.) *Soviet Education in the 1980s* Croom Helm, pp. 24-49.

2   See Mitter, Wolfgang (1979) *Secondary School Graduation; University Entrance Qualification in Socialist Countries. A Comparative Study* Pergamon

3   Grant, N. (1972) The USSR. In Scotford-Archer, Margaret *University and Society: A Comparative Sociological Review* Heinemann, pp. 80-102.

4   The comparison is not precise, as part-time courses last longer; but the general pattern holds.

5   There are constant complaints about the attitude of university-trained teachers, and some hot defences. This has been a recurring theme for decades. See Grant, N. (1972) Teacher training in the USSR and Eastern Europe *Comparative Education* 8 (1) 7-29.

6   The Russian word *nauka*, like the German *Wissenschaft*, has wider connotations than its English equivalent, science. The actual titles can vary according to specialist field — candidate of pedagogical sciences, doctor of medical sciences, etc.

7   Novosibirsk is very highly rated indeed in terms of natural and physical sciences, and shows signs of outstripping Moscow and Leningrad in some respects.

8   See Zajda, J. (1979) Education for labour in the USSR *Comparative Education* 15 (3) 287-300; Grant, N. (1982) Work experience in Soviet and East European schools. In Eggleston, John (Ed.) *Work Experience in Secondary Schools* Routledge and Kegan Paul, pp. 121-139.

9   Inequality of attainment and opportunity between town and country is still one of the most severe problems in the Soviet educational system; it has to do, among other things, with the size of the country and difficulties of communication, and staffing problems. It remains politically important, as a third of the population is rural.

10 Komsomol — literally, the Communist League of Youth (*Kom*munis-ticheskii *soyuz molo*dyozhi), the senior youth organization and, in effect, junior branch of the Communist Party.

11 See Matthews, Mervyn (1982) *Education in the Soviet Union: Policies and Institutions since Stalin* Allen & Unwin; Zajda, Joseph (1980) *Education in the USSR* Pergamon; Grant, Nigel (1979) *Soviet Education* Penguin.

12 The terminology can be confusing because of lack of precise equivalents. *Uchebnoe zavedenie*, literally educational institution, is often used to mean 'school' or 'institute' at this level; *uchilishche* is another word for school (*schkola*), but these are not interchangeable, *uchilishche* having more of an instructional connotation, while *shkola* has a more general one.

13 For a treatment of this level, see Neave, Guy (1976) *Patterns of Inequality* NFER.

14 Osnovnye napravleniya reformy obshcheobrazovatel'noi i professional'noi shkoly (*Pravda* 4 January 1984, pp. 1-2). Among other
things, the statement (from the Central Committee of the Communist Party) announces the lowering of the age of starting school from 7
to 6, and the shortening of higher educational courses for students
who have come through the secondary specialized or secondary *PTU*
routes; there is also a great deal about improving vocational training.
15 Oral communications, Moscow and Leningrad, October 1983.

Part 2
Processes for Change

6 Survival in a Harsh Climate

Gareth Williams

In the introduction to the interim reports of the SRHE Leverhulme programme of study I wrote, 'A fundamental question facing higher education is the extent to which consensual arrangements and assumptions that generally worked well during the long postwar period of expansion can cope with the much more stringent conditions likely to prevail in the 1980s and 1990s. Is there sufficient common purpose amongst the various institutions and interest groups that constitute the higher education system to permit the development of viable long-run policy objectives, or must higher education policy increasingly become merely the outcome of a struggle for survival and dominance among conflicting interests and ideas?' Unless the answer to that question is positive I am sure future governments will feel that they themselves must impose solutions on the warring factions.

The general issue is one which has been central to higher education policy in Britain for a long time − certainly since the state began to be deeply involved in the finance of higher education after the Second World War. What is the proper place of institutional independence in a modern, publicly financed system of higher education? What is the proper balance between autonomy and accountability? Is it possible for autonomous institutions to respond in a way that is consistent with the more general national interest − especially at a time of severe resource stringency?

Before coming to the central theme I want to comment on this underlying issue of resource stringency, for it has aroused some debate in the months since the publication of the final SRHE Leverhulme report. Were we correct to let the likelihood of continued financial stringency dominate our thinking? Was this not an excessively pessimistic extrapolation of recent trends?

The charge of excessive pessimism has been made on three grounds. First, there have been hopes that the British political climate will change and that a different government in the late 1980s will put higher education higher up on its public expenditure agenda. Second, there have been claims that because the middle-class birthrate declined much less than the working-class birthrate between 1964 and 1978, higher education will be affected much less by overall demographic trends than schools have been. Third, hopes have been expressed that participation rates within each social class will increase.

These claims were examined in considerable detail during the course of the SRHE Leverhulme programme of study. The key indicator is participation rates. These stagnated during the 1970s and many indicators of student demand were lower in 1980 than in 1972. The best evidence we were able to obtain showed that stagnation was associated with declines in the private rates of return to higher education, and that there was little likelihood of rates rising significantly in the foreseeable future. Any hopes of a spontaneous rise in participation rates is optimistic rather than realistic. The social class effect will offer some relief but this can be calculated. Williams and Blackstone (1983) accepted Farrant's (1981) calculation that differential birthrates could be expected to improve participation rates by about 12 per cent, suggesting a fall in student numbers between 1981/2 and 1995/6 of 19 per cent rather than 22 per cent.*

Some observers, such as the Royal Society working party (Royal Society 1983), who are concerned mainly with the universities, have attempted to derive comfort from the fact that the universities are particularly likely to attract middle-class students. This is true, but the issue then becomes a matter of how the decline in numbers should be allocated between universities and other institutions. There is little doubt that demand from school-leavers with 'A' level qualifications, and the demand for graduates by their future employers, would favour the universities at the expense of other institutions. One of the issues that must be resolved is whether protecting the universities and letting the brunt of any contraction be borne by colleges of higher education is in the national interest or that of students. This is the kind of problem it may be impossible to resolve by negotiation or contructive competition.

The hopes of a new dawn resulting from a change of government are unlikely to be realized for at least three reasons. First, there is no political party at present which appears to be putting higher education high on its political agenda; second, while political parties would probably respond to pressure of student demand (whether or not the Robbins criterion

---

*It should be remembered that peak student numbers will occur in 1985/6, so the total fall from the top of the peak will be about a quarter if the social class effect is taken into account, rather than a third if higher education follows the overall demographic trends downwards. These estimates correspond very closely to projections made by the Department of Education and Science (1983).

was explicitly accepted), this is unlikely to be forthcoming; third, the beliefs about higher education's contribution to economic growth and social equality which fuelled the expansion of the 1960s are not sustained by current interpretations of the evidence about the economic and social functions of higher education.

Our conclusion from all these considerations was summed up in the subtitle of the Williams and Blackstone (1983) book, *Higher Education in a Harsh Climate*. British universities, polytechnics and colleges will have to face a harsh climate for the rest of this century. The SRHE Leverhulme Report, *Excellence in Diversity* (Society for Research into Higher Education 1983), attempts to outline a strategy that will enable the essential features of a healthy higher education system to flourish even in these adverse conditions.

From the outset the main debates of the SRHE Leverhulme programme of study veered between two alternative strategies: a tightly controlled system with functions allocated between institutions and administered according to a detailed overall plan, or a market system in which competition amongst institutions and amongst students determined the structure of the system and the allocation of resources. People who had a clear personal vision of what higher education should be, whether of the right or the left of the political spectrum, tended to favour the planned solution; those who were less clear about the overall aims and purposes, but who saw higher education as a diverse network of interacting activities, tended to opt for market-type solutions, though there were wide differences of opinion about the extent to which the market should be subsidized and the mechanisms by which it should be subsidized.

Excellence in Diversity, as the title implies, sees higher education in terms of the second of these images and as a consequence places institutional autonomy at the heart of its strategy. However, institutional autonomy can never be unconstrained, particularly when it relies heavily on public funds and when the institutions are involved in activities which concern large numbers of the most able young people and hence have a substantial effect on the future of the nation. What then are the legitimate constraints, and what voluntary constraints might the institutions accept in order to forestall closer external regulation?

One false trail must be avoided. Institutional autonomy is neither a necessary nor a sufficient condition of individual academic freedom. Neave (1983) has shown how individual academics can be protected by law in universities and colleges that are subject to considerable external control. Conversely, a senate or academic board majority can be as restrictive of the freedom of individual academics (especially those not represented, such as research workers) as a central government department.

There are dilemmas which those of us with a strong belief in the professional freedom of academics must face. Does it extend to the right to teach students things that are believed by most other informed people to be wrong, obsolete or immoral? Are the claims of individual academic freedom altered when most of the resources necessary to sustain that freedom come through public funds? Important as it is, I do not intend to pursue the issue here. My present concern is with the claims of academic institutions, universities, polytechnics and colleges to be self-governing.

The justification for institutional autonomy must be extrinsic. It is possible to make a case for individual academic freedom as an end in itself. It is not possible to make such a case for the autonomy of academic institutions – even those that have been around longer than our system of parliamentary government. Autonomous institutions, particularly those financed from public funds, need to be able to demonstrate their capability of responding to needs outside themselves. The survival of an individual university or even a higher education system is not necessary if its functions can be better performed in other ways.

Ultimately the case must rest on the belief that knowledge is more efficiently created and disseminated if decisions, and particularly resource allocation decisions, are widely distributed. No one, not even a democratic government with a huge parliamentary majority, has a monopoly of truth.

The case for institutional autonomy rests ultimately on the belief that knowledge and understanding are more likely to expand as a result of incremental changes along a broad front rather than sharply focused developments in particular areas. *Excellence in Diversity* accepts this position, but the majority of its authors believed that members of society outside higher education institutions have the right to be reassured on three main counts: that academic institutions do in fact offer a diverse and flexible range of courses to potential students; that suitable academic standards are maintained; and that institutions are able and willing to respond responsibly to changing external circumstances.

The main proposals of *Excellence in Diversity* are underpinned by one or more of these three themes. The rationale for each proposal is discussed at some length in the accompanying volume *Response to Adversity* (Williams and Blackstone 1983). The proposals cover broadly four main areas: the pattern of courses, the maintenance of academic standards, the differentiation of institutions and the mechanisms of finance.

The proposals that have generated most interest in the press and most controversy within higher education are those concerned with the pattern of course provision, and in particular the suggestion that broadly based courses of two years might replace the three-year specialized Honours degree as the essential core of the higher education system.

Opponents of change have claimed that the British Honours degree course is the shortest in the world. This is not strictly true: Belgium, France, Japan and the United States all have initial courses of two years. In general, it appears that those countries with more or less open access for school-leavers are likely to give students the opportunity of a qualification after two or three years; while those whose higher education is more meritocratic or élitist, such as the Eastern European countries, tend to have much longer normal courses of study. My source for these claims is the UNESCO *World Guide to Higher Education* (1976), a manual that I recommend to anyone who wishes to make a serious contribution to the debate about how they manage these things in other countries. I will quote two extracts from the UNESCO guide, since they concern countries that we sometimes wish to emulate and about which misconceptions abound. First, Germany: (after reviewing various two-year engineering and other vocational qualifications) 'For studies that require a longer period one may reckon that the first level of study is very often reached after four or five semesters devoted to the study of the basic subjects and often somewhat broadly conceived as pluridisci-plinary.' Second, Japan: 'The first stage of higher education is divided into two phases. The first phase is devoted to an obligatory two-year course of general studies (social, natural and pure science, humanities) whatever the course envisaged for later studies.' One generalization I would be prepared to debate is that the basic structure of higher education courses has changed less in Britain during the past quarter century than in any other advanced country (apart, possibly, from Eastern Europe). This may be because our ancestors in their wisdom hit upon a degree structure that was ideal both for the restricted higher education system we had twenty-five years ago and for the much more open system I hope we shall have by the 1990s. They may have done so, but we should at least ask ourselves from time to time whether any radical changes are needed. That is the debate *Excellence in Diversity* has tried to start for the first time for twenty years.

Many of the criticisms of the report appear to be based on a misunderstanding of what *Excellence in Diversity* actually says. It does not recommend that two-year general degrees should be compulsory for everybody, as many critics have implied. It does offer a measured, though because of the nature of the report, necessarily brief, critique of the present system and possible alternatives. It concludes, 'a pattern of courses based on a core of two years' study leading to a variety of subsequent options would increase flexibility as well as having academic and economic advantages.' As a statement of fact, I remain convinced that the claim is justified. The key issue, however, is the nature of the subsequent options and the terms on which these would be available. That is the area in which, in my opinion, discussion should be concentrated. It may indeed be true, as some critics have suggested, that two-year initial courses would actually mean four-year degrees for a substantial number of students. It may well be that the expansion of knowledge in many areas does mean that those who are to get Honours degrees that are not idiotically narrow need to study for four years rather than three. If so, this needs to be argued through and a convincing case made.

So far, discussion of the pattern of undergraduate courses has been inhibited by the closing of ranks to protect the status quo, in which 80 per cent of the student load of universities and nearly 60 per cent of the full-time-equivalent students in public sector institutions are devoted to three-year Honours degree courses. I get very irritated by claims that at a time of demographic decline, universities and colleges might lose even more students than they otherwise would if a marketable qualification could be obtained after two years. This seems to suggest that students exist for the benefit of the institutions rather than vice versa, and that it is indeed true that considerable numbers of students who would be quite happy to complete their studies in two years are at present trapped on three-year courses.

One issue which clearly raises some hackles is the suggestion that a course of less than three years' full-time-equivalent study should be called a degree. The notion of a degree is clearly a powerful totem for many people. Several commentators who would not object to two-year core courses have expressed strong doubts about calling the qualification at the end a degree. My reaction to this line of argument is, 'That which we call a rose by any other name would smell as sweet.' To me the key issue is whether universities would offer the two-year qualification, and whether they would be prepared to accept students from other institutions on to the later years of three- and four-year courses with full credit for qualifications obtained elsewhere. If such credit transfer is possible, I would see no great loss in calling the two-year qualification a diploma or certificate.

The other key issue about two-year qualifications is the suggestion (not recommendation) that mandatory grants might be linked to two-year rather than three-year courses. It seems to me intrinsically no more undesirable that grants for the final year or two of Honours degree courses should be discretionary, than that, as at present, courses both below and above Honours degree level should qualify for discretionary grants while full-time Honours degree courses attract mandatory grants.

The next group of suggestions in the SRHE Leverhulme Report concern the maintenance of academic standards at a time when it is likely that institutions will be competing fiercely with each other for students. The signatories of the report were disturbed by evidence from the United States (especially Freeman 1981 and Trow 1982) which showed how excess capacity and competition between institutions can lead to declining standards and to a concern with student numbers regardless of the benefits students obtain from their courses. The group felt that the Council for National Academic Awards (CNAA) should continue to adapt its role so as to be able to continue to exercise a watching brief over the quality of provision in the public sector, and that the universities would be well advised to consider setting up some kind of academic review body for the university sector. It is gratifying that there have been developments along these lines in both sectors. The CNAA has announced a considerable extension of its 'partnership in validation', and the Committee of Vice-Chancellors and Principals has set up a sub-committee to examine arrangements for academic review in the universities.

The main thrust of the strategy of *Excellence in Diversity* derives, however, from its proposals for the reform of the finance of institutions. In a nutshell, the report proposes that major higher education institutions should cease to depend to such a large extent on a single financial channel (the University Grants Committee (UGC) or the National Advisory Body (NAB)) but should be able to obtain funds through a variety of mechanisms. The essential difference from present funding arrangements is that formulae for basic or core funding would positively encourage institutions to seek alternative sources of funding rather than discourage them. Again, there are distinct signs of movement in this direction, with the UGC ceasing to take such a strong line in penalizing universities that exceed student number targets, and the general encouragement of institutions to seek research grants and contracts for the sale of academic services through science parks and similar activities.

I myself follow Lionel Robbins and Clark Kerr in being convinced that academic institutions can be properly autonomous only if they have access to significant sources of funds independent of their main funding bodies. There has been some misunderstanding of this point, and a few observers have claimed that the SRHE Leverhulme group has proposed the privatization of higher education. This is certainly not the case. Page two of the report states quite categorically that higher education is 'an activity that must remain largely within the public sector'. However, there are many public sector channels, including the research councils, the government departments and the local authorities. We took the view that between them, and along with student fees and the sale of services to the private sector, these channels should account for about half the total income of universities, polytechnics and colleges. In this context I must add that I think it is a great pity that no Continuing Education Development Council has been established to succeed the Association for Adult and Continuing Education (ACACE). It is unlikely that the continuing education of adults will receive any significant priority unless there is some agency responsible for channelling funds specifically in this direction. In general, however, I think it is likely that this Leverhulme suggestion will materialize, and that by the 1990s we shall have a network of strong higher education institutions which receive only about half their total income in the form of guaranteed general grants through the University Grants Committee and the National Advisory Body.

Which brings me back to my initial theme – the place of institutional autonomy. A higher education institution is subject to three kinds of influence. It must be a haven for the individual scholar and should provide an atmosphere conducive to free inquiry and professional autonomy. It is a means of arriving at academic consensus. And it is the main channel for contact between individual academics and the outside world both with regard to funding and in respect of groups such as employers who have some legitimate interest in academic activities. The institution should create out of these influences a corporate identity which defines its particular place in the spectrum of higher education activities.

Excellence in Diversity endorses the idea, originally put forward by the House of Commons Select Committee (1980), that institutions should prepare and agree with their principal funding bodies mission statements defining their present and future role in the higher education spectrum. Such mission statements would locate the institution both for students and for funding agencies. An institution would be free to develop any activities within its agreed mission. Proposals to move outside the institution's accepted area of competence would need to be agreed with the appropriate funding body.

We concluded that 'the key to a higher education system that is able to offer excellence in diversity is restrained pluralism'. Institutions should have a substantial measure of independence, but should be exposed to external influences both through active lay governing bodies and through financial incentives which encourage them to respond to changing social and economic needs.

The essential features of a post-Leverhulme higher education system would be the negotiation of development strategies, the provision of long-term core funding of institutions to cover about half the total expenditure envisaged in their agreed development plans, and the provision by government and the private sector of funds through several different mechanisms so that individual institutions might develop their own areas of strength and not be totally dependent on the judgements of a single funding body. In such a system the debate about the pros and cons of the binary policy would become largely irrelevant. However, there would still be a need for some planning.

It is likely that some institutions will have to close or merge with others between now and 1990. External intervention is likely to be necessary to ensure that students do not suffer when doomed institutions struggle to avoid that fate. However, I am certain that the system we propose would help to ensure that the fate of individual academic institutions would be determined mainly by the abilities and efforts of their members and not by arbitrary political or partly informed academic judgements. Institutions would be autonomous, but they would need constantly to justify and earn their autonomy. That is the best we can hope for − or, indeed, ought to hope for − in the harsh climate of the 1980s and 1990s.

In conclusion, I can do no better than repeat the final sentences of *Response to Adversity* (Williams and Blackstone 1983). 'Our proposals are designed to take advantage of the opportunities given by falling numbers of school-leavers to develop at no extra cost a higher education system that is responsive to changing social and economic needs while maintaining quality and academic integrity. There is no comfortable response to adversity. What we propose would be invigorating. A healthier system would emerge that was equipped to meet the challenges of the twenty-first century.' I stand by these remarks.

References

Department of Education and Science (1983) *Future Demand for Higher Education in Great Britain* Report on Education No. 99, London : DES

Farrant, J.H. (1981) Trends in admissions. In Fulton, O. (Ed.) *Access to Higher Education* Guildford : Society for Research into Higher Education

Freeman, R. (1981) Response to change in the United States. In Lindley, R. (Ed.) *Higher Education and the Labour Market* Guildford : Society for Research into Higher Education

House of Commons (1980) *The Funding and Organization of Courses in Higher Education. Fifth Report from the Education, Science and Arts Committee 1979-80* London : HMSO

Kerr, C. (1980) *Three Thousand Futures: The Next Twenty Years for Higher Education* (Carnegie Council Final Report) San Francisco : Jossey Bass

Neave, G. (1983) The regional dimension: some considerations from a European perspective. In Shattock, M. (Ed.) *The Structure and Governance of Higher Education* Guildford : Society for Research into Higher Education

Robbins, L. (1980) *Higher Education Revisited* London : Macmillan

Royal Society, The (1983) *Demographic Trends and Future University Candidates* London : The Royal Society

Society for Research into Higher Education (1983) *Excellence in Diversity* Guildford : Society for Research into Higher Education

Trow, M. (1981) Comparative perspectives on access. In Fulton, O. (Ed.) *Access to Higher Education* Guildford : Society for Research into Higher Education

United Nations Educational, Scientific and Cultural Organization (1976) *World Guide to Higher Education* Paris : UNESCO

Williams, G. and Blackstone, T. (1983) *Response to Adversity* Guildford : Society for Research into Higher Education

7 The Leverhulme Recipe

Peter Scott

The final report of the SRHE Leverhulme inquiry was a substantial document with many recommendations for future policy and with much argument and evidence to support these recommendations. But the message of Leverhulme, a little unfairly perhaps, can be reduced to four main themes – wider access to higher education; the reform of courses within universities, polytechnics and colleges; greater diversity within the system; and stronger management at both institutional and system level.

To take each in turn. First, *wider access*. The difficulty here is that the experience of the 1960s and the 1970s is still so fresh in the minds of many people in higher education that the pattern of expansion in those two decades may be regarded as the only possible pattern of expansion in the future. Perhaps the most crucial difference between past and future patterns of expansion, however, is simply that the latter may not be an expansion at all if the measure is to be some crude head count of students in the system. Instead, access to higher education is likely to be widened by a process of substitution, as demographic decline leads to a reduction in the number of traditional full-time students, leaving room for the enrolment of more non-traditional students. Higher education is unlikely to prove an exception to the general rule that nature abhors a vacuum. Institutions worried about possible cuts and closures probably abhor it even more! Yet higher education has probably not yet come to terms with the great difference between the widening of access by a process of expansion – which leaves the traditional core of the system unscathed – and the widening of access by a process of substitution – which may lead to a shrinking of that core. For some the latter is likely to appear to be a much more radical process and one which may potentially threaten traditional academic values to a degree that was not experienced in the 1960s expansion.

This is particularly significant as demographic decline will not have the same effect on all parts of higher education. In general terms the colleges of higher education will be the hardest hit and the universities the least affected, with the polytechnics somewhere in between. So the universities – or at any rate some universities – may be able to cope by raising their entry standards rather than by substituting non-traditional students. As the latter course may appear to many in universities to be a potentially subversive process, the temptation may be very great. Several of the technological universities have already followed this path in their efforts to meet the much reduced student targets imposed on them by the University Grants Committee (UGC) in July 1981. But whatever the detailed responses of individual institutions, it is clear that not all of them are going to be equally interested in (or be forced to be interested in) recruiting the mass of non-traditional students that often gets lumped under the description 'continuing education'. Instead we are likely to see a highly differentiated response.

A third point that must be borne in mind when the widening of access to higher education is being considered is that it is very easy to become a prisoner of classifications – and higher education is itself a rather circumscribed classification that may blind us to what is happening in the rest of the post-school system. Again it is all too easy to be mesmerized by our own experience during the very different circumstances of the 1960s or by the much more spectacular expansion of higher education that took place in the United States at the same time. Just because on the other side of the Atlantic twenty years ago the main block to educational progress seemed to be at 18-plus college level, it does not follow that the block is to be found in the same place in Britain in the 1980s. Indeed, there is a case that is so strong that it has become almost platitudinous for arguing that this block is to be found at a somewhat lower level, among 16-plus secondary school-leavers. And in fact the justice of this argument has been accepted by two successive governments of very different political complexions. The result has been the explosive growth of the budget and operations of the Manpower Services Commission (MSC) which have changed the face of further education. Yet for too many people in higher education none of this expansion counts because it seems to be happening in the wrong place or because the barriers we have built up between higher education and further and school education make it almost invisible. The idea that the main thrust of the expansion of post-school opportunities might take place at an almost sub-secondary level through the operation of the MSC rather than at the elevated level of higher education is both unfamiliar and uncongenial.

So the widening of access may well be an important feature of the 1980s, as the SRHE Leverhulme Report recommends. But unless we take into account these three factors – substitution rather than expansion, the differential impact of demographic decline on individual institutions, and the probability that the main expansionary action may take place in further rather than higher education — we are likely to form a very misleading impression of the shape of this wider access.

Second, *the reform of courses*. Inevitably perhaps, a lot of attention has been focused on the Leverhulme proposal that two-year Pass degrees should become the normal undergraduate course for the majority of students. This proposal has provoked a fair amount of controversy and dissent. But it may be a mistake to concentrate too much on the precise details of the solution proposed by Leverhulme to a problem that is generally acknowledged to exist and to require a solution. That problem is the domination of undergraduate education in British universities (absolutely), polytechnics and colleges (substantially) by the three- or four-year Honours degree, normally studied full-time and in a narrow specialism. This was regretted by the Robbins committee twenty years ago and the reasons for that regret have increased rather than diminished. Looking ahead to the maybe very different student constituencies of the late 1980s and 1990s the almost total supremacy of the Honours degree seems even less appropriate. So Leverhulme may have come up with the wrong answer but was certainly asking the right question. Sometime during the 1980s we are going to have to come to grips with the rigidity of the present forms of undergraduate education in Britain (or England and Wales, as Scotland still deserves, although only just, a verdict of 'not proven'). There is a range of available solutions — introducing a first/second/third cycle pattern on the French model, although the government will fight against any system that may lengthen undergraduate study and so increase the student grants bill; favouring two-year diplomas at the expense of three-year degrees as the National Advisory Body for Local Authority Higher Education (NAB) has tentatively explored; inventing new types of qualification rather as the Diploma of Higher Education was invented ten years ago; creating a seamless web of courses and qualifications through a system of credit transfer and accumulation. The critics of Leverhulme's proposed two-year degrees, if they accept that undergraduate education is insufficiently flexible, have a duty to be more than negative and to join in the movement for reform.

It is interesting to note how much postgraduate education has changed over the last twenty years. Its entire centre of gravity has shifted from research degrees to taught courses. Indeed it would not be too much to suggest that postgraduate education has come to terms with the great expansion of higher education between 1950 and 1970 far more effectively than undergraduate education, where its impact would have been expected to be more considerable and certainly more direct. This suggests that the Honours degree is a powerful representation of the underlying values of higher education to a much greater degree even than the PhD. Maybe Leverhulme underestimated the difficulty in proposing the substitution of two-year Pass degrees for three-year Honours degrees because it failed to recognize the fundamental and therefore powerful values embodied in the latter. As a result their preferred solution may appear a little superficial and facile. But that is not an argument for abandoning the challenge to reform undergraduate education, only for renewing this effort at a different level. The task for the 1980s therefore should be to excavate the fundamental values expressed by our present forms of undergraduate education and examine them in the light of the changing role of universities, polytechnics and colleges. Certainly any attempts at reform that remain almost entirely mechanical and ignore these values are unlikely to get very far.

Third, *greater diversity*. One of the remarkable features of the Leverhulme programme was that the majority of its participants arrived with the prejudice that the binary policy was an anomaly and should be swept away − but left with a grudging acceptance that imperfect as it was this policy was some kind of crude guarantor of institutional diversity. They may not have liked the present admittedly arbitrary division of higher education into a university and a polytechnic and college sector, but they liked the prospect of a unitary system even less. The reason was simple and obvious: the very messiness of the binary policy tends to fudge the distinction between higher and further education, while a unitary system would inevitably create a sharp apartheid between the two. At a time when the nature of higher education's constituency might radically change with a strong movement towards continuing education, clearer demarcation of the boundary between higher and further education struck few people as a sound policy. As the 1980s unfold, polytechnics and colleges certainly and universities probably will offer courses which ten years ago they might have regarded as inappropriate in the middle of the Gadarene rush to full-time degrees.

In the six months since the publication of the SRHE Leverhulme Report the emphasis on institutional diversity has been further sharpened. The prospect that money for research will be separately earmarked from money for teaching has come much closer. It has strong if still surreptitious goverment support. Although the natural instinct of most universities is to resist such earmarking because it is so clearly an invasion of their institutional autonomy, the evident decay of the dual support system has convinced many, particularly in science faculties and universities with the strongest research reputations, that some change is necessary. The polytechnics and colleges naturally have to support the debunking of the dual support system because it is the only way they are going to get any separate money for research at all.

Of course any earmarking of research money would lead to far-reaching changes in the present structure of higher education. It would certainly lead to more equitable treatment between the university and non-university sectors. Research is the universities' great alibi in justifying their more generous funding. If it were accounted separately, there would be a strong movement towards establishing common unit costs for teaching across all higher education and funding institutions accordingly. Any observed inequities would then have to be explicitly rather than as at present vaguely justified. A second important change, a little further down the road perhaps, would be to debunk the myth that British universities form a homogeneous sector of broadly equivalent institutions. The substantial differences of quality and of research commitment, which today are only informally acknowledged, will be made explicit by the earmarking of research money. The result might not be the stark three-tier university sector that is the nightmare of the Association of University Teachers (AUT). In Britain we are unlikely to see the overt development of either research universities at one end of the university spectrum or liberal arts colleges at the other. But the differential reputations of individual universities are likely to be made more explicit with significant consequences for the career opportunities of their academic staff.

All this is not going to happen overnight. In the first place a half-way house compromise will probably be reached with the UGC 'indicating' how much money it has assumed a university will spend on research, while still leaving the university free to spend its recurrent grant in the old free way. But even this modest change would immediately highlight a universities' pecking order in a manner that may be very low-key but would nevertheless be a formal acknowledgement of significant differences. Nor does the evidence of the last twenty years, and in particular the reaction of the universities to the UGC's 1981 decisions, suggest that many universities would be brave enough to ignore the UGC's 'indications', although it may take until the end of the century to establish unambiguous earmarking. So the prospect is that the binary policy will remain in operation and that the university sector will become more highly differentiated.

Fourth, *stronger management*. The SRHE Leverhulme Report paid particular attention to this theme. It was attracted by the idea of institutions drawing up mission statements and it proposed that a centre for higher education policy studies (which would have a secondary role as a staff college for institutional leaders) should be established. This emphasis on stronger management is likely to be expressed at three levels: system, sector, and institution.

For the system as a whole the case for effective co-ordination of sectoral (and institutional) policies and for creative strategic policy making gets stronger every year. Leverhulme was ambivalent about recommending the establishment of what has come to be called 'an over-arching body' to co-ordinate the work of the UGC and the NAB. Part of this ambivalence probably arose from a misconception of the likely role of such a body and a natural reluctance to recommend the creation of yet another quango. But the job of a national commission for higher education would not be to meddle in or second-guess the detailed decisions being taken by the UGC and the NAB, but to tackle effectively the twin tasks of co-ordination and forward thinking which at present are ineffectively tackled by informal and normally bilateral discussion between the UGC, the NAB, and the Department of Education and Science (DES). A brief glance through the twenty-eight questions which the UGC has put to the universities, or the issues raised by the NAB in its consultative paper, *Towards a Strategy for Local Authority Higher Education in the Late 1980s and Beyond*, should be enough to convince most people that there is a wide range of important policies which neither body by itself is competent to answer.

At the sectoral level the main focus of interest is likely to be on the UGC. The NAB is a new and still interim body, although its success so far has been such as virtually to ensure its survival as a permanent part of higher education's policy furniture. The UGC is a different case. Somewhat in decline during the 1960s and 1970s (because it had so little to do but gently nudge expansion along), the committee reasserted itself in 1981 amid great controversy by taking important decisions about the future shape of the university system that were free of government direction. This had two results: first, it provoked a chorus of protests within universities about the legitimacy and competence of the committee; and second, the goverment decided that this show of independence would be the committee's last. The UGC as a result now faces two tasks, to build up its competence and legitimacy in the eyes of the universities and to accept that in future the DES will advise the UGC rather than the other way round. In a sense the UGC has been turned round. It no longer faces Whitehall but instead faces the universities. One possible implication is that however strong the case may once have been for staffing the UGC with civil servants, that case is much weaker today. The staff of the UGC now needs to be much more immersed in the detailed operation of universities, because it is in negotiation with individual universities that the bulk of the committee's work will consist in future, and because it is important to retain and where necessary rebuild the confidence of the universities in the UGC. The logical conclusion would seem to be that the UGC should be established as an independent agency and cut its immediate links with the DES, and recruit a mixed staff of civil servants and those with experience in university administration.

At the institutional level stronger management may be expressed in two ways. First, there is likely to be a readjustment of the balance of power between councils and senates. The convenient fiction that councils looked after the money and kept out of academic affairs, while senates decided the academic policy of universities, may cease to be tenable in a time when money is short and managerial and academic decisions cannot easily be disentangled. The 'donnish dominion' embodied in senates may be substantially qualified. This at any rate is what should happen. But so far it has not. In most universities the contraction that followed the 1981 cuts has been managed by tightly-knit management teams — vice-chancellor, registrar, a few senior professors. Councils have tended to keep their noses out, except in some semi-judicial, passive, court-of-final-appeal role. Why? One reason may be that in the years of 'donnish dominion' the lay dimension of university government atrophied to such a degree that in many cases it became effectively moribund. With the possible exception of eager accountants serving as treasurers, most lay people involved in university government appear to regard their participation in honorific terms. The unfortunate result for universities may be that having 'turned off' the lay influence it may be very difficult to 'turn it on' again. Yet all the evidence points to a new and pressing need to re-establish community links.

Within universities stronger management may be inimical to academic democracy. We may see an intensification of the already established trend towards the creation of a top management team on a semi-industrial model. The polytechnics and colleges have meanwhile always been closer to that model of organization with their well developed directorates. Looking even further ahead we may even see the gradual evolution of an American style of higher education government, in which the administration is firmly in charge and the faculty is reduced to a subordinate role. But such developments are not inevitable. It is possible to combine stronger management with academic democracy. But this will require a considerable readjustment of attitudes that have flourished in universities particularly during the 1960s and 1970s. First, ordinary professors and lecturers will have to become more involved in higher education policy, or else the field will be left to the academic bureaucrats. Second, they will need to cease to be so introverted and begin to pay more attention to the actual role of the university in present-day society, which may mean giving much more weight to lay voices. Third, they will have to be prepared to accept the responsibility, and occasionally the odium, for tough and unpopular decisions. For if they do not take them, others will — and without scruple or sensitivity.

It may be that in the changed circumstances of the 1980s with the urgent need for stronger management the traditional distinction between council and senate no longer makes much sense. It tends to set lay against academic interests in higher education government. It confuses by encouraging minorities to refuse to accept majority decisions. It creates an atmosphere of 'them' and 'us'. It leaves vice-chancellors and university administrations serving ambiguously competing masters. Perhaps the best solution might be to merge councils and senates to produce a streamlined mixed lay and academic body that could reconcile the competing but equally legitimate claims of stronger management and academic democracy.

8 Public Expenditure Constraints

Peter Brooke

Since 1981 the government's policy towards the funding of higher education has been one of restraint. Universities are just coming to the end of a three-year period up to 1983-84 during which their grant in respect of home students was cut by 8.5 per cent. They lost further income in the same period because their fee income from overseas students did not make up for the withdrawal of subsidy. The combined effect of the two policies on individual universities has varied substantially as the University Grants Committee (UGC) imposed differential cuts in support.

Reductions in local authority higher education have followed a slightly different pattern. The plans which are just emerging from the new National Advisory Body for Local Authority Higher Education (NAB) imply a 10 per cent cut between 1982-83 and 1984-85. These plans represent the first stage of a restructuring process which is likely to lead to a degree of concentration on the major and more cost effective institutions. The planned level of support for local authority higher education will, as in the universities, require substantial reductions in academic staffing.

Expenditure both in the university and public sectors in future years will be held within cash limits which reflect the government's pay and price assumptions. Cost increases will not necessarily be financed by extra money even if they are outside the control of institutions. Strict economy in expenditure will be required. The government is committed to a review of higher education provision for the period after 1985-86, when 18-year-old demand will have peaked.

Against a background of a forthcoming period when conventional demand would be contracting seriously and public expenditure on higher education would have to be justified all the more in terms of its contribution to future needs, the early part of this year saw publication of the final report of the wide-ranging programme of study into higher education organized by the Society for Research into Higher Education and financed by the Leverhulme Trust. This was probably the most systematic review of higher education policy by an organization outside government that has ever been undertaken.

Many of the aspects of higher education addressed by the SRHE Leverhulme Report are also part of the agenda on which the Secretary of State has asked for advice from the University Grants Committee, and of the committee's exercise to consult all universities. A similar exercise has been put in hand by the National Advisory Body for Local Authority Higher Education. I would however like to look in more detail at the principal aspects of higher education which the SRHE Leverhulme Report addresses, and to share with you current government thinking on these.

Access and Levels of Participation

So far as access is concerned, the government hopes that it will continue to be possible for all those who are qualified and willing to enter higher education to find a place somewhere, although not necessarily at the institution or in the subject of their choice. We are at present planning provision at about the lower level of demand projected in *Report on Education No.99*, which the Department of Education and Science published last April. But to achieve this there will have to be a continuing search for economy in every aspect of spending. There is a responsibility on the authorities of every institution to examine and re-examine where savings can legitimately be made. For the future, we shall be keeping the level of provision under review in the light of the demand that actually materializes and of further advice from the University Grants Committee and the National Advisory Body.

This said, however, I do not believe it is in the interests of the taxpayer, of institutions and of students themselves that courses should be provided at public expense which do little to equip students to find valuable and rewarding employment. A good start has already been made on shifting effort within higher education towards vocational courses, but I have little doubt that this should go further. Within this movement there is the additional possibility of making greater use of 2-year Higher Diploma courses, which offer good employment prospects and low cost to student and provider. Those with lower qualifications should think carefully before being tempted into spending (indeed should perhaps be strongly discouraged from spending) three years doing degrees in subjects which may well not bring them a job at the end of them. We hope that the National Advisory Body will continue to give priority to 2-year Higher Diploma courses in their planning exercises and that employers will maintain their acceptance of this kind of qualification. I recognize that any move in this direction should be accompanied by greater opportunities for those with 2-year qualifications to enhance or update them later.

We would wish to see some experimentation in less specialized degree courses. A number of institutions already adopt a multi-disciplinary approach to some degree subjects. We hope to encourage this trend as part of diversifying provision. The demands of higher education have tended to place strong pressure for specialization in sixth-form studies. Although we have made it clear that 'A' level examinations in the General Certificate of Education will be retained, we are concerned about the large proportion of able pupils who cease serious study outside their chosen specialisms after the age of 16 and we are exploring ways of broadening the curriculum of 'A' level candidates.

While we await the results of the consultative exercise, we are not at present convinced of the case for a 2-year Pass degree for the generality of students, followed by 2-year specialization for a much smaller number. It seems to be at least the majority view that for the majority of students the 3-year single or combined Honours degree provides the best preparation and training, and the best value for money. We do not think that a general change would necessarily make the best use of academic and other resources in our institutions. There would be a great deal of pressure for the norm to become a 4-year course and for grants to be extended accordingly. Few academics would feel that, in many scientific subjects, it would be possible to provide a useful training in a broader, less specific 2-year course.

Quality and Validation

It is a major concern of the government that despite the present financial climate quality and standards should be maintained and enhanced within higher education. The Committee of Vice-Chancellors and Principals (CVCP) has set up a working group to study the universities' methods and procedures for maintaining and monitoring academic quality and standards. I understand that the group will start by looking at activities related to undergraduates and at methods and procedures of external examining. The chairman of the CVCP has made it known that he believes it is possible to monitor and buttress quality without the creation of some central validating body akin to the Council for National Academic Awards (CNAA) in the local authority sector of higher education. The CNAA itself is currently engaged on a process of self-appraisal with a study into longer-term developments set up in 1981, and more recent initiative on the costs of validation.

But, as well as maintaining standards, the government also wishes to see institutions designing courses in such a way as not to deter entrepreneurial spirit but to ensure that graduates leave institutions able to make an immediate contribution. We are examining whether there is any way in which the government can help ensure that coherent signals from employers about what sort of graduates they really need are passed to institutions and to potential students.

Outside Income for Institutions

Turning to funding mechanisms for institutions and for students, there seems to be a wide spectrum of agreement that it would be desirable for institutions themselves to earn more of their income from outside government. The government is considering the recommendations of the report of the Advisory Council for Applied Research and Design (ACARD) on encouraging even stronger links between higher education and industry. We need to recognize that working with industry is no easy task for institutions, and I congratulate those who have worked hard to establish good relations with industry – I am sure that such links are of great benefit both to the institutions themselves and to their industrial partners. But although contract activity is valuable – indeed essential for the growing together of higher education and industry that is vital to our economic recovery – it does not of itself replace public funds devoted to the teaching and other basic functions of the university unless it creates, or can be exploited for, profit. If universities are to become less dependent on public funds they will also need to raise money through private and corporate giving. There is little tradition in this country of philanthropic donations to higher education institutions from large enterprises and prosperous graduates – but this is where institutions will have to look to generate increased non-specific funding.

Research Funding

A great deal has been written about the way university research should be funded. There appears to be some consensus emerging for an increase in selectivity in the funding of research both within and between institutions. This is a major policy matter which is under discussion with the UGC and the research councils. It is one of the aspects highlighted in the UGC's consultation exercise with universities and we shall all await with much interest the response of the universities to the various questions about research posed by the chairman of the UGC.

Student Support

So far as student support is concerned our system remains generous in comparison to what is available in many other countries, despite the need in recent years to reflect the general public expenditure climate when setting the level of the award. Public expenditure constraint must be expected to continue for the next few years, and to play an important part in setting the future level of the grant. The structure of the awards system reflects policy on the provision of, and access to higher education, however, and for the future this will be determined in the context of the decisions which are taken about the overall development of higher education in the light of advice from the UGC and NAB.

Centre for Policy Studies in Higher Education

The SRHE Leverhulme Report also raised the question of the establishment of a centre for higher education management and policy. The present lack of an independent focus for professionally conducted higher education policy studies is apparent. The government would be attentive to what might come out of such enterprise; and, while I can hold out no hope for government funding for it, we hope that institutions will think about whether they would wish to give support from their existing resources or can obtain some private funding. I suppose that many members of the Society for Research into Higher Education will be amongst those who would contribute greatly to a policy studies centre.

Responses to Demographic Change

Turning now to the next decade in higher education, the implications of the demographic trend are I think clear. Even if qualified demand for higher education continues to be met, there is likely to be a fall of some 15-20 per cent by 1995 in the number of students in higher education. I appreciate there is argument about the precise scale of the fall. The issue is so important to policy-making that I welcome the fullest and most rigorous debate on it. Whatever the fall, however, the opportunity may well be taken to increase certain other types of participation. I am sure there would be general agreement that participation should not be increased at the expense of standards by allowing the normal minimum qualification for higher education to be eroded significantly.

The rationalization of the higher education system to ensure that, as numbers fall, higher education continues to be provided in efficient and economically viable institutions is a major challenge to the government, to the University Grants Committee, to the National Advisory Body, and to institutions themselves.

I acknowledge that a great deal of thought needs to be given to where and how reductions in places should be made and in particular to what might be the most constructive balance between provision in the various

sectors of higher education. It may for example be argued that closure of
a university makes no academic sense while institutions in the public and
direct grant sectors catering for students with lower qualifications
remain open. But some may believe that it is desirable to maintain the
excellence of the university system by not allowing entry qualifications to
fall as overall demand for higher education decreases. I fully recognize
that closures of institutions form only one of a number of possibilities for
adjusting to the demographic trend. And I appreciate that we have to
take account of many other factors besides movement in demand, such
as the absolute needs of the country for skilled manpower irrespective of
the size of the qualified pool, and the claims for continuing education.
However, it is important, particularly given the increasing pressures on
public expenditure, that we do not shrink from discussing options
because we do not like the sound of them.

With the setting up of the National Advisory Body for Local Authority
Higher Education, the government for the first time has in place
mechanisms which should allow for the rational management of the
higher education system as it faces the challenge of declining numbers.
Development of the relationship and the partnership between the NAB
and the UGC and central government is something which will be tested
in the fullness of time. NAB itself of course is up for review during 1984
and that will be the time to take stock of current progress. The
consultation programmes currently in train initiated by the National
Advisory Body and the University Grants Committee will at least give
institutions the opportunity to assess the future realistically and publicly
to make their contribution to the way the system should be developed.
The SRHE Leverhulme reports are proving an invaluable asset to this
debate.

9 Rethinking Professional Development

Haydn Mathias and Desmond Rutherford

The future for higher education is one of uncertainty and challenge. There is uncertainty about the future level of financial support, the value of research and the quality of teaching, the demand for places, and even about the precise contributions of individual institutions. Some universities are unlikely to retain their traditionally protected positions as centres of excellence in academic research or in teaching essentially academic courses to a highly selected and homogeneous student body. The momentum for change is inexorable. To meet this challenge, institutions will need to take the professional development of their academic staff — their most expensive resource — much more seriously and more systematically than has previously been the case.

Here we analyse the SRHE Leverhulme propositions for the professional development of teaching (Bligh 1982) by drawing on the model of innovation processes developed by Becher and Kogan (1980). We will outline specific recommendations for practice that need to be implemented to ensure that the priority is given to the development of teaching that will enable the higher education system to face an uncertain future with enthusiasm and confidence.

Innovation Processes and Professional Development

Becher and Kogan describe the structure of higher education in terms of four distinct levels : central authority ; institution ; basic unit (approximating to departments) ; individual. At each level they identify two processes of interaction : the normative mode, which focuses on the maintenance of values, and the operational mode, which focuses on the execution of tasks. The normative mode is further divided into intrinsic and extrinsic elements. Interaction between adjacent levels occurs in the normative mode through the expression of judgements and in the operational mode through the allocation of tasks and resources. The resulting eight-cell matrix (Figure 9.1) provides an elegant but necessarily over-simplified model of the key structures and processes in higher education.

Figure 9.1   Structures and Processes in Higher Education

Mode ＼ Level	Individual	Basic unit	Institution	Central authority
Normative	VALUES -- judgements of quality	-- VALUES -- judgements of quality	-- VALUES -- judgements of quality	-- VALUES
	⋮	⋮	⋮	⋮
	development	development	development	development
	⋮	⋮	⋮	⋮
Operational	TASKS -- allocation of resources	-- TASKS -- allocation of resources	-- TASKS -- allocation of resources	-- TASKS

This model is undoubtedly general in its formulation. The distinctions between 'intrinsic' and 'extrinsic' values at each level may be conceptually neat but are practically difficult to separate. There is an assumption of a hierarchical process of judgements passing down from higher to lower levels even though the negotiative nature of decision-making is fully recognized by the authors. Similarly the model suggests that only adjacent levels interact although, again, it is acknowledged that the same individuals may find themselves working at different levels in the system. However, the model's simplicity does provide a refreshing clarity of perspective which opens up new ways of viewing and understanding the higher education system much as Bloom's Taxonomy of Educational Objectives (Bloom *et al.* 1956) did for assessment.

A predisposition for change is created when the equilibrium between the normative and operational modes is disturbed and values and tasks conflict. Becher and Kogan characterize innovations and developments in higher education depending on whether there is an external or an internal impetus to change, whether they are preceded by a change in values (ie normative to operational) or in tasks (ie operational to normative), and whether they challenge or confirm existing norms. A number of examples of various types of change at different levels in the system are analysed and some conclusions about the characteristics of each type can be drawn from these.

Most successful changes seem to take place at the basic unit or departmental level. Becher and Kogan emphasize the pivotal role of the basic unit in facilitating or inhibiting change as an inevitable consequence of the considerable autonomy it enjoys. Some kind of external pressure or power is usually needed. However, the nature of this external power seems more effective when it is diffuse (eg market pressures) or takes the form of incentives for growth and expansion. Prescriptive pressure seems ineffective except when it directly threatens survival. Thus external pressure emphasizing normative to operational change, which is evolutionary rather than radical in character, seems to be most successful. On the other hand, internally generated initiatives tend to be associated with operational to normative change and, again, are evolutionary and relatively slow-moving in character.

Becher and Kogan say of professional development (and student counselling):

> In both instances – student counselling and staff development – the campaigns have come and gone, leaving behind an identifiable residue but somehow failing to transform the status quo in quite the way their proponents must have wished. (p.129)

They argue that professional development was a movement generated by interest groups external to institutions which placed its main emphasis on change in the operational mode but which failed to establish significant change in existing values and norms. However, as we have pointed out, operational changes would be more likely to be successful if internally initiated, preferably with basic unit support and institutional incentive. These conditions were not prominent in the case of professional development. Following Becher and Kogan's analysis, the external impetus for professional development should have emphasized a normative to operational approach, but successful changes in this case are usually associated with diffuse external pressure or incentive. Such pressures and incentives have been applied in the past (Matheson 1981) but have tended to be too prescriptive (eg the Prices and Incomes Board's efforts to reward teaching financially) or have been lacking in conviction (eg the agreement between the University Authorities Panel and the Association of University Teachers on probation). A further difficulty is the essentially radical nature of professional development which brings into question the competence of academic staff and so, inevitably, provokes resistance.

As Bligh has pointed out, institutions have not exercised their power to underline the importance of the professional development of teaching. There are neither extrinsic rewards (Bligh 1982, p.75) nor sanctions for poor teaching (p.80). Participation in professional development activities is for the most part, certainly in universities, voluntary and unrewarded, with the inevitable consequences that these policies imply. Bligh, like Becher and Kogan, identifies the lack of institutional support for teaching as the key factor which explains the limited impact of professional development:

> The perceptions of academic staff can only be changed by institutional policies to reward teaching being explicitly stated and evidently, if not openly, implemented. (p.75)

From Propositions to Practice

It is obvious to us that specific recommendations need to be implemented at the central authority, institution, basic unit and individual
level in order to ensure that the proper priority is given to the
development of teaching. It is to these recommendations that we now
turn our attention. Bligh puts forward recommendations for central
authority initiatives but cautions that professional development cannot
be effectively promoted by a 'highly centralized and authoritarian
system' (Bligh 1982, p.86). He argues for an independent national body
responding to demand, providing co-ordination and focus, offering
courses, pursuing research, and promoting and reviewing policies. Such
a body would be financed by the interest accrued on a levy on
institutions, the capital being used to pay institutions according to the
time spent by their staff on centrally-organized activities, although,
paradoxically, fees for such courses would also be charged.

There is much to be commended in these recommendations. However, attempts to apply extrinsic financial rewards to professional development have been resisted in the past and have ultimately failed. As a
strategy, the recommendations can be seen as operational to normative
in character (ie operating through resource allocation) but as Becher and
Kogan's analysis implies, such changes – to be successful – need to be
internally rather than externally initiated except where external pressure
is 'inexorable'. However, they can also be viewed as normative to
operational in character (ie through policy advocacy and review) but this
would seem to require a greater level and more sensitive influence of
external power.

In their analysis of central authority power Becher and Kogan note
that this is severely constrained by the moderating effect of institutional
and basic unit representation on central bodies and by the limited
opportunities available to influence resource allocation, most of which
represents relatively fixed salary and other running costs. However, this
picture has changed. Government intervention in the guise of efficiency
and public accountability has broken through the protective barrier of
the University Grants Committee (UGC) to influence higher education
policy more directly. Levels of staffing, the question of tenure, the
balance of subject offered in any one institution and the promotion of
research in certain subject areas reflect this highly directed interventionist line. Universities are facing inexorable external pressures for change
in these areas from the central authority level as well as less threatening
pressures and incentives in the areas of continuing education, overseas
student recruitment and part-time degree courses.

It would seem to us that such a climate of uncertainty, where existing
values and practices are being challenged and unfrozen, can provide

significant opportunities to promote effective policies for professional development. Central authority power, if skilfully handled, can be used to bring about change of a more enduring nature. We would, therefore, go further than Bligh, while noting his cautions, in arguing for greater central initiative and intervention in the promotion of professional development. For example, as well as calling for a clearer policy statement, institutions might be required to set aside a proportion of their income for professional development and account for its use on a regular basis through a form of audited self-evaluation. They might also be required to demonstrate as part of the accountability process that appointment and promotion criteria more positively recognize activities in teaching as well as in research and that opportunities for professional development have been taken advantage of. In these respects we agree more closely with the propositions put forward by Lindop *et al.* (1982) in the same volume as Bligh's recommendations (particularly propositions 1.06,1.08,1.17,1.22 to 1.25,2.03 and 2.14).

The need to respond in a more coherent and co-ordinated manner to external and accountability pressures, together with the lack of staff mobility, will lead to increasing institutional influence over the lives of its members. Bligh's propositions on the institutionalization of professional development in many ways recognize this changing situation. However, he is careful to emphasize the need for continuing sensitivity to local and individual circumstances although this does lead to a certain degree of ambivalence in his position. One of his main propositions is for the establishment of a central professional development committee with 'institutional authorization at the highest level' (Bligh 1982, p.78) coupled with a responsiveness to local needs. Many such committees already exist but their recommendations and initiatives are regularly ignored both by basic units and by individuals, reflecting the current lack of status accorded to professional development. However, the type of committee suggested by Bligh would have much wider functions and powers and include receiving regular professional development plans; initiating, developing and evaluating professional development activities; and allocating relevant resources.

This proposition begs many questions (eg of implementation, membership, accountability and administration) and its all-embracing nature suggests a claustrophobic paternalism which many academics would find alien. If we accept that some form of stronger central institutional body is desirable, then the gains to individual, basic unit, and institution need to be more clearly spelt out, as does the nature of the power it would possess.

As a 'normative' to 'operational' change the proposition benefits from a consonance with existing values in that similar yet weaker bodies already exist. However, as an internally-generated change it appears too radical in Becher and Kogan's terms to achieve success. It would need to be backed by an external source of power or incentive from central authority level of the kind we have already described: ie accountability, resource control and criteria for appointments, tenure and promotion. Without such backing from or links with the central authority level, it is difficult to see how this proposition, as the many similar propositions which have gone before it, would be readily accepted at the institutional level.

At the basic unit and individual level Bligh's propositions offer mainly description and analysis rather than recommendations. Overall, his main recommendations lie at levels above the basic unit for providing a context for professional development which would create a climate and conditions where teaching would be valued and rewarded. Bligh views the basic unit, the social and working group with which academics primarily identify, as the main instrument for professional development. The critical role of the basic unit as a determinant of change is also stressed by Becher and Kogan. There is a need for change to accord with the values of the basic unit and to be recreated by those it affects. However, these authors also see the basic unit as being essentially conservative and highly resistant to change.

Although the basic unit is undoubtedly a powerful group it is easy to forget that it is composed of highly individualistic professionals with a fair degree of personal autonomy in both teaching and research who work together as a rational basic unit for only some of the time. Their main driving force is personal reputation and esteem in their academic work recognized not only by their basic unit colleagues but by the extra-institutional professional and other groups to which they belong or which they value: their priorities are not necessarily those of the basic unit. As both Bligh and Becher and Kogan indicate, the professional development of teaching can pose a threat to their self-esteem since it implies that the essentially private activity of teaching becomes open to public scrutiny and to the judgement of those who are apparently more expert. The initiation and implementation of change at the basic unit and individual levels, therefore, do need, as Bligh is at pains to point out, a significant degree of understanding and sensitivity.

The Institutionalization of Professional Development

Although the acceptance of change by the basic units and the individuals which comprise them is a crucial factor for success, we would agree with the general implication of Bligh's propositions that change has to be initiated at higher levels in the system to create a driving force and climate whereby teaching is valued and rewarded. In times of expansion this strategy is probably ineffectual, as some of Becher and Kogan's examples demonstrate. However, a period of contraction and disruption to the system, where central authority and institutional influence begin to challenge the more traditional sources of academic security, offers positive opportunities to move and 'refreeze' the equilibrium of values and practices to a new position. In other words, it is possible to create a context which provides the previously and largely missing external source of pressure and incentive in Becher and Kogan's model of change. The initiatives at central authority and institutional levels already described themselves contribute leadership components which are also decisive factors in change.

The head of department is a key leadership figure at the basic unit level, and indeed at the institutional level, but is one which is in need of professional development as Bligh suggests. Much more has to be done in the immediate future to clarify and develop the role of the head, not only for the sake of professional development but also because this role has now become significantly more complex and demanding (cf Startup 1979, Becher 1982). However, in some aspects of professional development the head of department, who is a colleague as well as leader, may well be too close to the situation to be effective (Bligh 1982, p.76) and a more distant yet connected source of leadership at a higher level needs to be available. Although central institutional figures fulfil this role, they are possibly too remote in their influence and understanding. This leaves an institutional role which has grown more by historical accident than by design, namely, that of the dean of faculty. The role of dean has probably even greater potential for development in management and organizational terms than that of the head of department (Morgan and Davies 1982) and is one which could potentially fulfil an important professional development leadership role as it occupies a unique position between institutional and basic unit level.

Responsibility for professional development at basic unit and individual level is vitally important if it is to have meaning and value. However, professional development also requires a tangible local organizational framework if it is not to become a transitory phenomenon characteristic of self-help schemes. We suggest two ways in which this might be achieved whilst allowing a large measure of autonomy and freedom of action to exist. Both are based on a concept of audited self-evaluation accountability (Open University 1982). First, within a set of broad guidelines each individual would submit to, and in consultation with, his head of department or dean an annual report of activities and plans which would include research, administration and teaching. These reports would serve as a basis for discussion of the professional development needs of an individual as well as evidence to be submitted in support of applications for tenure or promotion.

Second, at the basic unit or faculty level we suggest a local professional development committee which would then organize activities tailored to local needs. These might include developing existing teaching skills, organizing seminars to introduce new ideas, undertaking reviews of the curriculum and promoting teaching innovations and experiments. Such group-based activity would draw teaching out of its individual and private world and make it more clearly a common responsibility. Funds for the local programme would be available from the central professional development committee's budget to which the local committee would have to account within a broad rather than detailed set of guidelines.

Although in some institutions this kind of local committee scheme has been tried, with perhaps disappointing results, in the situation we envisage there would be an accountability chain in the most general sense all the way up the system to central authority level which would provide an appropriate power context. The Council for National Academic Awards (CNAA) in the polytechnic sector potentially offers such a context; in the university sector the UGC will have to provide the stimulus as a matter of urgency. Viewed in Becher and Kogan's terms as a 'normative' to 'operational' change strategy, it satisfies the conditions of the presence of an external source of power or incentive, is consonant with local values, and is evolutionary in character in as far as basic units work through an open committee system which is essentially under the control of its members within broad lines of accountability.

Conclusion

We have attempted to scrutinize Bligh's major propositions for the professional development of teaching in terms of a model of innovation processes derived directly from higher education. We seem to have used the term 'power' quite frequently since the model identifies it as an essential component of change but alongside other decisive factors. This is an important point. Power in itself is not sufficient to bring about change in professional development and in many ways is incompatible with the concept. However, it is a necessary, and up to now largely missing factor which influences the impact and effectiveness of professional development. Viewed in another way it is the complement to responsibility in that it represents the accountability dimension of professional freedom of action. Paradoxically, the greatest opportunities for the advancement of professional development present themselves at a time of contraction and survival. Periods of expansion have a habit of diffusing effort and absorbing initiatives within current values and practices. Severe disruption, on the other hand, can cause the necessary cracks in the system leading to the unfreezing and disequilibrium which are a precondition for change.

It is under these conditions, as the balance of power shifts decisively towards central authority, that values and practices are directly questioned and challenged, and are susceptible to change. What follows, however, is important. A sustained driving force is necessary to shift the equilibrium of values and practices to a new position and hold it there until re-freezing takes place. This is not to argue for disruption as a strategy for change but rather to recognize that positive change can come about through disruptive circumstances. Professional development is at a low ebb and is not likely to re-emerge as a concept of consequence if left to the mercy of random forces. If professional development is to have a significant future, we are convinced that bold initiatives and positive advocacy have to be made now before the system settles into a modified configuration.

References

Becher, T. (1982) *Managing Basic Units* A report of the IMHE Special Topic Workshop, Paris 29 November - 1 December (the Institutional Management in Higher Education Programme of the OECD Centre for Educational Research and Innovation).

Becher, T. and Kogan, M. (1980) *Process and Structure in Higher Education* London : Heinemann

Bligh, D. (1982) The professional development of teaching? In Bligh, D. (Editor) *Accountability or Freedom for Teachers?* Guildford : Society for Research into Higher Education

Bloom, B.S. *et al.* (1956) *Taxonomy of Educational Objectives, Handbook 1 : Cognitive Domain* New York : David McKay Inc.

Lindop, N. *et al.* (1982) Teachers and staffing. In Bligh, D. (Editor) *Accountability or Freedom for Teachers?* Guildford : Society for Research into Higher Education

Matheson, C.C. (1982) *Staff Development Matters* Norwich : Co-ordinating Committee for the Training of University Teachers

Morgan, J.L. and Davies, A.W. (1982) The politics of institutional change. In Wagner, L. (Editor) *Agenda for Institutional Change in Higher Education* Guildford : Society for Research into Higher Education

Open University (1982) *Approaches to Evaluation : Audited Self-Evaluation* (Course E 364, block 2, part 4) Milton Keynes : Open University Press

Startup, R. (1979) *The University Teacher and His World* Farnborough : Saxon House

10 Sources of Academic Resistance

William Fleming and Desmond Rutherford

Why have the 'Recommendations for Learning' drawn up by Donald Bligh for the SRHE Leverhulme programme of study provoked little or no reaction among academics? Why have only the most vaguely-worded recommendations commanded general assent? Why have specific recommendations unleashed a barrage of hostility and criticism? We do not believe that the fault lies with the recommendations. We believe they should have provided a much-needed stimulus to future development in teaching and learning in higher education. Yet reaction to them is likely to reinforce the widely-held opinion that they refer to matters best left to individual academics.

Theory-of-Action

We will here analyse those recommendations, together with their supporting arguments, that were concerned with 'The need for more professionalism'. We will draw on the Theory-of-Action perspective, both as it was originally developed by Argyris and Schon (1974) and as it has since been conceived by Heller (1982), who pointed out that it has particular relevance to the problems confronting higher education. He emphasizes that academics have considerable insight into the problems they face and recognize a range of possible solutions. Yet their difficulties in solving some problems are sometimes overwhelming: there is insight but not effective action. To explain this he argues that, on analysis, the actions of most individuals and organizations, including academics and their institutions of higher education, can be seen to be informed by tacit 'governing values' of which they are largely unaware and over which they have little control. The governing values, together with the corresponding behavioural strategies, constitute a first model of Theory-in-Use (Model 1), given in Table 10.1. Academics whose actions are informed by Model 1 are both secretive and

Table 10.1   The Model 1 Theory-In-Use

GOVERNING VALUES	BEHAVIOURAL STRATEGIES	EXAMPLES OF SPECIFIC ACTIONS	ANALYSIS CATEGORIES
Define your goals in private with the minimum of consultation	Design and manage the environment unilaterally	Make up your mind on each issue privately	Unilateral decision
		Act on your view	Unilateral action
		Avoid public discussion which might refute your view	Advocacy without inquiry
Maximize winning and minimize losing to achieve your goals	Own and control the task	Seek responsibility for tasks	Control task
		Cajole others into agreeing with you	Control others
Minimize generating and expressing negative feelings	Unilaterally protect yourself	Withhold your own feelings and so avoid personal confrontation	Protect self
		Speak in abstractions to limit your accountability	Unillustrated attribution/ evaluation/inference
Be rational	Unilaterally protect others from being hurt	Don't express negative feelings about others	Withhold information
		Keep others from exposure to blame without their knowledge	Protect others

competitive. They decide privately what goals they want to achieve and work purposefully towards them. They seek to manipulate and control colleagues and students and to increase their own influence and power. At the same time, they avoid personal confrontations that could become emotionally charged. The evidence for the pervasive nature of Model 1 is well documented, and we have some evidence for it of our own, from an analysis of what on the surface seemed to be a 'good' seminar (Fleming and Rutherford 1983).

The consequences of Model 1 are generally both unwanted and unintended and bring an escalation of existing problems as well as creating new problems. There are two reasons for this: first, academics who seek to achieve their unilateral and undiscussable goals by controlling and manipulating others provoke either increasing resistance or superficial compliance; secondly, inferences and evaluations of colleagues' ideas, behaviour and competence are neither made explicit nor are they tested, with the inevitable result that errors and misunderstandings are perpetuated and compounded rather than resolved. One of the greatest difficulties is that our governing values and corresponding strategies are so thoroughly absorbed that we are unable to recognize their causal role in our ineffectiveness. Moreover, problems can only be solved within the parameters of this model when governing values remain unquestioned and unchanged.

Table 10.2   The Model 2 Theory-In-Use

GOVERNING VALUES	BEHAVIOURAL STRATEGIES	EXAMPLES OF SPECIFIC ACTIONS	ANALYSIS CATEGORIES
Production of valid information	Advocate your own personal ideas/opinions and invite inquiry/dispute/ confrontation	Express your own ideas and invite reactions	Advocacy with inquiry
	Express and test your opinions of/reactions to the ideas/actions of others	Do not withold negative feelings but explain these	Evaluation with data.
		Refute incorrect statements made by others but give evidence	Confrontation with data
Free and informed choice in decision-making	Work with others and share power in order to solve common problems	Co-operate rather than compete with others	Co-operation
		Do not attempt to control/ manipulate others	Openness
Commitment to decisions made and to their evaluation	Emphasize directly observable data	Refer to concrete examples to support your views	Advocacy with data
	Protect self and others jointly with an orientation towards growth	Confrontation on difficult issues	Confrontation with data

Although our actions in general are guided by this model (1) of Theory-in-Use, values and strategies that we proclaim in public — our Espoused Theory — may be quite different. In other words, we may claim in all innocence and with our deepest conviction that we act in one way — according to our Espoused Theory — yet, in practice, our actions are informed and determined by a quite different Theory-on-Use. To take a straightforward example, an academic may claim to seek student reaction during a lecture but rarely looks at his audience or gives the students an opportunity to ask questions. The differences between his Espoused Theory and his Theory-in-Use, if identified and explored, could provide a very powerful impetus to change.

It is said that academics whose governing values are directly opposite to those of Model 1 are informed in their actions by a sub-set of it (Model 1a). In decision-making situations such academics appear diffident and indecisive, guided by pragmatism rather than conviction. Their relationships with others are characterized by a frankness which is often tinged with criticism and sarcasm. While Model 1 and Model 1a strategies can solve problems of a routine nature they cannot solve the type of non-routine problems that arise in a time of crisis.

Heller goes on to describe a second model of Theory-in-Use (Model 2) whose governing values and strategies are given in Table 10.2. Academics whose actions are informed by Model 2 are both open and co-operative. They seek to work with others to explore problems, to gather information, to reach decisions, to plan actions and to evaluate the consequences. They do not shrink from necessary but productive confrontations with others even at the risk of provoking heated arguments and bruised feelings. They are able to reflect on the causal role of their governing values and to change them when needed.

Heller argues that the values and strategies of Model 2 enable academics to co-operate with each other and to solve their common problems, especially at a time of crisis and change. However, it is extremely difficult for people to change governing values that are linked with strategies that have been acquired over many years and which they mistakenly believe to have served them well. Such values and strategies are generally so well learned and so much part of automatic behaviour that even an intellectual and emotional commitment to change from Model 1 to Model 2 may not be sufficient.

Rhetoric

In the analysis which follows we show that the radical recommendations and supporting arguments listed by Bligh under 'The need for more professionalism' are based on Model 2 values. Some of these may command the general assent of academics at the level of Espoused Theory. But certain of them conflict with the Model 1 values that typically inform the actions of academics. Our thesis is that Bligh's recommendations could only be followed up in a 'Model 2 world' and that the world of academia, despite its Espoused claim to the contrary, acts predominantly according to Model 1 – increasingly so during a time of recession. Resistance to the sort of radical change suggested by Bligh can therefore be confidently predicted. We will also argue that because Bligh's recommendations are, in the main, presented without a detailed strategy for implementation, their impact, as Heller has emphasized, will be minimal.

Recommendation 1 is that 'the design of courses and the processes of teaching, learning and assessment be more open that they are at present, and subject to regular peer review.' Bligh argues that for this recommendation to be effective, 'a process is needed of working together openly, honestly, without presenting a front and without fear of humiliation'. This process would obviously require such skills as are postulated in the second model of Theory-in-Use: the ability to *cooperate rather than compete* and the confidence in personal relationships to *surface and confront threatening issues*. Peer review is defined by Bligh as 'a process of professional observation, discussion and judgement... by teachers of teachers.' Here the emphasis is very much on the *production of valid information* and a willingness to *test inferences and evaluations* derived from that information – which are again Model 2 strategies. At the level of

Espoused Theory, the generality of academics may be willing to support this recommendation or, at least, to withhold doubts and criticisms. After all, few will wish to prevent (other) teachers working together in the positive way that seems to be implied, and of course many will point out in all sincerity that this is already accepted practice in academic life. However, if the recommendation had included specific proposals for action then perhaps the many unsuspected deviations academics made from Model 2 would have been more apparent. Peer review may be open, honest and non-threatening at the level of Espoused Theory. Nevertheless, in practice, the increased exposure increases vulnerability, and Model 1 values and strategies come into play as a way of reducing the threat and defending both individuals and the system. Information is more likely to be withheld, distorted, or expressed in abstractions, in order to *control the task* and *protect self* (Model 1). The implementation of Recommendation 1 therefore becomes increasingly difficult. Staff would be quite incapable of involving themselves in any meaningful form of professional peer review. It is hardly surprising that few examples of it have been reported (see Mathias and Rutherford 1983 for an analysis of the history of the Course Evaluation Scheme at the University of Birmingham and an alternative explanation for its early successes and eventual demise).

Recommendation 1.1 is that curricula in higher education 'neglect neither practice nor theory, and that they take account of the needs both of society and the individual.' It would be too harsh a judgement to suggest that this recommendation is little more than meaningless rhetoric. However, it is phrased in so general and innocuous a manner that few academics will regard it as worthy of more than passing consideration. Because the recommendation does not advocate specific proposals for action, most academics will have little difficulty in encompassing its spirit within their Espoused Theory. Nevertheless, if there was ever the possibility of implementing it resistance would be quickly mobilized, probably under the guise of 'academic freedom'. Academics guided by Model 1 strategies such as *unilateral decision* and *control task* would be most likely to regard prescriptions for course development as a threat to their autonomy and would act accordingly.

Recommendation 1.2 that 'Courses should be manifestly student-centred' is again drafted in such a vague manner as to command general support among academics at the Espoused Theory level. The concept that a university is 'a place of learning for both students and staff' finds ready acceptance among academics. However, although this recommendation is in itself acceptable, the methods by which Bligh suggests it is made operational are much more problematic. The first of these (Recommendation 1.2a) proposes that 'Teachers in higher education should explain clearly to students the aims, structures, procedures, requirements and methods of assessment (if relevant) of their courses' and that these should be 'open to criticism from students and staff alike'. Many staff would argue that this is standard practice in their depart-ments, with students' comments being welcomed through their repre-sentatives on appropriate departmental committees. We are suggesting that while such openness does occur at the Espoused level, the practice of assessment, for example, is still characterized by Model 1 strategies and values, the assumptions behind which are not questioned. The line beyond which 'academic authority' exercises *unilateral control* over the task is clearly drawn in practice, even if not articulated. The line is not likely to become 'open to criticism', ie discussable, in a way which is committed to gathering valid data about its underlying values and effects and to abandoning it should a better alternative be suggested. This very clearly demands the Model 2 skill of being willing to *advocate your own ideas* (and opinions), *invite inquiry* and *change* them in the light of discussion. Academics programmed with Model 1 values and strategies are likely to view this recommendation with trepidation as a very serious threat to their own control of the course and, perhaps worse, as opening up the 'hornets nest' of student criticism. In practice then, this is extremely unlikely to occur as two of the most potent Model 1 strategies are to *control the task* and *protect self*.

Similar comments and reservations about defining and controlling the task apply Recommendation 1.2b, which proposes that 'Teachers should help students to take maximum responsibility for their own learning'. This appears to envisage a much greater degree of autonomy for students in their learning but not to the extent that teachers should 'renounce their responsibility for students' learning' (a Model 1a strategy). Boud and his co-authors (1981) have argued that currently accepted methods of teaching in higher education create despondency, stifle creativity and foster disenchantment among students. They offer some alternatives which provide a much greater degree of student autonomy; but it is likely that their arguments and suggestions are both too radical and too strident to have much impact on the mainstream of academic practice.

Recommendation 1.2c includes an explicit criticism of courses which focus 'upon the exposition of a series of topics by teachers'. This suggestion is aimed at replacing the lecture system, on which so much teaching in higher education is based, with more task-centred and project-based courses. However, the lecture is the one teaching method which most naturally corresponds to Model 1 values and strategies. Typically, the teacher defines the aims and objectives of the lecture without consultation with his students *(unilateral decisions)*, allows them little opportunity to interrupt or ask questions *(advocacy without inquiry)* and controls the situation to maintain his own authority *(protect self)*. As a consequence, academics can be expected to be highly committed to the lecture as a method of teaching and to react most strongly to criticisms of its use.

Recommendation 1.2d proposes that 'Styles of teaching should be developed such that working relationships between teachers and students are valued by both'. At the level of Espoused Theory all teachers and students would no doubt support the notion of effective working relationships. Yet these are very difficult to establish and maintain on the basis of Model 1 values and strategies, especially at times of crisis and threat. The problem of effective working relationships is one not only between teacher and students but also among teachers themselves, especially in large institutions. The result, according to Hogan (1980) is that, in general, institutions are no longer capable of reaching a consensus over common goals and that:

> Many of our larger organisations now look remarkably like feudal systems with great departmental barons competing for ever larger shares of the spoils to support sectional interests. (Hogan 1980, p.130)

Recommendation 1.3 is a plea for 'Institutional reviews of their assessment procedures'. Bligh offers a brief and spirited criticism of the 'crudity' of many assessment procedures but, unfortunately, offers no concrete proposals for carrying out such 'reviews'. The difficulties involved for a department, never mind an institution, in reviewing its assessment procedures in a way that goes beyond the usual academic rhetoric are, as we have implied, virtually insurmountable. If such reviews were attempted the Theory-of-Action would predict that the underlying governing values would remain tacit and unchallenged. It is unlikely therefore that consideration of the more fundamental issues of relationships in teaching, learning and assessment to which Radley (1980) refers would emerge as a basis for future action.

In Recommendation 2 (Professional Improvement) Bligh suggests the appointment of staff 'to have special expertise in the study of teaching and learning of their subject' who would 'with their colleagues, work on the design and management of courses'. In addition, 'Professional development units should concentrate upon the education and training of such specialists and ... new staff.' These are controversial suggestions that the generality of academic staff will find unacceptable, even at the level of Espoused Theory. Again, these two recommendations will appear to many academics to strike at the heart of academic freedom and the implication that there is a general body of 'knowledge of the principles of course design, research into teaching, learning and assessment methods' that can be applied to particular problems in particular disciplines is not widely accepted. Academics programmed with Model 1 values and strategies will be highly resistant to relin-quishing the almost total control and ownership of their courses that is implied by working with these new 'specialists'. An extended role for professional development units with an emphasis on 'education and training' implies a lack of competency among academics that they would certainly resist (as we have already argued, *protect self* is one of the most potent Model 1 strategies). Rutherford (1982) has suggested that the role of those involved in professional development units is essentially supportive and enabling rather than prescriptive as implied in these recommendations.

Reaction

Initial reaction to Bligh's recommendations at our own university was extremely hostile. Most were passed over as being of common sense and hardly warranting further discussion (which, of course, is consistent with debate at the Espoused Theory level). Recommendations 1.2c (criticism of the lecture as a method of teaching), 2.1 and 2.2 (professional improvement) were severely criticized as our analysis has predicted.

It would appear that similar sentiments and reservations were expressed at a conference in November 1982. The convener's report (Stodd 1982) mentions that the recommendations headed 'Professional Peer Review' 'commanded general assent and were seen to represent good academic practice.' However, concern was again expressed about Recommendation 1.2c and 'several comments argued that there was a valid place for exposition.' Many reservations were also expressed about Recommendations 2.1 and 2.2. Stodd's report also hints at the 'insight but no effective action' paradox that we referred to earlier.

Conclusion

The consultative process that produced the 'Recommendations for Learning' can be readily classified as Model 2 strategy: the recommendations themselves are consistent with Model 2 values. The difficulty is that the prevailing Theory-in-Use model among the generality of academics is Model 1. Thus, as we have argued in this paper, those recommendations which propose specific actions will conflict with Model 1 and will be rejected; those more general — and less threatening — recommendations may command assent at the level of Espoused Theory. The inescapable conclusion is that the 'Recommendations for Learning' will have little impact on academic practice.

The Theory-of-Action perspective provides an elegant analysis for the unfavourable reception that Bligh's recommendations have received. Yet, to some at least, his arguments are persuasive and — especially with regard to students — humane. Academics cannot afford to be complacent about the current status of teaching and learning in higher education. There is much that needs to be done and this is well recognized. The Theory-of-Action perspective explains why not enough of this concern and insight has been translated into action, it also explains why, where 'change' has come about, the underlying values and relationships have remained unaffected: for example, where 'continuous assessment' has in practice been 'continuous examination'. The task of re-orientating the governing values that inform academics' behaviour from Model 1 to Model 2 is a tremendous, perhaps an impossible, challenge. Yet this, we argue, must be the focus of professional development in the future

References

Argyris, C. and Schon, D. (1974) *Theory in Practice:Increasing Professional Effectiveness* San Francisco : Jossey-Bass

Bligh, D. (1982) Recommendations for Learning. In Bligh, D. (Editor) *Professionalism and Flexibility in Learning* 11-12. Guildford : Society for Research into Higher Education

Boud, D. (Editor) (1981) *Developing Student Autonomy in Learning* London: Kogan Page

Fleming, W. and Rutherford, D. (1983) Professional development: from insight to action. In *Improving University Teaching: Ninth International Conference* 384-394. Maryland, USA : University of Maryland

Heller, J.F. (1982) *Increasing Faculty and Administrative Effectiveness* San Francisco : Jossey-Bass

Hogan, D. (1980) New directions in the study of innovation *Royal Air Force Bulletin* 18,127-134

Mathias, H. and Rutherford, D. (1983) Decisive factors affecting change: a case study *Studies in Higher Education* 8,45-55

Radley, A. (1980) Student Learning as social practice. In Salmon, P. (Editor) *Coming to Know* London : Routledge and Kegan Paul

Rutherford, D. (1982) Developing university teaching: a strategy for revitalization *Higher Education* 11,177-191

Stodd, G.J. (1982) *Follow-up Conference. Teaching and Learning in Universities, Polytechnics and Colleges* Unpublished report

Part 3
Expectations and Experiences

11 The 'Expectations of Higher Education' Project

Maurice Kogan

In 1980 the Department of Education and Science (DES) invited my department to mount a research project which would throw light upon the expectations that different groups possessed of higher education. They wanted research which would help policy makers by exposing the range of thinking about what was expected of the higher education enterprise. Few surprises emerge from this complex and difficult project, which does, however, like much research before it, serve to warn against some of the more simple-minded tenets of faith about what the economy needs and what higher education can provide.

The Expectations of Higher Education survey will be fully reported in a synopsis and in typescript accounts of each of the main sub-projects now being run off by the DES. It consisted of four main parts which varied in their methodologies. The *survey of student expectations* was based upon a questionnaire to which 3800 students responded. It is still being written up and references to it here will be of a tentative nature. The largest and most important component of the project, the *expectations of employers*, was conducted through 201 taped interviews with employers involved in the recruitment policies and practices in 139 firms. The sub-project on *institutions providing higher education* consisted of a case study of a college of education, a university and a polytechnic and was based on a total of 130 interviews with staff and 22 interviews with students. And, finally, there was a *survey of careers advisers* based primarily on questionnaires.

Before I speak about the implications of the studies I should make plain my relationship to the project. I was one of three directors, the others being Norman Lindop and Harold Silver, but I was the grant holder. My own role has been to make sure that all parts of the project were written up and made available in a reasonably synoptic form and that their policy implications were drawn out. The running of the project and the methods adopted in it were the largely autonomous decisions of

99

the project convenor, Mrs. J. Roizen, who is also the principal author of the employers' survey. I believe the issues raised in the research and for further analysis are important and although the methodologies and findings are not mine, I use it to signal issues which ought to be discussed publicly.

Main Themes

The expectations project must be set in the context of a long history of policy statements and assumptions about the relationship between higher education and the needs of the employment market. The ways in which education seems to meet employment needs are complex and various. Here we can follow Buley's classifications[1]. Higher education might add value to the formation of reinforcement of quite general characteristics in employment recruits. Or it might produce 'finished goods' in the sense that specific knowledge and skills adaptable to specialized employment are provided. Or, again, the 'basic raw materials approach' assumes that higher education enables employers to select potentially able employees through the screening facilities which it provides. In practice, of course, all three modes might operate at once in some kind of loose coupled hierarchy. Constraints upon employers' freedom, however, are obvious. They have to recruit certain kinds of graduates to fill vacancies where specific skills and knowledge training are imperative; and the costs of training within industry affect the degree of eclecticism with which employers can approach the task of recruitment. Moreover, and this point can be inferred from the employers' survey, observers of labour market patterns such as Pearson[2] have noted a stratification in which employers seek very high level quality graduates as potential recruits for the most senior forms of general management, a second level, which might also include people of very high ability but will be more concerned with the recruitment of specifically trained professionals and specialists, and a third, more general and catch-all category which will include recruitment for less senior management roles.

One of the fascinations of the study is, however, how one complex block of institutions interacts with a second. The variability of employers' needs is capable of setting up equal variability of response in the providing institutions. Thus the 'added value' approach sits comfortably with the feeling expressed by academics in our institutional studies that in helping students to develop academic interests and as individuals, they are, at the same time, meeting a major demand from the employment market. That is an assumption reinforced by many of the statements in our employers' study and puts into question the extent to which institutions need to manipulate the balance between different kinds of courses according to the different employers' approaches towards recruitment. The changing balances of courses can be analysed in those terms as well as in terms of the development of academic disciplines from the perspective of academe itself.

A further set of points then concerns the extent to which there are mechanisms and processes by which the two sets of institutions find relationships with each other. Here our study of the careers advisers and of other devices both within higher education and employment and between them become relevant.

Finally, we note the ways in which students, concerned as they are about employment prospects as well as with the other values which higher education might advance on their behalf, find accommodations within these complex interactions of employment demands and institutional offerings.

Major Implications of the Study

The first major implication of the study was that simple-minded attempts to equate the needs of the employment market to specific and highly instrumental modes of training and education do not conform with what employers or students or higher education institutions believed to be useful. Whilst some employers certainly found shortcomings in higher education, for the most part they seemed well pleased with its eclecticism and flexibility. The reader of the sub-projects gets an overwhelming sense of the complexity of wants, needs, demands and expectations and the fact that mechanisms have been set up intuitively to meet them. The research thus replicates findings from similar research elsewhere, from Japan for example.[3]

Secondly, the employers and institutional studies confirmed that demands for graduates were difficult and diverse to aggregate. They varied not only between employment firms but also within them.

Because employers might follow the different approaches just referred to, they had several visions of the desirable qualities in graduates which, again, however, could not be clearly defined or elaborated let alone aggregated. Even employers located in the same production or service sector differed in the type of graduates they sought to recruit and these could vary, of course, according to the occupation or function for which recruitment was undertaken.

If, then, employers' demands were various, the authors of the employers' study pointed to a hierarchy of preferences among different higher education institutions as sources of recruitment. In crude terms, and I will state a few reservations later, universities were preferred to polytechnics, and the colleges of higher education hardly entered employers' consciousnesses at all. Within the university sector, Oxbridge was sui generis and a few other highly esteemed universities were sources for regular recruitment. The indifference to the products of polytechnics expressed by some respondents was related not so much to what happened in the courses as to the assumed academic quality of their intakes. Here the screening hypothesis is strongly endorsed. Yet not all recruiters looked for graduates with very good degrees: some preferred to recruit at the middle level of the degree range. Notions of academic excellence were not, therefore, sustained unalloyed. But academic ability was prized and was the factor underlying the differential status accorded to different institutions. Many of the 139 firms where interviews were completed recruited from a relatively small core of institutions, although some might visit many more.

As a result, to quote Roizen and Jepson:

> ...public sector higher education does not... appear to have achieved the status intended for it.... Most employing organisations continued to attach the highest importance in selecting graduates – or at least in short listing them – to the 'A' level grades they achieved three or four years earlier. It was thus the nature and qualification of students at entry, and the generalised status of institutions associated with this factor, which figured as the principal component of institutional identity in employers' minds.... The effect of this (was) not balanced by any general perception of the special, academic, vocational or social value of a public sector degree.

At the same time as they prized academic ability, employers prized other personal attributes associated with higher education. While many employers valued particular skills such as numeracy, ability to work in groups and to write reports, many were less concerned with what was taught on degree courses than with the development of general and personal qualities, with graduates who had met a variety of people, for example, or who engaged in extra curricular activities, or who were 'outward bound' types. A number of respondents emphasized the importance of practical abilities, pragmatic intelligence, commonsense and commercial awareness in graduates. Some of these qualities might be related to practical work in case studies, work experience, being taught by those with work experience, or work experience unconnected with the course. These preferences do not sit easily with the fact that employers preferred university graduates to those from polytechnics.

At this point a reservation must be stated. In the Brunel study the employers from large firms were situated at a national headquarters and sufficient account could not be taken of regional or local recruitment or certain kinds of recruitment within the same or other firms. And the sample may not have picked up enough of the specialist occupations into which roughly a third of graduates go.[4]

Shortage of Graduates

Employers spoke to few absolute shortages of applicants except in specialist areas. Generally, recruiters suffered from too many rather than too few applicants. Their problem was sorting them out. As we have seen, to them the most serious shortage was that of high ability graduates.

Some companies distinguished between distinctive broad occupational streams associated with degree subject requirements and occupations not demanding specialist pre-requisites. Certainly some specialist occupations led to demands for specialist degree preparation. But there remained wide variation in the qualities looked for in graduates even within occupational streams. Thus firms of accountants embodied varying attitudes towards qualifications. Some looked for business studies or accountancy degrees. Others emphatically recruited able people from whatever discipline. Computer firms displayed a similar variability.

The Value of Higher Education

What value did employers ascribe to higher education? A few employers believed that they must come to higher education if they were to get good recruits, and thus seemed prepared to ignore, or to take for granted, any value that might be added by higher education.

But few had doubts about the value added by higher education. They valued it because it helped them screen their sources of young able recruits. They prized it because of its ability to identify and enhance academic ability. They prized it because it enhanced personal qualities.

There were explicit comments approving the opportunity that higher education gave to students; in one accountant's terms, the opportunity 'to study a subject because they love it....' When asked about the advice they would give students about their choices of subject, some employers felt the students would be best studying something they were interested in or good at.

Yet some employers expressed doubts. Some were unsure about specifying the value added by the experience of higher education. For one employer, university experience compared unfavourably with technical college experience. Indeed, some non-recruiters of graduates doubted the value of a degree course for the sorts of jobs within the company. A member of a firm of accountants recruiting non-graduates thought that recruits for their foundation courses compared favourably with graduates because they were more malleable. They were 'at least as good, if not better, than many graduates'. He thought there had been a swing back to the non-graduate. A minority were more definite in their criticisms of higher education. 'Universities have still not grasped that people... are going to come (into employment) to make things, that it must meet a price and make the delivery date, you have to direct people to do it.' But this was not the majority view.

Student Expectations

The project was intended to match student expectations and, to a more limited extent, their experiences, to those of employers and the providing institutions. We had evidence, for example, from our study of the polytechnic that its staff assumed that a large number of polytechnic students would have preferred to go to university. This assumption is, of course, substantiated by previous studies by, for example, Whitburn *et al.*[5] A study by the Committee of Directors of Polytechnics found that a little under half of applicants to polytechnics also applied to universities. Preliminary findings from the Expectations of Higher Education survey of students indicate that a rather larger proportion of final-year undergraduates had applied to universities before entering their present courses. Of these, many would have preferred to enter a university.

The survey of students' expectations is still being analysed and I must therefore dwell upon its provisional conclusions in tentative terms and without the use of specific figures. These shortcomings will be remedied shortly when the survey is completed and released in its soft cover form by the DES.

We were concerned to ascertain the extent to which students on entry had specific vocational intentions. The survey shows, but note that it recorded students' statements of their expectations on entry when they were already in the final year of their courses, that students in similar disciplines in both universities and polytechnics had similar career goals on entry. But there were differences in degree: for example, students entering engineering courses in polytechnics were more 'decided' towards particular occupations than were their university contemporaries who were 'inclined towards' them rather than decided. Again, cutting across the binary line, students who can be described generally as being in the arts or social studies areas responded that they needed time or wanted to pick up skills from their higher education experience before opting for an occupation. The tendency was strong among, for example, the historians in universities. Yet among social studies students there were some who entered polytechnics in order to pick up particular qualifications leading to certain occupations.

Other job-related preferences emerged stronger among those in sandwich courses, this being largely accounted for because they were in engineering subjects, and among males in both sectors. This again can be accounted for by the fact that there are more women in social sciences and arts subjects.

We need to probe the figures a bit more closely in order to be certain how far the stronger career goals present among polytechnic students is accounted for by the presence of part-time and older students.

A second group of findings will concern students' perceptions of what employers look for. Perhaps inevitably and naturally, these students, all in the year when they would be seeking employment, in both polytechnics and universities, assumed that appearance at interviews, quality of the written application and good references were very important. But turning to the actual qualities which students thought employers valued, students from both sectors rated very high the motivation of applicants in terms of both what was sought and what should be sought. As part of this, both sets of students, with the university respondents slightly more than those from polytechnics, thought employers were looking for leadership potential.

The employers' study showed how they regarded the sector of origin as important in recruitment. An overwhelming number in both sectors felt that the sector was important to employers. A higher proportion in the universities maintained that it should be. Other messages had got home, too: students were clear that employers rated Oxbridge highest, for example.

The majorities were still strong, but less so, when students were asked whether they believed 'A' level scores to be important to recruiters of graduate employees. Slightly more of the university students thought they were regarded as important by employers than did those of polytechnics. But many more university students than those at polytechnics thought that they ought to be important.

It will be seen, then, from these very provisional results that students understand well the kind of assumptions built into the processes of recruiting graduates. At the same time, polytechnic students, not unnaturally, were not so willing to accept the appropriateness of some of the criteria being applied.

Institutional Case Studies

Three institutional case studies were undertaken, and the first issue was the extent to which institutions had self-identities which would affect their working with the labour market. By self-identities we mean dominant perceptions of the functions that they perform or ought to perform. Here we follow Clark[7] on collective historical experience, and Entwistle[8] on notions of what an institutional title might denote.

Individual institutional identities were made up of their different perceptions of distinctive kinds of academic excellence, of the research functions performed, and the courses offered. So were the kinds and qualifications of students recruited. They had different views about the value added by the education which they provided, about the importance of external markets and about the amount of work experience that should be part of the course. Those perceptions of acceptability to employers affected the nature of the courses developed and were reinforced by the institutional arrangements.

Institutional identities are not made up simply of the perceptions of those within the institutions. As we have seen, employers also had a strong notion of institutional identity which affected employment practice. They derived their perceptions of institutions from direct contact, mostly through the recruitment of graduates. And because employers did not feel bound to make contact with the whole range of universities, let alone polytechnics or colleges, there is, in Roizen and Jepson's term 'a built in conservatism, in which employers have in the past recruited mostly from the universities, in some cases from a few universities....' Polytechnic teachers did indeed hope that as their graduates entered employment that bias based upon selective knowledge might change.

The Responsiveness of Institutions

Members of providing institutions shared the employers' difficulty in aggregating the diverse demands made upon them. They were generally confident that a first degree course in an acceptable discipline enhanced employment prospects whether or not the career specifically related to the undergraduate specialism. They emphasized the need to retain the integrity of their subject area while increasing the range of options available to students. They assumed that employers did not necessarily want specific courses of study to meet specific needs but evidence of general intellectual ability.

Of the three institutions, the university emphasized the importance of maintaining the quality of its intake and the academic content of the course; it was not their function simply to provide vocational training. In this, the university opinions were consonant with the preferences of employers.

The polytechnic was committed to applied and sandwich courses, with an evident market orientation in mind and with an eye to providing something competitively different from the universities. Some departments made deliberate attempts to orientate courses towards the needs of industry and employment and away from theory.

The college of higher education, a former teacher training institution, now emphasized 'training people for jobs with people', to provide industry with good managers for which the subject of study was not of paramount importance. They too were thinking about their most plausible markets.

Thus all three institutions felt that they made their graduates employable by emphasizing the general educational purposes of their courses. Some of the strongest statements of commitment to employer needs came from particular departments in the polytechnic. But all three institutions were moving away from academic specialization through joint and combined courses in the university, multidisciplinary subjects in the polytechnic, and no single Honours course at all in the college of education.

Thus while sustaining an institutional identity and their own educational academic concerns the institutions believed that they were providing an education consistent with the qualities which employers stated, in our survey, they were looking for.

Contacts Between Employers and Education

Many employers mentioned the lack of integration, co-operation and mutual understanding with higher education. Some criticized universities and several commented that institutions generally did not bother to find out what employers needed. A few employers argued that industry needed to make its requirements clearer. The polytechnic institutionalized its contacts with employers more than the other institutions through committees at departmental or faculty levels on which employers were represented.

Yet, in both sectors, it was informal contacts that were mentioned as effective: opportunities occurred through such arrangements as the Co-operative Awards in Science and Engineering or work placements. Consultancy, research, old boys and previous experience in employment outside the academic world were mentioned as important sources of information about industry and other areas of employment. The main contacts between employers and careers advisers were informal.

Employers expressed no great wish to be involved in course design and planning and it was less active participation than increased mutual understanding and knowledge about higher education that seemed desirable.

Careers Advisers

At the boundaries between institutions and employers are the careers advisers. Their role requires the maintenance of linkages and the offering of a brokerage function between employers, institutions and students. Yet the power belongs to the academics who regard the advisers as somewhat marginal. Recent difficulties in securing employment have, of course, caused greater significance to be placed on them in some institutions.

Many have been employed outside education before. But employers may be 'suspicious of their academic connections and they differ from employers in some of the emphases they think desirable in their work. Employers may prefer them to be more directive in the advice which they give students. Advisers are cautious and have to strike a balance between prescribing and offering direction-free advice.

Conclusions for Policy

Generating conclusions from across four somewhat disparate studies is hazardous. Let me chance my arm, however.

First, whilst many of those interviewed hoped for improvements in existing arrangements, for the most part employers and institutions and, by inference, many undergraduates, sponsor the degrees of freedom to which higher education now meets the needs of the employment market. If provision had been created to meet student demand in a somewhat incremental fashion rather than through systematic planning, the study does not show that employers seek radical change.

This does not, of course, pre-empt the question of whether employers are right to thus sponsor eclecticism. It must be for others to say whether employers adequately specify the needs of their firms or of the economy. But the studies also confirm the practical and logical difficulties of higher education planning in that employers find it difficult to aggregate their needs at any particular time and that, correspondingly, institutions can only make the most general guesses about who will require what from their courses. Instead, employers have notions of 'the best graduates' in which there are complex mixes of high level academic work, social training and individual personal development.

Thus employers look to higher education to select able young people for them. They also look to higher education as the primary source of training in some specific knowledge and skills for particular occupations. But they support educational experiences which, almost irrespective of the course of study, create flexibility, enhance personal development and build up individual motivation. And what employers and institutions want seems, at minimum, not to be in conflict with what students want.

Studies such as this do not lend themselves to precepts upon which social engineering and central government planning can comfortably be based. But there are issues for the more general and political consideration. First, it does seem bizarre and socially inequitable that employers' power to recruit helps to accentuate the divisions already implicit in what is virtually a tripartite system of higher education. It is bizarre and socially inequitable that graduates from those institutions which have been built up, at enormous social expense, to meet employer and social needs, the polytechnics, to say nothing of the colleges of higher education, should find their graduates excluded from some key recruitment processes such as the employers' milk rounds. It is exceedingly costly for employers to attempt to recruit from all institutions but the result is that they simply may not know the potential of those which do not figure among their traditional recruitment groups. The cost effectiveness of going to well known and large universities must be recognized. But long-term social costs are involved in ignoring large segments of the graduating population who still, by international standards, come from a relatively small segment of the total age group.

Secondly, and finally, there are research questions that remain. Essentially, such studies as these now discussed are concerned with the outcomes of existing institutional relationships. My own disciplinary inclinations lead me to believe that more studies of the how and why are desirable. The extent to which higher education is permeable and responsive is partly a question of how institutions create the curriculum, select students, and how far those processes are the product of internal academic norm setting and how far they bear the impress of changes in stated or informed needs and wants in the external social and employment environments. Issues of authority and power are never far behind questions of policy outcomes.

References

1 Buley, A.L. (1972) Defining the parameters. In Jevons, F.R. and Turner, H.D. (Eds) *What Kind of Graduates Do We Need?* Oxford University Press

2 Pearson, R. (1981) *Graduate Employment and Careers* IMS Report No. 30, Institute of Manpower Studies

3 Umakoshi, T. (1982)*Expectations of Higher Education: A Japanese Case* Unpublished paper given at OECD Conference, Hatfield Polytechnic

4 Pearson, *op.cit.*

5 Whitburn, J., Mealing, M., and Cox, C. (1976) *People in Polytechnics* Society for Research into Higher Education

6 CDP (1982) *Polytechnic Degree Course Applicants: A Summary of Those Seeking Entry to Full Time and Sandwich Courses in October 1979* Committee of Directors of Polytechnics

7 Clark, B.R. (1981) *Academic Culture* Yale Higher Educational Research Working Paper, Yale University

8 Entwistle, N.J., Percy, K.A., and Nisbet, J. (1971) *Preliminary Report to the Joseph Rowntree Memorial Trust: The Social Implications of Educational Change. Vol. II, Aims and Objectives* University of Lancaster

Commentary

William Taylor

We are all very grateful to Maurice Kogan for giving us the benefit of some of the preliminary findings from the important study that he and his associates have been undertaking. In discussing his paper, it seems to me that we could usefully focus on three areas. The first of these concerns the implication of the findings of the study for the curriculum of higher education.

As I understand what has been said, the work suggests relative weakness in the linkages between the content of higher education courses and the exercise and utilization of particular kinds of knowledge and skill, even within occupations that might be labelled, to coin a phrase, 'technological and vocational'. There are various ways in which those responsible for course design and teaching in higher education have sought to strengthen such linkages. One is to analyse the job requirements of particular occupations in great detail, and to choose course content closely related to those requirements. The greater the variability and unpredictability that exists in the job concerned, the more difficult this task becomes. Higher education, almost by definition, prepares individuals for work that is not very readily definable or predictable in its nature and thus there are limits to the extent to which such targeting of content is possible or desirable.

Another approach is to identify a core content of essential skills and knowledge likely to be relevant in almost all occupational settings in which graduates of various diploma and degree courses find themselves, and to build curricula around this core.

A third reaction is to argue that students will benefit most from a much more general programme of study, designed to 'develop the powers of the mind', or to 'inculcate attitudes favourable to hard work, team effort, conscientiousness, accuracy, responsibility, personal ambition, trainability'. Patrick Nuttgens has commented that some such approaches are based on the apparent assumption that if people are not trained to anything in particular, they will be able to change from one kind of incompetence to another without difficulty. An emphasis on trainability comes through quite strongly in the statements of some of those whose views are reported in the study with which we are concerned. I would like to offer a couple of observations on this emphasis.

One reason for stressing trainability may have less to do with the relation of the content of courses to the nature of work requirements than with certain contemporary characteristics of employment. For example, a greater concern with internal promotion may arise from the job security that current legislation confers. If it is difficult to 'let people go' (to use the American euphemism), then it is necessary to be very careful about who is recruited. That being so, there may be advantages in creating a pool of people with a high level of general competence, able to acquire relatively quickly those special skills that are needed within the enterprise. In other words, trainability facilitates internal selection and staff deployment.

Another reason for the high value attached to general credentials may be the way in which the process of hiring is undertaken within large firms. In many cases, personnel specialists identify a short list of potential candidates and present these names to the head of department concerned. The personnel specialist needs to be able to defend the choice he has made. Why pick out this particular six from the two hundred who applied? A good Honours degree from a high status institution is more readily legitimated in this respect than other less visible criteria.

A second set of implications of the study concern the organization of higher education. It seems that the polytechnics and higher education colleges still have some way to go before they establish themselves fully in the judgements of some of those directly concerned with personnel selection. Before we assume that, because some employers today appear to pay more attention to universities, other institutions have somehow got it wrong, we should think about those proportions of the employer population who themselves have experience of higher education in general, and of non-university higher education in particular. Should we really be surprised if people undervalue those parts of the system that did not exist at the time they were themselves receiving higher education? The considerable efforts that polytechnics and colleges are making to get across the distinctive nature of what they are doing may be a little while yet before bearing fruit.

A third set of implications have to do with placement. Not all employers are good at identifying the qualifications and experience that best match the recruitment needs of their existing workforces, let alone those of future intakes. Anyone who has had the job of actually having to write a job specification knows that it is much more difficult than it sounds. There are also weaknesses in what might be called the signalling system, by means of which the world of work makes its requirements known and educational institutions adapt their responses. Inertia in the capacity of institutions to respond can protect against the effects of fashion, but can also compound labour shortages in important fields. In this respect, we have to be sure that mechanisms for the logistical and academic approval of new courses balance, on the one side, considerations of effective resource utilization and standards with, on the other, those of adequate speed of response.

Another factor in the weak linkages between education and employment, especially as far as older age groups are concerned, has to do with the extent of occupational mobility in the working population. The proportion of those ten years into their careers who still work in the jobs for which they were originally trained is in some fields surprisingly small.

Another aspect of the placement factor is the significance that employers attach to certain 'signals' as compared with others. When recruitment takes place prior to degree results being available, weight tends to be attached to 'A' level results, and also, I have been told, to the average UCCA scores of the institutions in which candidates have studied and of the subjects they have chosen.

As one final point, in suggesting aspects of placement for discussion it would be wrong to omit reference to the quality of the careers advice available to students. Not all academics attach as much importance to the work of their own careers advisory services as they should, particularly at a time when, although graduates remain in a stronger employment position than their less well qualified contemporaries, the task of finding work appropriate to their skills and potential is by no means always easy.

12 Student Experience of Learning

Paul Ramsden

Struggling to get out from beneath most discussions of autonomy and accountability in higher education is the issue of students' experiences of teaching and learning. Are there real differences in the academic ethos and impact of more and less autonomous institutions? Is the binary system doing what it was intended to do – as far as students are concerned? Is there evidence of a connection between good undergraduate teaching and research excellence, in terms of student experience? Do students in universities learn better than students in polytechnics? These questions are of pressing relevance in the context of concern with quality assurance in higher education and the future of the binary system.

The character and functions of the polytechnics and the universities are, at least at first sight, very different. There are really two categories of difference, one horizontal and the other vertical. In the first place there are differences compatible with the aims of binarism. Thus British universities continue to emphasize scholarship, disinterested and free pursuit of knowledge, critical thinking. Their staff are generally appointed for their research excellence, and are protected through the concepts of academic autonomy and tenure. The lecturers are accountable largely to the 'invisible college' of professionals in their discipline. In contrast the polytechnics stress a 'service' function; their main concern is with preparing undergraduates for careers, and not a great deal of research is undertaken. The courses are overseen by many external groups, including the Council for National Academic Awards (CNAA) and local bodies. Their staff are more accountable to the management group within the institution, and are more likely to have professional experience and qualifications outside education. So far the differences can be summarized as accountability + utilitarianism versus autonomy + inquiry (see Table 12.1).

The other category of differences is essentially concerned with quality. There is no doubt that the polytechnics are second chance, lower quality

Table 12.1   'Horizontal' Differences between Universities and Polytechnics

UNIVERSITIES	POLYTECHNICS
Research emphasis	Teaching emphasis
No CNAA, HMIs, LEAs, etc.	CNAA, HMIs, LEAs, etc.
Scholarship	Relevance
Monitoring	Matching
Staff more accountable to their peer group (the 'invisible college')	Staff more accountable to management
AUTONOMY + INQUIRY	ACCOUNTABILITY + UTILITARIANISM

institutions for many students. Entry qualifications are lower, and fewer good degrees are awarded. The view is shared by employers; the recent Brunel survey (see Chapter 11) confirms previous reports that university graduates (even in 'irrelevant' subjects) are preferred. The poly graduate is more likely to be without a job at the end of his or her course. The inferior image is given further support from peer reviews. A recent review conducted by *The Times Higher Education Supplement* revealed that very few polytechnic departments were thought to be at the top of the list for research or teaching. Moreover, polytechnic staff are on average less well qualified, earn less, have substantially heavier teaching loads, and do not have the same employment safeguards. And no one who has worked in both types of institution could deny that universities are better resourced in terms of the things that make academic life comfortable – no matter what objective calculation of units of resource may be preferred (see Table 12.2). Incidentally, there is only an occasional acknowledgement of these quality differences in the SRHE Leverhulme volumes.

Table 12.1   'Vertical' Differences between Universities and Polytechnics

UNIVERSITIES	POLYTECHNICS
Higher entry qualifications	Lower entry qualifications
Higher quality departments	Lower quality departments
Staff well qualified	Staff less well qualified
Staff better paid	Staff worse paid
Staff more autonomous	Staff more controlled
Resources low	Resources abysmal
Liked by employers	Less liked by employers
FIRST RATE	SECOND RATE

Taking the two sets of differences together, we can make quite a few predictions about student learning and experiences of teaching. Student learning in the polytechnics would be expected to be of lower quality than in the universities. Polytechnic students might be expected to emphasize a process of learning involving narrowly reproducing material within the context of job-related skills; university students, exposed to an environment emphasizing academic autonomy and scholarship, ought to be interacting critically with their subjects and developing more general skills of critical thinking and understanding. Having lower entry qualifications should mean that the polytechnic students display poorer study habits. The polytechnic students would be expected to be more interested in gaining qualifications for future employment, and possibly to be more competitive and achievement-motivated. Polytechnic courses ought to be seen to be more vocationally relevant, more clearly structured, and better taught, in accordance with the polytechnics' emphasis on 'relevant' education and commitment to undergraduate teaching.

Student Learning and Perceptions of Teaching

The accuracy of these predictions can be examined by comparing them with the results of a national survey of over 2000 polytechnic and university students in a total of sixty-six academic departments or units carried out in 1980. The situation may, of course, have changed since then.

The main results of the survey have been fully reported elsewhere (see for example Ramsden and Entwistle 1981; Entwistle and Ramsden 1983). The investigation used an inventory to assess students' approaches to learning on four main dimensions. The first two, the meaning and the reproducing orientations, have been identified in many recent studies of how students learn. Similar to the idea of a 'deep' approach to studying, the meaning orientation implies that students are trying to *understand* what is being learnt by relating it to previous knowledge and personal experience. This is a demonstrably more effective approach than *reproducing* (similar to a 'surface' approach), which implies that students make minimal attempts to pass assessments by concentrating on what is thought to be essential. This narrow approach often means that students end up 'learning' only facts, details or procedures divorced from analogy and application. Needless to say, the former approach is academically and practically more desirable.

The other two study orientations are strategic and non-academic. These are almost opposite to each other. Neither seems specially attractive. The first is about using competitive, sometimes even ruthless strategies to ensure that you do better than other students, with the intention of gaining good qualifications for future employment. The second is concerned with disorganized study habits, negative attitudes to academic study, and an unfortunate tendency to jump to unsubstantiated conclusions. The four orientations are not mutually exclusive: every individual has a score on each.

Students' experiences of teaching were also examined in the study. A course perceptions questionnaire was used to look at, among other things, students' perceptions of teaching effectiveness, the clarity of the goals and standards of their courses, how vocationally relevant their studies were thought to be, and whether they felt part of a cohesive group of learners.

Results

We had previously reported (Ramsden and Entwistle 1981) that there were marked differences in students' orientations between the three main subject areas (science, social science, and arts) included in the survey. In this analysis, statistical controls for these effects were therefore included. When the results are examined against the expectations, the first thing we find is that there are many similarities between university and polytechnic students. The effects of subject areas are often much stronger than those of institution type. In spite of the lower entry qualifications of the polytechnic students in the sample, they report that they are as well organized and positive about studying as the university group. They are no more likely, either, to concentrate on memorizing and reproducing what they are learning (see Table 12.3).

Table 12.3   Hypotheses and Observations concerning Students' Experiences

PREDICTED	OBTAINED
Polytechnics higher on 'reproducing'	No difference between universities and polytechnics on 'reproducing'
Polytechnics higher on 'extrinsic/ achieving'	Polytechnics higher on 'extrinsic/ achieving'
Universities higher on 'meaning'	Polytechnics higher on 'meaning'
University students better at studying	Polytechnic students better at studying
Polytechnic courses more vocational	Polytechnic courses more vocational
Polytechnic courses better taught	Polytechnic courses better taught
Polytechnic courses more clearly structured	Polytechnic courses more clearly structured

There are, however, statistically significant differences on the strategic and meaning orientations. The polytechnic students in the science and arts faculties are more strategic — more concerned with extrinsic motives for studying, more competitive, and more aware of the 'assessment game'. This seems to fit the more utilitarian image of the polytechnics. Surprisingly, though, there is also some evidence that student learning in the polytechnics is of a higher quality than in the universities. Polytechnic students in all three faculties score higher on the meaning orientation scale. Something seems odd here: the university students ought surely to be more concerned with academic values and deep approaches to studying.

There are also significant differences on the course perceptions scales. As predicted, the polytechnic students think their courses are more vocationally relevant. They are also thought to be more clearly structured, to have clearer assessment standards, and to be located in a better 'social climate' – their students talk to each other more about academic work and are more likely to meet socially. There is an impression here of a context of learning in which staff and students are working together towards common aims. Perhaps most interestingly of all, the teaching is thought to be better in the polytechnics, in accordance with their emphasis on undergraduate education.

Implications

These results come from a relatively small sample of polytechnics and they concern only full-time students reading for first degrees. That makes it unwise to place too much confidence in the findings, or to assume that all polytechnic students are like these. Nevertheless, there are some intriguing policy implications. It does seem to make sense to argue that students in polytechnics are probably of similar quality to those in universities, despite their lower school-leaving qualifications. (This is, incidentally, evidence that the introduction of a wider range of criteria for entry to higher education would be less disastrous than some people suppose.) It appears that employers' attitudes to polytechnic graduates are based on a misunderstanding. It is ironic that university students, with no better study habits, and less 'relevant' courses, are more likely to find employment. Whatever the advantages of the binary system may be, the emphasis it places on polytechnic graduates as second-class citizens in the eyes of potential employers is not one of them.

How can we explain the apparent anomaly that the university students, although studying in an academic environment that stresses scholarship and critical thinking, are indeed less likely than their polytechnic counterparts to display an 'academic' approach to studying – interest in what is learnt for its own sake and an active attempt to understand what is being studied? Part of the answer may lie in students' experiences of teaching in the two groups of institutions. There is a statistical relationship between departments with perceived good teaching, choice over subject-matter, and high scores on the meaning orientation. There is interview evidence that the relationship is a functional one: good teaching really does seem to encourage deep approaches to studying (see Entwistle and Ramsden 1983).

If polytechnic teaching is better, why? Perhaps the poly students are less critical and discriminating. A more likely explanation is that polytechnic staff spend more time on undergraduate teaching than their university colleagues. The overseeing of courses by the CNAA, which to university eyes is extraordinarily demanding and strict, might also help to produce better taught and more clearly structured programmes. The SRHE Leverhulme recommendations for a review of the external examiner system in universities seem to be supported. The suggestion that the connection between good teaching and research activity may only be fortuitous (see Williams and Blackstone 1983, pp. 85-87) also appears to be well-founded. There is no simple transfer of the scholarly spirit of an academic department to the learning of its undergraduates.

Another reason for the apparent superiority of the polytechnics in teaching may be that most of them have educational development units, whose functions include encouraging staff to try new teaching and assessment methods, and running initial training programmes for new lecturers. Concern for professional development of teaching, as opposed to staff members' academic development in their subject fields alone, is altogether rarer in universities. The inescapable inference is that efforts to improve teaching have worthwhile effects on student learning, and the SRHE Leverhulme programme's recommendation for more generously resourced professional development activity is strongly sustained.

Conclusion

On the evidence presented here it seems fair to say that commonly-held prejudices concerning the relative quality of undergraduate teaching and learning in universities and polytechnics are questionable. Yet there are entrenched opinions about what constitutes an acceptable academic environment on both sides of the binary line. Polytechnics often appear to have an irrational fear that increased autonomy, whether at institutional level or for their staff, will compromise the relevance and attractiveness of their courses. Universities are deeply suspicious of increased accountability in the shape of organizations such as the CNAA, while the idea of professional development aided by educational advisory units is anathema to many staff.

It may be unhelpful to inform both sets of institutions that there are international examples that belie their fears. One group is afraid of more control, the other of more freedom; the rigidity of the binary line prevents them from learning from each other. Somehow or other, if we want the best possible undergraduate education, they need to be encouraged to feel that they are working towards the same ends.

Note

The full results of the research on which this paper is based are published in *Higher Education* 12 (6) 691-707.

References

Entwistle, N.J. and Ramsden, P. (1983) *Understanding Student Learning* London: Croom Helm

Ramsden, P. and Entwistle, N.J. (1981) Effects of academic departments on students' approaches to studying *British Journal of Educational Psychology* 51,368-383

Williams, G.L. and Blackstone, T. (1983) *Response to Adversity* Guildford: Society for Research into Higher Education

13 What were Universities For?

John Darling

This document has not yet been written, but will be issued in ten years' time by a government agency which is to be set up shortly.

MINISTRY OF TECHNOLOGY AND PROFESSIONAL TRAINING
December 1993

This review memorandum is issued by the Ministry to coincide with the closure of the last of Britain's universities. It is worth recalling that only ten years ago it was universally assumed that these anachronistic institutions would continue indefinitely. The last decade has seen their unnecessary activities brought to an end with a speed and efficiency which rival the disposal-rates of other terminations of unwanted institutions like the House of Lords. The recent conferral of knighthoods on the Ministry's rationalization consultants reflects general credit on everyone who worked so hard on the closure operation.

The Ministry can also take satisfaction in the successful development of its own courses in law, medicine, and engineering, as well as in the building of the Central Laboratory for Scientific and Technical Research on the former site of the terminated British Museum. These arrangements ensure that the few worthwhile activities of the university system will continue, but that instead of being subject to haphazard development by individualist enthusiasts, they are directly harnessed to society's needs.

This historic victory for progress began in 1981 when experimental pruning of university departments was carried out on a scale that made most educational cuts look like pin-pricks. The next step was to close half the country's faculties of arts and social sciences. This produced the important discovery that such a reduction made no measurable difference whatever to the nation's well-being. Although arts faculties claimed to supply many school-teachers in the days when these were in demand, in reality schools employed these 'graduates' only out of kindness, for what they had been taught at university generally bore little relation to school requirements. Many teachers of English, for example, had spent a whole year studying Anglo-Saxon but had acquired no competence in the arts of interpretation, register, or creative writing.

Only when the Ministry's valuators moved in to make inventories of arts faculty equipment was it discovered that whole libraries consisted of books which were scandalously out-of-date and which had occupied expensive shelving systems sometimes for centuries. (Some ancient universities, incidentally, were founded by the Christian church rather than the state, which probably explains a thing or two.) The revelation of so much costly irrelevance so enraged the British tax-payer that he demanded the closure of the whole university system, with its few useful functions being brought under responsible control.

This brought to an end the scandalous practice of allowing lecturers to spend their time (and the public's money) on *whatever investigations seemed to them of interest or value*. The interests of some dons rarely extended further than themselves, their colleagues and their own institutions, and a Society for Research into Higher Education had to be formed to cater for those who devoted their time to such incestuous investigations. Admittedly, in the final stage of their existence, the more rational university departments did research work for the government and other public bodies, but there was always an unacceptable risk of co-operation falling below the required level of compliance with necessary central directives.

The institutionalized recalcitrance of university teachers – now scarcely credible – was often disguised as the over-rated virtue of 'independent thinking' – generally an excuse for a shameful combination of eccentricity and conceit. One F.R. Leavis, for example, had attempted earlier in the century to portray the university as representing a cultural tradition 'having an authority that should check and control the blind drive onward of material and mechanical development with its human consequences' (Leavis 1943). It is now a great relief to be rid of the impudence of those who received generous salaries from public funds only to assume the mantle of social critic. Clearly a society like ours cannot reasonably be expected to finance either the fostering of an out-moded 'humanism', or the harbouring of dissent from progressive values.

Ironically, the university contained within itself one of the causes of its own destruction, for it was unable to agree on a clear definition of its own objectives. Some maintained that truth and knowledge should be pursued for their own sake, while others argued that universities should produce tangible benefits. Some exalted the role of researcher, while others stressed that universities were primarily teaching institutions. In the 1960s the term 'multiversity' was coined to indicate that these places no longer had a single unifying aim. Yet, in reality, confusion about the purpose of universities was nothing new. What was new was an increasingly rational society in which such confusion was unacceptable.

Indicative of the uncertainty surrounding academic proceedings is the story of a young man who, when being interviewed for a place at university, was asked why he wanted to become a student. 'To obtain the benefits of a liberal education', he replied. 'And what is a liberal education?' asked the professor. 'That is what I hope to discover if I get in', was the reply.

Attempts to justify the existence – and even the expansion – of universities were made in this country in the 1960s in a document known as the Robbins Report, which portrayed education, and particularly higher education, as an investment. This specious claim is still worth exposing. Here are the seductively misleading passages.

> We do not believe that modern societies can achieve their aims of economic growth and higher cultural standards without making the most of the talents of their citizens. This is obviously necessary if we are to compete with other highly developed countries in an era of rapid technological and social advance...
>
> Judged solely by the test of future productivity, a community that neglects education is as imprudent as a community that neglects material accumulation ...
>
> On a broad view of history... the evidence is very strong. The communities that have paid most attention to higher studies have in general been the most obviously progressive in respect of income and wealth. (HMSO 1963)

Although the Robbins Report correctly sees the production of wealth as the test of any institution's worth, the argument contains two mistakes. First, while higher education and wealth have usually gone together, the former is a symptom rather than a cause of the latter. This is because, in the days when education was highly prized, and before leisure had been properly separated from intelligence, a country which became prosperous would use its surplus wealth to build universities to meet the demand for higher education (much as we in the 1990s are investing our national profits in a sixth, and shortly a seventh, television channel). Second, higher education, far from accelerating technological development, often militated against it. At university, many students acquired a distaste for what they learned to view as the materialistic philosophy of industry, while others found their years in these academic play-pens quite debilitating. As Paul Chambers of ICI once pointed out: 'Life at a university with its intellectual and inconclusive discussions at the postgraduate level is, on the whole, a bad training for the real world, and only men of very strong character surmount this handicap' (West 1970).

The point was put even more bluntly by the personnel director of Spillers Dog Food and others who declared that aspiring managers would get a better preparation in the army.

> Of course we don't expect a young man from the army to be fluent in Medieval French Literature or a master of Micro-Biology. But in our experience as employers, we've found that a Short Service Commission in the Army equips a man to make the change to business management very easily. For both jobs are concerned with the handling of people and getting the best out of them, often in trying situations. (*The Times* 1974)

The gap between the utilitarianism of what Chambers rightly called 'the real world' and the philosophy of the ivory-tower blocks became increasingly obvious. In an attempt to bridge the gap, the Association of University Teachers adopted as its defensive slogan 'Britain needs its universities'. But in an increasingly open society, people saw and heard more about universities than they had in the past, and what they learned they did not like. Television had grasped the potential of the university as an appropriate setting for the portrayal of youthful sexuality. One programme, 'The History Man', achieved great success by meeting the country's need for pleasurable tut-tutting. In 1983 one foolish university gave the BBC freedom to film any aspect of her affairs. Inevitably, student life was portrayed on the screen as one long spasm of social intercourse in smoke-filled bedrooms – and, as every voyeur understood, there is no smoke without cannabis. In 1985 the AUT finally recognized the 'Britain-needs-its-universities' slogan as an unconvincing attempt at donnish patriotism, and misguidedly replaced it with the more up-to-date and individualistic message 'Wake up with a university lecturer'. This set the seal on the image of the university as a cornucopia of illicit pleasures.

There had been a slow but dramatic reversal in the public standing of universities between 1950 and 1980, a change which can be demonstrated by comparing two university novels by Kingsley Amis – *Lucky Jim* published in 1954, and the less well-known *Jake's Thing* which was published twenty-four years later. Jim and Jake are both historians of a kind; both stories are farcical concoctions involving matters of the heart and associated areas of the anatomy; but the outlook of each novel is quite different.

Lucky Jim immediately caused a stir not just by its satirical spirit (which was then unusual) but because the institution Amis was sending up was the university. Parents approved of universities, teachers likewise, and it was assumed to be a good thing to attend one. At that point, the wider public had never set its collective foot inside one and so had no reason to suppose it to be anything other than a worthy and admirable institution. Thus the portrayal of universities as ludicrous, phoney, pernicious and absurd was an outrageous (and profitable) novelty. Droves of graduates were only too happy to part with a few bob for the pleasure of being told that their *almae matres* were in fact ladies of doubtful virtue. Jim, a young assistant lecturer, finally sees through the whole charade and gets out of university for the relatively sane and worthwhile world of business.

By the time we come to *Jake's Thing* at the end of the 1970s, Amis has clearly changed his tune on things academic. In the earlier novel, an article that Jim writes is portrayed as part of a farcical academic paper chase; but Jake's books on colonization in Ancient Greece are treated quite seriously, even as his life's justification. The university, or at least Jake's traditional, all-male, Oxford college, is presented as a bastion of sanity against the rest of the world – and it is the 'real world' which is now seen as comprising all that is ludicrous, phoney, pernicious and absurd.

Mockery of conventional wisdom is the stock in trade of the satirist: the professional iconoclast has to take a deviant view. The irreverence of *Lucky Jim* was a success precisely because universities were then highly esteemed. Amis's rancorous defence of traditional university values in *Jakes' Thing* must therefore be seen as a significant pointer in the later period to the low standing of universities – a position from which, it is gratifying to record, they never recovered.

Universities had gradually come to be seen as centres of leisure. Dons who protested that it was very exhausting leisure did nothing to improve matters. What the public had discovered was that university teachers spent very little time teaching. Teachers saw their students for only a few hours a week, and the teaching year lasted for only twenty-five weeks, leaving expensive accommodation lying empty for much of the year. The numbers in classes were often unbelievably small, and yet this was proclaimed as an institutional virtue. University teachers seemed quite ignorant of the successes of the monitorial school system in the nineteenth century, and of the equally impressive record of continental universities which relied on a teaching system of large formal lectures. Dons spoke fondly of the need for Socratic relationships with students which enabled them to teach by conversation and questioning. It was not lost on critics that this style of teaching first evolved in a slave-based economy where the young of the prosperous part of society had too little to do.

Echoes of this privileged leisure were often found in universities in the form of lavish provision of sports facilities, dance halls, and centrally-heated halls of residence maintained by armies of domestic staff. To add insult to injury, the children of these cooks, cleaners and porters were effectively excluded from universities even though their parents helped to finance these institutions through taxes. The offspring of manual workers were never admitted in significant numbers, and though over the years there was increasing sensitivity about this, the situation

continued fundamentally unchanged. University education consequently came to be recognized as that intolerable phenomenon, a minority
interest paid for by the majority.

One major stumbling block to self-reform had proved to be the sheer
weight of tradition in these self-styled bastions of rationality. Being quite
insensitive to the dangers of old-age, universities openly paraded their
antiquity, and one of the more pathetic features of the eighties was the
sight of Aberdeen University preparing to 'celebrate' (*sic*) its 500th
anniversary in 1996 - a festivity which mercifully never came to pass.

All deviations from academic tradition invariably faced strong opposition. In the nineteenth century when University College, London was
founded by atheists and patronized by non-conformists, Oxford and
Cambridge spear-headed the opposition. In the twentieth century Keele
University was another radical departure which was eyed with the
greatest suspicion by the academic world, while the idea of a university of
the air which would be open to all was consistently derided by dons and
by the academic press. The *Times Educational Supplement* was startled
to discover that it would be open to clerks and housewives (TES 1963)
and it lampooned the proposal as 'building new academies in the sky',
'the sort of cosy scheme that shows the Socialists at their most endearing
but impractical worst' (TES 1966).

Only the so-called 'new universities' proved immediately acceptable,
no doubt because their allegedly innovative stance against single-subject
degrees merely reflected the long experience of the Scottish universities.
In structure these short-lived institutions were mock-collegiate, and
tended to be based in towns like York which lived off their past. A
sensible proposal to site one of them in Scunthorpe predictably made
little headway.

So even if universities had had the nous to sense the rising tide of
public animosity, it is improbable that they would have been capable of
making radical changes. They believed that opposition was limited and
temporary, and mistakenly identified government as the hostile force
instead of society as a whole. Only in what came to be known as the
Leverhulme years did universities belatedly acquire a vague sense of the
need for change. The response of the academics was characteristic: they
held a prolonged series of seminars at someone else's expense.

In retrospect, universities seem to have been, for self-styled centres of
intellect, extraordinarily optimistic and surprisingly stupid. Right up to
1980 they persisted in seeing the University Grants Committee as a
'buffer' between themselves and the government. They continued to
expand their operations well into the 1970s, and in 1983 Leverhulme
was still calling for increased participation in university courses. Despite
an increasingly unfavourable environment, their great antiquity and

sheer magnitude made the universities confident of their future. But they forgot about dinosaurs.

Acknowledgements

Some of this material has previously appeared in the *Times Educational Supplement, Scotland* and in *Scottish Educational Review*. Reproduction is by kind permission of the editors.

References

HMSO (1963) Committee on Higher Education (Chairman, Lord Robbins) *Higher Education Report* Cmnd.2154. London: HMSO 8,204,206

Leavis, F.R. (1943) *Education and the University* London: Chatto and Windus. Quoted in Powell, J.P. (1974) Universities as social critics *Higher Education* 3,150

The Times (1974) Advertisement 11 January. Quoted in Dore, R. (1976) *The Diploma Disease* London: Allen and Unwin, 30

Times Educational Supplement (1963) Editorial 13 September

Times Educational Supplement (1966) Editorial 4 March

West, E.G. (1970) *Education and the State* London: Institute of Economic Affairs, 103

Part 4
Structure and Policy

14 Giving and Taking Quality Advice

Peter Knight

I will address a few remarks in a personal capacity to an issue that has not been examined very much in the current discussions. This is the use of advice on 'quality', particularly in the recent National Advisory Body (NAB) planning exercise. Now, NAB is an unsophisticated body, and the planning exercise that it concluded towards the end of 1983 was (if I use polite adjectives) primitive and crude. Part of the rationale for that exercise was that it made judgements on the basis of quality, whatever that means.

In talking about quality, NAB has fallen into a trap. Firstly, in the debates in the board, the word 'quality' is only used with reference to degrees and postgraduate work. It is not used to talk about a substantial and important part of the public sector: that is the sub-degree work, such as Higher National Diplomas and Certificates. Quality appears to have been captured by the degrees. Secondly, there has been no attempt at any stage to discuss what is meant by quality. Are we talking about pass rates? Are we talking about failure rates? Are we talking about the youthfulness and dynamism of the staff? Or are we talking about the age and the wisdom of the staff concerned in teaching those courses? No, what we are talking about (and I am sorry if this is a cynical view) is using 'quality' as a way of hiding judgements which are actually taken on more grubby and pragmatic grounds.

Now, if you're going to use quality as a rationale (pseudo or real) for decisions, somehow or other you have got to get advice about quality. Here I'm going to use a four-letter word which is popular in the public sector; I'm sure you'll know this word; in order not to offend sensitivities I will spell it; it's spelt CNAA. Now, NAB needed the Council for National Academic Awards (CNAA) to provide academic advice, and I'm sorry if my analysis of the situation is cynical, but when the question was first raised, 'Where will we get academic advice from? Who can possibly provide it?', one organization certainly seemed to run around yelling,

'Me, sir, me: I'll tell you, I'll tell you whatever you want to know.' That effectively was the starting point of the CNAA as perceived by at least some members of the board of the National Advisory Body. Now, in the debates that followed, there was a little bit of a drawing back from that position. Perhaps the council of the CNAA realized that there were dangers in following this path. Perhaps the CNAA should not become the academic arm of the National Advisory Body. Perhaps caution should prevail, rather than enthusiasm. So, as the planning exercise moved on its inexorable way, and data got fed into the vast abacus of the computer that lives in the offices of NAB at Metropolis House, the question of what advice one would get from the CNAA remained an open issue. Would they say anything? In fact, they did say some things: not a lot, but they took about fifty pages of A4 to say it, and they provided a detailed comment on almost every institution's plans in which they made judgements about quality.

Now, those judgements about quality were couched in what can only be described as 'weasel words', and one needed to decode them with great care at that weekend in Eastbourne when the NAB board held its residential meeting. The weasel words go like this. If you are referring to a course, and you see a comment from the CNAA, 'This course is of particular and unique quality': O.K. 'This course is a course of quality': chancy. And then, the words which I do remember, 'There are no grounds of quality per se for the maintenance of this course': thumbs down! I may have paraphrased a more sophisticated presentation, but it was of that type. In the confusion which arose out of the residential weekend, by and large I think the CNAA got away with it. But there was another trap waiting around the corner for them, and that trap was the débâcle over town and country planning. Now, I'm a member of the NAB board, so I will happily do the mea culpa, it was my fault. The board simply did not know what criteria it was going to apply to town and country planning, and when it did apply certain criteria it didn't like the answer. Therefore it changed the criteria, and the NAB committee didn't like the answer! The one key thing in terms of quality advice which emerged was that the CNAA listed by institution, in order of quality, the town and country planning courses. They put them in Category 1, Category 2, Category 3, and the message came out clear: if decisions were being taken on quality grounds, occupying Category 3 was an exciting and rapid way to premature retirement.

When the decisions were taken on town and country planning, interestingly, the criticism wasn't directed to NAB (which had actually taken the decisions); the arguments tended to be about whether or not the CNAA should have provided the advice. Not whether the advice was right or wrong (although that debate could also take place), but whether in principle that advice should have been provided by a validating body which had only engaged up to that time in threshold, rather than quality validation. So, the mental image that one had of the CNAA's involvement in town and country planning was of them sitting and knitting as the tumbrels rolled by, taking town and country planning courses to their ultimate fate.

You will have gathered from my comments that I have reservations about the CNAA's role, and it's probably time for me to articulate those reservations perhaps more forcefully than I have done so far. I think the involvement of the CNAA (or, indeed, the Business and Technician Education Council, if it chose to go down that path) in providing quality advice to the National Advisory Body is unacceptable, for two reasons. Reason number one: the CNAA is incompetent to provide that sort of advice. What the CNAA does at course level is to provide a threshold system of validation. It is 'yes' or 'no'; the course has achieved the quality, or the course has not achieved that quality. An essential component of this threshold validation system is that there ought to be honest and open dialogue between the course team and the visiting party from the CNAA. That dialogue cannot take place in anything other than threshold validation, because staff would not be prepared to admit their weaknesses if that admission would get them over the threshold but into the category of courses of low quality consigning them to some future oblivion. The process of threshold validation, if it is to succeed (which it has done in the past), is not a process which will allow the CNAA easily to give advice on quality and ranking. There is also a logistic problem. By and large, courses are reviewed on a five-yearly basis. We live in rapidly changing times, course leaders change, resourcing changes, staffing changes. Information based on review visits which took place a few years ago are out of date and irrelevant. The system can and will have changed such that continuity of advice does not exist, and no confident statement about quality can be maintained.

Reason number two (here I choose my words with care and pick a delicate phrase) is that for the CNAA to provide such quality advice is corrupt. Of course, it is corrupt in the nicest possible way. The system of CNAA validation is a system of peer-group review, and the strength of peer-group review is that the people who are undertaking that review should be disinterested personally in the outcome. Therefore, if I (and I am a member both of the CNAA board and of one of its committees) am visiting a course, the only issue either in the forefront or in the back of my mind, should be the quality of that course and the experience which the students will gain from it. Suppose I know that the CNAA is undertaking a quality judgement, and that this quality judgement will find its way into a ranking which could in future determine which course should open and which course should close. Then, if my own institution (as it almost inevitably will be) is offering a similar course, an issue on the hidden agenda of every validation meeting will be whether the course is going to be approved and be in competition for survival with those courses which the members of the validation panel are responsible for running. That is corrupt in the sense that it is an unacceptable use of a peer-group review system because the future employment of people on the panel may rest on the decision which is taken to validate or not that course. In short, I'm not satisfied with the advice that might be provided to NAB by the CNAA, whether it is actually going to be provided by the subject boards, or whether, because of the speed of the response which NAB requires, the advice would be given by officers of the CNAA, who would then be put in an invidious position.

Now, this is all very well, but it's worth considering for a moment why we're in this mess. We're in this mess because the issue really is not about quality, and it's not about validation; it's about politics and it's about power. I think that there is a view in the CNAA which says that by becoming the academic arm of the National Advisory Body the CNAA would be able to play a leading role in shaping the system for the future in a way perhaps many of the people involved in it would wish it to do. It might lead to a more secure future for the council if the council thought that there were serious threats (and there may well be) that institutions, particularly the polytechnics, would obtain the rights to award their own degrees and diplomas, and be less dependent on the council. Perhaps security for the CNAA does lie in becoming the academic arm of NAB. The question now in terms of politics is, given that the council has chosen this particular path, whether it can be stopped.

Interestingly, I don't think anybody in the system actually likes the CNAA. It's rather like that magnificent metaphor about not insulting the alligator until you've crossed the river. If you're in an institution and subject to quinquennial and course reviews, you know you're going to have to cross that river every five years. You can never insult the alligator! It doesn't mean to say you have to like it. So, nobody has tended to be rude or critical of the CNAA. Nobody actually likes it, and what happens to us all is we tend to get sucked into its processes. And its processes are rather enjoyable, let's admit it. As a member of the CNAA board or panel, it is pleasant: you get to stay at four-star hotels; you enjoy looking at other courses; you learn; you meet colleagues; it's an exciting stimulating experience, but that doesn't mean to say that the supporting structure is actually one which should be maintained.

My concluding remarks are quite simple. I would like to incite people to insurrection. I genuinely believe that there is an opportunity for the institutions to say that the CNAA has got to change, because we, the institutions and the individual members of the CNAA, are not going to accept the path down which the council has decided to go. The institutions have never flexed their muscles, they've never argued against the council, and perhaps it is a test of maturity for the public sector that that time has now come. So, I urge you to take part in this popular uprising. You have nothing to lose but partnership in validation! I think we have everything to gain, because I genuinely believe that if we fail to change the CNAA we will actually be heading for a form of academic corporate state which will reduce the freedom available to colleges and improperly interfere with the provision of higher education in this country in the 1990s.

15 Innovation through Collaboration

Graham Stodd

This is an outline of a regional initiative to promote innovation in a contracting and ageing higher education system. It involves dialogue and co-operation between a university, a polytechnic and a voluntary college of higher education. But the suggested general strategy is not dependent on this specific though imaginary proposal.

Let us suppose that maps in the offices of the Department of Education and Science, the National Advisory Body and the University Grants Committee show that the region of Northex has three major institutions of higher education: the University of Northex, Scunchester Polytechnic and Eastdale Voluntary College of Higher Education.

The university was created in 1965, achieving a reputation for innovation in terms of its curriculum and of its interface with the community. It was able to innovate because, in its early years, it succeeded in recruiting a number of mid-career academics who were keen to develop new course structures, to develop interdisciplinary approaches and to facilitate student learning. Eighteen years later, many of these original innovators have retired or have run out of steam and the younger founding academics have obtained promotion elsewhere.

The polytechnic resulted from the amalgamation in 1969 of a technical college and a school of art. In 1976, following the reorganization of teacher education, it took in a local teacher training college, although initial teacher training has now been phased out. The polytechnic was intended to create a 'new and flexible interface with industry, commerce and the local community, providing a bridge between further and advanced further education.' In its early years it tried strenuously to achieve this aim, but administrative, human and validation pressures brought about a process of 'academic drift'.[1] The majority of its courses are now only at degree level and nearly 75 per cent of the students are full-time. Its courses are validated by the Council for National Academic Awards (CNAA).

The college of higher education was one of the earliest denomination-al teacher training colleges and has its courses validated by the University of Northex. During the 1960s, with active encouragement from the university, it developed some innovatory courses in its teacher training programme, including an experiential foundation course. There was a change of principal in 1973 and the college developed a range of BA degrees, following the national decision to contract teacher education. Roughly 50 per cent of its students now follow the BA programmes. In the process of diversification, a significant number of staff took advantage of the Crombie redundancy scheme and were replaced by younger well-qualified subject specialists to teach the new BA degrees. In 1978, the college developed a new BEd degree, following the phasing out of the Teachers Certificate qualification. This new degree was far more structured and less innovatory than the previous degree, and some staff argued that the college, as well as the polytechnic, had experienced 'academic drift'.

In 1981, the vice-chancellor of the university wrote to the principal of Eastdale College, asking him to comment on an article[2] about the future of the colleges of higher education. This article argued that the colleges of higher education had developed BA degrees which were not distinctively different from those available in the universities and

Figure 15.1   Projection of the 18-year-old Population of Great Britain

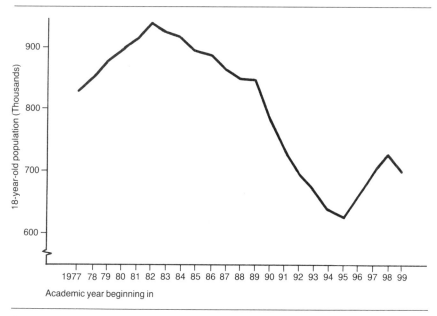

Source Future Demand for Higher Education in Great Britain Report on Education No. 99, Department of Education and Science, London, 1983

polytechnics. It was likely, therefore, that they would start to experience serious recruitment problems in the latter part of the 1980s, as the size of successive eighteen-year-old student cohorts declined (see Figure 15.1).

The article proposed that a small group of institutions should develop an alternative paradigm of higher education involving the credit accumulation of a profiled qualification, by a mixture of part-time and full-time study, set in the context of lifelong learning. Implicit in the scheme was a broadening of the traditional content of higher education, to include such elements as community development, human potential studies, an individually negotiated project, and independent study. The distinctiveness of the proposal was claimed to lie in its emphasis on the development of the individual's emerging vocational, intellectual, social, emotional and other needs at the point in his life when they were appropriate.

The principal replied that he was already aware of the author's views, having received an advance copy from a fellow principal. Indeed, his vice-principal, charged with the responsibility for academic development, had attended an informal consultation, involving a small group of voluntary colleges, to discuss the ideas. In addition, the paper had been considered by an appropriate committee in his own college.

Although there was some truth in the arguments presented, he judged that his college was unlikely to move in this direction. Some 64 per cent of his staff were aged forty or over and felt that they had changed enough already in responding to the demands of diversification and the contraction of teacher education. In addition, the advent of the BA degrees had given them what they perceived to be an additional status in the academic world, which they might lose in the proposed development. More crucially, they felt that such a development would be too much of a gamble, without clear evidence of support at the national and local level. The principal felt that the proposal would receive little support from the DES because it would make it more difficult for the department to control student numbers, due to its extreme flexibility. He also felt that the scheme would present extremely difficult validation problems, because student intakes would lack homogeneity; the credits would not necessarily form a coherent whole; the students' experience of higher education would not necessarily be integrated and the content of the credits would not necessarily imply extended progression. Finally, his discussions with fellow college principals made him feel that they were being forced to concentrate their energy on short-term survival rather than on the medium and longer-term development of their institutions.

The vice-chancellor was privately disappointed by this predictably cautious and conservative reply, but did nothing further until 1983, when four important documents[3,4,5,6] were published in a matter of a few months. He invited the director of Scunchester Polytechnic and the principal of Eastdale College to join him for a regular series of whole-day discussions about the future of higher education in the Northex region. They were joined at one of the meetings by the director of education for Northex, a national officer of the voluntary colleges, and observers from the Department of Education and Science, the National Advisory Body, the University Grants Committee and the Council for National Academic Awards.

In November of 1983, they published the following joint consultative paper:

This paper results from a series of extended discussions, which have taken place since the summer and is now circulated to colleagues in the university, the polytechnic and the college of higher education, for discussion and comment. At present, it is a personal analysis of our common problems but, if there is some agreement that the suggestions should be explored in greater detail, a more formal group will be set up.

Our institutions have received, during 1983, four important documents[3,4,5,6] which formed the starting point for our discussions. Although divided by the binary line of the universities and the public sector they were, in fact, relevant to all institutions. Between them, these documents raise major questions about the way higher education will develop in the decades ahead. They pose questions about course structures, curriculum, accreditation, continuing education, institutional co-operation, credit transfer, innovation, distance teaching, and other issues including cost-effectiveness and staff development.

In our judgement, the region of Northex will need a more flexible and varied provision of higher education by the twenty-first century than at present. In essence, although there are clear differences between our three institutions, the majority of our students enter at eighteen and follow full-time degree courses of study.

Our society is undergoing rapid change, and it is clear to us that recent developments in technology will lead to an increasing demand for mid-career retraining; to a contraction of the size of the nation's work force; to delayed entry into work and earlier retirement; to more time for leisure pursuits. We suggest that our institutions should play a central role in supporting these changes and that this will mean a significant shift from full-time to part-time education and the development of an integrated pattern of sub-degree and degree-level awards across our institutions.

So far, we have concentrated on the structure of our courses, but we also considered their content. In 1981, the Royal Society of Arts supported a manifesto which appeared in a number of papers[7] and was signed by a significant and influential cross-section of the leaders of our society. It criticized the education system for not providing an 'education for capability' by its present emphasis on 'analysis criticism and the acquisition of knowledge', at the expense of problem-solving, doing, making and organizing in a constructive and creative manner. There is probably some truth in this criticism and we are struck by the similarity of the assumptions, which underlie most of the courses in all three institutions. We suggest that it will become desirable to respond to these criticisms and develop some courses which possess a different mix of underlying assumptions.

In addition to considering the structure and content of our courses, we also considered our teaching and administration systems, with particular reference to the likely impact of new technology. We are all aware of the rapidity of developments in this field, but we suggest that they will, in the longer term, change the higher education system beyond recognition. Word processor, video cassette and disk, micro-processor, cable television and satellite broadcasting all possess potential which needs to be explored and exploited in the decades ahead. In terms of our own region of Northex, they offer a potential for developing a closely integrated system linking and rationalizing the provision within our three institutions and freeing resources to support a stronger system of distance teaching and continuing education.

The analysis so far suggests the need for major change in the higher education system of Northex, but we have to face the reality of our present position. All three institutions are faced with the prospect of a major decline in the number of eighteen-year-old entrants over the next fifteen years. All three institutions are faced with a long-term decline in the traditional levels of funding and income, with a demand to be cost effective. All three institutions are faced with the problem of a large number of mid-career staff who are unable to move to promotion (49 per cent of the university, 60 per cent of the polytechnic and 64 per cent of the college staff are over forty years old). Given this reality, there is obviously a danger that Schon's[8] 'dynamic conservatism' will set in, making significant change almost impossible.

This conservatism goes against the traditions of our three institutions which have all, in different ways, seen themselves as creative in the past. We recognize, however, that although during the 1960s they each started to develop distinctive styles of higher education, this creativity lost its edge in the 1970s, and our institutions started to lose their distinctiveness. We have observed this same process at work in many of the new universities set up in the 1960s and, at a different level, in a number of primary and secondary schools.

We feel that there is a general lesson to be learned about institutional creativity, which we can perhaps apply in the future. In order to explain it, we would like to draw a tentative analogue from the field of nuclear physics, involving the interaction of particles in a reactor. It would appear that some institutions succeed in developing what might be called a critical mass of staff energy, which, in its interaction, sparks off a major innovation. This innovative energy appears, however, to have a creative 'half life' of between ten and fifteen years, during which the creativity gradually burns itself out (see Figure 15.2).

Figure 15.2   Hypothesized Relationship between Creativity and Academic Drift in Institutions of Higher Education

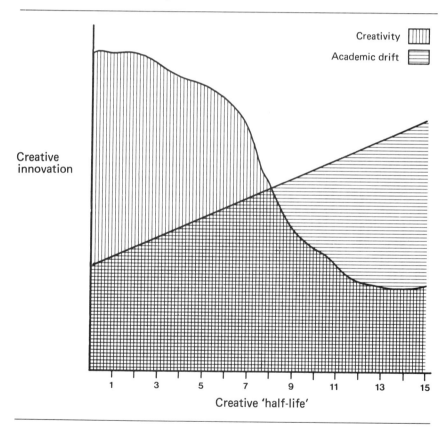

In the light of the above analysis, we wish to suggest that, in the next decade, our three institutions initiate a co-operative and integrated plan to develop a higher education network appropriate for Northex in the twenty-first century. This paper only suggests a broad outline, which would need to be filled in later.

First of all we suggest that the university and the Council for National

Academic Awards, as validating bodies, agree to co-operate in drawing up a regional academic plan. In the course of our discussions we considered the emerging potential of credit accumulation, credit exemption and credit transfer, and we recommend that we review our courses and regulations to facilitate developments in this area, establishing a firm interface with the credit structure and philosophy of the Open University.

Secondly, we recommend that Eastdale College should become an experimental open college, concentrating on short-cycle higher education courses of two years' duration. In our judgement, the college will need to change fundamentally by about 1990, as the size of the 18-year-old cohorts declines; it is therefore appropriate to initiate change now.

We suggest that the college should consider developing a course structure, based on the concept of credit accumulation, allowing for full-time/part-time or mixed mode study, set firmly in the province of continuing education. In order to facilitate this, we recommend that an approach be made to the Department of Education and Science to consider sponsoring a pilot scheme in Northex, involving an alternative pattern of student funding, which would enable students to take full advantage of the mixed mode route of credit accumulation. This would probably include some mixture of credit vouchers, student loans, commercial sponsorship and Manpower Services Commission support and would not preclude the continuation of a limited number of traditional three/four-year full grants. In addition, we suggest that negotiations should take place with a group of local and national employers in order to obtain sponsorship for students, either in terms of employment of the short-cycle graduates or in the funding of part-time student/employees.

Credit accumulation possesses an inherent flexibility, which would enable some students to cumulate four credits into a Diploma of higher education in two years and others, by working an extended academic year, to cumulate six credits into a Pass degree in two years. Eastdale College would be 'short-cycle' in the sense that students would only remain there full-time for two years, but many might return there, in part-time mode, to complete their studies.

We have noted the criticisms of the Education for Capability movement and the potential of 'profiled accreditation' enabling non-traditional subject matter to be introduced into higher education. We hope that Eastdale will explore this concept of profiled accreditation.[9]

It is clear to us that some colleagues in the polytechnic and the university might wish to be involved in such an innovation; equally we recognize that colleagues in Eastdale might have serious reservations.

We are therefore proposing to enter into detailed discussions with interested parties, to enable staff to move either temporarily or permanently between our institutions and, indeed, for some to work in more than one. This will naturally involve discussion of conditions of service, pension rights, re-location allowances and other matters.

Finally, in order to exploit the full potential of the new technology, we are proposing that we should develop a clear regional policy, centralizing some services and establishing a high quality cable network to enable development of interactive teaching, information retrieval, communication and administrative systems. In addition, we suggest that Eastdale should become a centre of high activity with regard to new technology and that the university and polytechnic should mount a major research project to monitor the development.

It is an open question whether an innovative development will take place in this region of Northex, but the issues presented would appear to be common to many institutions. Such a development might enable an alternative style of higher education to emerge. The main intention here has been to explore the need for intervention to produce significant innovation, particularly in the colleges of higher education. The idea of a regional development is felt to have particular potential.

References

1 Pratt, J. and Burgess, T. (1974) *Polytechnics: a Report* London: Pitman
2 Stodd, G.J. (1981) The colleges of higher education and the academic time bomb *Journal of Further and Higher Education* 5(1)3-9
3 National Advisory Body for Local Authority Higher Education (1983) *Towards a Strategy for Local Authority Higher Education in the Late 1980s and Beyond*
4 Council for National Academic Awards (1983) *Future Development of CNAA's Academic Policies at Undergraduate Level*
5 Society for Research into Higher Education (1983) *Excellence in Diversity: Towards a New Strategy for Higher Education* Guildford: Society for Research into Higher Education
6 Letter from Chairman of the University Grants Committee (1983) *The Times Higher Education Supplement* 11 November, p.12
7 Royal Society of Arts (1981) Education for capability *The Times* 9 February, p.2
8 Schon, D. (1971) *Beyond the Stable State: public and private learning in a changing society* London: Maurice Temple Smith
9 Stodd, G.J. (1983) Profile based professional development *Journal of Further and Higher Education* 7(1)83-92

16 Course Length and Content

Derek Bosworth

The length and content of courses have formed a continuing focus of debate amongst both academics and policy makers. Abstracting from the detailed (and often scholastic) considerations of alternative syllabuses in each subject area, I shall here pursue the more general issue of whether changes in length and content may result in more vocationally orientated courses with higher rates of return to the individual. The question of the optimal length of degree course was certainly raised during the 1960s (Pippard 1969). More recently, however, we have seen calls both for an extension and for a contraction in the length of courses. Academics have tended to resist proposals to reduce (or supported proposals to increase) course length on grounds of maintaining or improving the level of scholarship. The Finniston Report (1980) argued for longer courses to improve the quality of engineering graduates. Paradoxically, the Finniston proposals came at a time when increasing pressure to economize (in the face of government cuts in the education budget and adverse demographic trends) was resulting in a more serious scrutiny of two-year degree courses. Not only have the University of Buckingham and the polytechnics taken initial steps along the road towards shorter courses, but more general proposals of this type are contained in the SRHE Leverhulme Report, *Excellence in Diversity* (pp. 8-12).

The economic consequences of the various policy options have not been fully explored. The question posed here is: What is best for the student from a financial viewpoint? It is demonstrated that the answer turns on what happens to the magnitude and timing of the various income and expenditure streams arising from the investment in higher education under the various options. While reasonable estimates might be made about the costs, the impact on graduate income is more a matter of conjecture. However, some relevant data exist about graduates' views on course length and content. A preliminary review of these survey responses appears to indicate what might be interpreted as a compromise policy option involving a two-year core course with additional course options that can be 'bolted-on' at a later stage in the individual's career. However, despite the potential benefits that are likely to accrue from delaying certain components of the degree course, the high opportunity cost of interrupting an individual's career at a crucial moment appears to imply the need for a different method of teaching these later elements, based on the new information technologies.

Economic Consequences of the Options

In this section, we analyse the effect of changes in length and content on the net present value of the investment in higher education (NPV). The examples assume a male student who, just prior to his eighteenth birthday, decides whether to continue into higher education (though the calculations can be easily adjusted to allow for alternative assumptions). A three-year course is taken as a benchmark by which to judge the change in NPV arising from extending (to four years) or reducing (to two years) the length of degree course.

From the student's point of view, extensions to the length of course imply a higher opportunity cost in the form of income foregone. For an individual deciding on the relative merits of moving from a three-year to a four-year degree course, the gains can be expressed as the change in NPV (or ΔNPV) as shown in Equation 1:

$$\Delta NPV_1 = \sum_{t=22}^{65} \frac{\Delta GE_t}{(1+r)^{t-18}} - \frac{(GE_{21} + C_{21} - G_{21} - V_{21})}{(1+r)^3}$$

In this formula, 'ΔGE' denotes the change in graduate earnings; 'GE' denotes the graduate earnings that would have been received under the three-year course; 'C' denotes the costs of education borne by the individual; 'G' denotes the student grant; 'V' denotes the value of vacation earnings; 'r' denotes the discount rate; and '21' denotes the age 21. (Further explanation of the derivation of all of the formulae discussed in this paper may be obtained from the author.) It is likely that the graduate earnings lost because of the additional year of study and the costs of education borne during that year would exceed the value of the additional year's grant and the additional vacation earnings; thus, $(GE_{21} + C_{21} - G_{21} - V_{21}) > 0$. For there to be an overall increase in NPV, the discounted net losses incurred in a fourth year of a degree must be more than offset by the resulting higher discounted income stream; that is, $\Delta GE_t > 0$.

There are however a number of ways in which the length of a course might be reduced. Three such options are outlined in the final SRHE Leverhulme report (*Excellence in Diversity* 1983, pp. 8-12).

1 Honours degrees could be awarded in a shorter time by lengthening the academic year, utilizing the existing vacations for teaching
  purposes.
2 Two-year courses could be introduced alongside the existing
  Honours degree (as with the Diploma in Higher Education
  introduced in 1973).
3 A new two-year (Pass) degree could be introduced in all institutions, including less material of a less specialized nature, and
  resulting in a more flexible qualification that could be more widely
  available (see also Bosworth 1982).

A fourth option might be to find a means of compressing the same
amount of material into a shorter space of time with unchanged
vacations. The second option is dismissed in *Excellence in Diversity* (p. 9)
on the grounds that it has little chance of success when traditional three-
and four-year Honours courses supported by mandatory student grants
continue to dominate provision in universities and colleges. The fourth
option may simply be argued to be technically unfeasible given existing
traditional teaching technologies and methods. Here I will therefore
concentrate on the first and third options.

There is one important difference between the length of course in
terms of the number of weeks of teaching and the time that it actually
takes to obtain a degree in a system of higher education that only teaches
for three-quarters of each year. It has been argued that the saving in
costs to higher education would be small if the loss of vacations for staff
were compensated by an equivalent amount of study leave. In addition,
the more intensive use of buildings and equipment would be at least
partly offset by their unavailability for other activities such as conferences (*Excellence in Diversity*). Nevertheless, the SRHE Leverhulme Report
omits to note the potential saving in grant from the final year of study,
though the difference between the value of a grant and unemployment
benefit (in what were previously vacations) should also be taken into
account.

The change in NPV experienced by the student as a result of moving
from a three-year to a two-year course can be approximately expressed
in Equation 2:

$$\Delta NPV_2 = \frac{GE_{20} + C_{20} - G_{20}}{(1+r)^2} + \sum_{t=18}^{19} \frac{G_t'}{(1+r)^{t-18}} - \sum_{t=18}^{20} \frac{V_t}{(1+r)^{t-18}}$$

$$+ \sum_{t=21}^{65} \frac{\Delta GE_t}{(1+r)^{t-18}}$$

In this formula, 'G' is the new grant given during the old vacation
periods, and V is the lost vacation earnings (or unemployment benefit).

If we are willing to assume that $G_t' = V_t'$, then the function simplifies to Equation 3:

$$\Delta NPV_2 = \frac{GE_{20} + C_{20} - G_{20} - V_{20}}{(1+r)^2} + \sum_{t=21}^{65} \frac{\Delta GE_t}{(1+r)^{t-18}}$$

The nature of the change in NPV thus appears to depend crucially on what happens to the graduate earnings stream. One possibility is that the whole graduate earnings stream is simply brought forward by a year (for example, the graduate now received the income which would otherwise have been earned at age 24 or age 23). Assuming that income streams do not turn down in later years of life, it follows that $\Delta GE_t > 0$ for all values of t. It may also be assumed that there is a net loss associated with the final year of a three-year degree; that is, that $GE_{20} + C_{20} - G_{20} - V_{20} > 0$. From this one may anticipate that $\Delta NPV_2 > 0$ (that is, that there would be a net benefit in opting for a two-year degree course). If, on the other hand, the graduate earnings stream remained constant, then $\Delta GE_t = 0$ for all values of t and the final summation term of Equation 3 would disappear. In this case, one may still anticipate that $\Delta NPV_2 > 0$, but the net benefits would be smaller.

In so far as financial considerations influence the decision to enter higher education (McMahon and Geske 1981; Williams and Gordon 1981; Bosworth and Ford 1981), any such gains may be reflected in increased numbers of applications for places. However, a number of caveats should be noted. First, there is the question of whether the compression of a given amount of material into a shorter overall period might adversely affect student performance (and thereby the quality of graduate output and the size of the earnings streams). The move would certainly put most pressure on those least able to bear it, notably on the poorer students or the mentally and physically weaker. Second, the move might affect the non-pecuniary benefits of higher education (for instance, in so far as the long vacations are seen as a perk and enable students to maintain social contact with distant relatives and friends, and so on). Third, there is the fact that certain courses (for instance, in engineering) already use the vacations for industrial training, effectively removing the option of compressing the teaching period. Whether, in reality, this is such a barrier depends on the net disadvantages of moving from a 'thin' to a 'thick' sandwich course. (The perceived advantages of thin over thick might, as they stand, indicate that such a move would be looked upon unfavourably. On the other hand, the reduction in the period during which the student is 'locked away' in academia might reduce some of the disadvantages of thick sandwiches. See Bosworth 1982.)

The alternative option to be considered here is that of reducing the length of course by cutting back on the amount of material taught.

Although the underlying reasons are slightly different, Equation 3 is still valid. However, in this instance, if as suggested by human capital theory education has a positive influence on earnings streams, then the reduction in the amount of material taught will mean that ΔGE_t is likely to be negative. Whether the change in NPV (that is, ΔNPV_3) is positive or negative now depends crucially upon the impact of the reduced length of course on the size of income loss.

Survey Evidence

Given the sorts of questions raised about the options for changing the length of courses, it seems essential to establish what the resulting impact will be on the individual's employment opportunities, career progression, and income streams. However, such options are largely untried in the United Kingdom, and without direct observations we seem doomed merely to speculate on the outcome, aided only by simulation exercises. While the experience of other countries may be of some interest, such evidence is all too easily dismissed as misleading or irrelevant when taken out of its own social, economic, and political setting. In this section, therefore, we turn to the more direct evidence based on the views of graduates now in employment concerning the length and content of courses.

A review of the literature revealed that a considerable amount of research has been undertaken on the question of 'ideal' versus 'actual' content of science and engineering courses. Two types of evidence are available: criticisms of courses by ex-students and comparisons of subjects studied with those used in employment. Unfortunately, most of the research focuses on scientists or engineers and, within these groups, on the balance in teaching between subjects which are 'mainstream' for the discipline and other disciplines or peripheral skills (such as managerial studies and report writing for engineers, and numeracy for social science, arts, and humanities graduates). The results are thus somewhat limited. There are other, technical problems associated with this type of research (for instance, in designing appropriate questions, in sample selection, and in the interpretation of results). Nevertheless, this body of information is quite revealing, potentially helpful in the context of educational planning, and probably deserving of considerably great research effort.

Surveys of graduate employees have been carried out by Berthoud and Smith (1981), Cairncross (1980), the Council of Engineering Institutions (1978), Gerstl and Hutton (1966), Grinter (1955), Hopkins (1966), Hutton (1978), Johnstone (1961), Jones (1969), and Lawrence and Hutton (1981). Gerstl and Hutton (1966, pp. 62-65) summarized the results of the Grinter Committee (1955) in the United States and the

British Association (1961) in the United Kingdom as follows: 'although present courses at universities and elsewhere seem broadly satisfactory in their technical content they do not produce complete scientists having breadth of education in non-technical fields or skill in technical communication.' Similar surveys in the social science and arts and humanities fields might well reveal a certain dissatisfaction with the more technical skills taught. Here, the recent large survey of employers (Kogan 1981, p.4) reveals complementary evidence of graduate weaknesses in the ability to write reports, lack of industrial experience, and lack of numeracy.

A natural conclusion might be to spend more time on non-scientific subjects, particularly in the area of communicative skills (amongst scientists and engineers) and in numeracy skills (amongst social scientists, arts and humanity students). Bearing in mind the typical range of tasks carried out by individuals at various stages of their careers, such a move would appear to make courses more vocationally oriented. While the other authors did make such recommendations, some reservations were expressed. In particular, there was evidence to suggest that Britain's actual performance in this respect was not very different from West Germany's. In addition, there is always the question of 'scholarship' to consider.

Recommendations for changing content always produce pressure on the length of courses, if only because lecturers find it easy to add new material but extremely difficult to delete old material. In the case of the United Kingdom, where three-year (taught) courses still dominate, the non-science and technology components discussed above were considered to be in addition to existing 'mainstream' courses. Hence the authors recommended the introduction of four-year courses into the United Kingdom, in order to produce 'more complete' scientists and engineers and to maintain academic standards in the 'mainstream' subjects (Gerstl and Hutton 1966, pp. 63-64; Lawrence and Hutton 1981, p. 135). In the case of the United States, on the other hand, the recommendation of the Grinter Committee (1955) took place in a country where four-year courses were already the norm. In that paper, the four-year 'norm' was rejected, at least in the inflexible form suggested by other authors.

The rate-of-return formulae point to the possible adverse effects of a move to longer courses unless there are associated, off-setting, income-increasing effects. Here the surveys provide some indications of whether graduate employees feel that a change in the length of course would have been beneficial. The evidence in the Jones Report (1969) does not give an unqualified 'yes' either to a straightforward shortening or to a lengthening of course. Opinion seems divided and, at first sight, the results seem to be contradictory. Nevertheless, the differences are associated with quite distinct groups: there are academics and related individuals who feel there is a need to increase the amount and depth of material taught in their specialist area, requiring a longer course; there are individuals who have moved into occupations (and the first rungs of their careers) directly linked with their degree subject, who feel that they could have almost certainly managed more than adequately with a smaller knowledge base, which could have been provided by a shorter degree course; and there are those whose career paths have taken them into new fields, who feel the retrospective need for a broader-based education on roughly the same length of course.

Lifetime Education

It seems possible to reconcile the length and content requirements of these different groups by altering the structure of higher education in the following manner: (i) by building the foundation of higher education on a shorter common core of 'mainstream' subjects; and (ii) by adding on 'additional' subjects at a later stage in the individual's career, where this later choice depends largely on the career path that is evolving for the individual or which the individual plans to follow. Thus, the additional 'bolt-on' courses might provide, for example, mainly 'more of the same' for those planning to follow academic careers, or mainly non-science/ technology disciplines for those moving into management.

Following this scheme, an individual who moved on to a less than dynamic career path would probably find two 'core' years quite ample and would not have wasted additional years 'locked into' higher education. An individual who progressed on his or her career path towards specialist functions within the firm would take an additional period of education; those moving into, say, key positions in specialist research and development functions would concentrate on additional 'mainstream' subjects, while those progressing towards management would focus more upon non-science/technology subjects. On the other hand, higher education could filter out academically strong individuals who planned to go into academia. Such individuals might be required to take a further specialist course, prior to taking a postgraduate qualification. There seem to be important reasons in many subject areas for allowing such individuals to spend a period in employment outside higher education, after taking their 'core' courses. In so far as academia wished to recruit amongst managers (who had completed the basic 'mainstream' courses and a course in mainly non-science specialisms), it might also require them to complete an additional specialist 'mainstream' course. Likewise, an academic with three or more years of 'mainstream' subjects under his or her belt, but wishing to enter a managerial position in industry, might be required to complete a further course in non-science/technology subjects.

The advantage of a scheme of this type is its much greater flexibility: first, in terms of length, in that those who need most education would receive it, unlike the present system which has, at least in the past, tended to equalize the length of course; second, in terms of the timing of education, in that individuals would be allowed to take courses at roughly the time at which they became important in their career paths (which would in turn ensure that only those who required tuition in specialist subjects received it, and that this tuition was of the latest vintage and provided as it became needed); and, third, in terms of course content, in that the overall degree would now be built up from a number of 'bolt-on' components.

The change in NPV caused by moving from a traditional three-year course to a two-year course with, say, a two-year, 'bolt-on' option can be specified in Equation 4:

$$\Delta NPV = \frac{GE_{20} + C_{20} - G_{20} - V_{20}}{(1+r)^2} + \sum_{t=21}^{T-1} \frac{\Delta GE_t}{(1+r)^{t-18}}$$

$$+ \sum_{t=T}^{T+1} \frac{G_t + V_t' - GE_t' - C_t}{(1+r)^{t-18}} + \sum_{t=T+2}^{65} \frac{\Delta GE_t'}{(1+r)^{t-18}}$$

This is now comprised of two marginal decisions, one at age 18 and one at age T (where $19 < T < 64$). If we can ignore, for a moment, the comparative content of the first two years under the two-year versus three-year courses, then this approach includes the traditional three-year course as a special case. If the additional 'bolt-on' course takes a single year, rather than two years (as assumed in Equation 4), the first and third terms cancel out, and the second and fourth terms add together to form the single net income stream, which is in effect zero (as we are dealing with the difference between a one-year course taken immediately after a two-year course, and an identical third-year course). Thus, unless the change in curriculum content and timing during the 'two plus one' three-year course were adversely to affect the income stream in comparison to its 'continuous three-year' counterpart, then this scheme would be at least as good for the student. The indications of the survey evidence are that the flexibility to take the additional course at the most advantageous time in the individual's career and the opportunity to take the type of course which was most appropriate and up-to-date would make the returns to this option higher. If this is the case, we are moving towards the concept of lifetime learning.

Conclusions

The main question about such a scheme is whether the individual would wish to undertake courses at a later stage in his or her career. Certainly, with traditional grant-giving mechanisms and existing teaching methods, past experience suggests that a very small proportion of individuals would go back into education full-time or relocate in order to do so. The costs of income forgone are higher (particularly if the individual has to give up a permanent job) and the number of years of earning lifetime left to recoup the investment becomes progressively smaller as the age T increases. Nevertheless, it should be borne in mind that this course structure was designed to enable those for whom the return is sufficiently high to undertake further education. On the other hand, there appear to be strong grounds for looking at the way in which mature students could be better catered for by the higher education system in a way that would raise the rate of return to later courses. One such approach might be through sabbatical periods for employees with the investment costs shared between the individual, the firm, and the government. An alternative, which is discussed at length elsewhere (Bosworth 1982) is the introduction of part-time, distance-learning techniques based on the new advanced information technologies, which could reduce the cost elements of the equation substantially for the individual.

Acknowledgement

I have drawn on the results of research undertaken during a project funded by the Technical Change Centre (Bosworth 1982) and a project on Loughborough students funded by Loughborough University (Bosworth and Ford 1983a, 1983b, 1984).

References

Berthoud, R., and Smith, D. (1981) *The Education, Training, and Careers of Professional Engineers* Prepared for the Committee of Inquiry into the Engineering Profession by the Policy Studies Institute. London: HMSO

Bosworth, D.L. (1982) *Higher Education and Technological Change* Report to the Technical Change Centre, London

Bosworth, D.L., and Ford, J. (1981) *The Pattern of Student Demand for Places* Paper presented to the second SRHE Leverhulme seminar 29 June - 1 July 1981, Middleton Hall, Gorebridge, Midlothian

Bosworth, D.L., and Ford, J. (1983a) *The Supply of Loughborough Students: A Survey of 1982 Entrants* Report to the Loughborough University of Technology, Loughborough

Bosworth, D.L., and Ford, J. (1983b) *Income Expectations and the Decision to Enter Higher Education* Paper presented to the SRHE 1983 Annual Conference, Loughborough University of Technology, Loughborough

British Association (1961) *The Complete Scientist* London: Oxford University Press

Cairncross, A. (1980) *Science Studies: A Report to the Nuffield Foundation* London: Nuffield Foundation

Council of Engineering Institutions (1978) *Survey of Professional Engineers 1977* London: Council of Engineering Institutions

Excellence in Diversity: Towards a New Strategy for Higher Education (1983) Guildford: Society for Research into Higher Education

Finniston, M. (1980) *Engineering Our Future* Report of the Committee of Inquiry into the Engineering Profession. London: HMSO

Gerstl, J.E., and Hutton, S.P. (1966) *Engineers: The Anatomy of a Profession* London: Tavistock Publications

Grinter, L. (1955) Final report on evaluation of engineering education *Journal of Engineering Education* 46(1) 26-60

Hopkins, A.D. (1966) *The Training of Professional Metallurgists* Birmingham: Department of Metallurgy, University of Aston

Hutton, S.P. (1978) Opinions on the social science content of the ideal engineering course *Proceedings of the Zweiter Internationaler Kongress fur Ingenienausbildung* Technische Hochschule, Darmstadt

Johnstone, E. (1961) A survey of chemical engineering education and practice *Transactions of the Institution of Chemical Engineers* 39, 263-279

Jones, D.T.L. (1969) *The Education of Scientists for Industry: Report of a Survey of Views of Professional Scientists* Guildford: Society for Research into Higher Education

Kogan, M. (1981) *Project on the Expectations of Higher Education: Employers Expectations*. As Bosworth and Ford 1981

Lawrence, S., and Hutton, P. (1981) *German Engineers: The Anatomy of a Profession* London: Oxford University Press

McMahon, W.W., and Geske, J. (1981) Financing education: Efficiency and equity. In W.W. McMahon (Ed.) *Educational Finance* New York: Allyn Bacon

NAB fudges the future (1983) *The Times Higher Education Supplement* 18 March, p.1

Pippard, B. (1969) The educated scientist *Physics Bulletin*

Williams, G., and Gordon, A. (1981) Perceived earnings functions and ex ante rates of return to post-compulsory education in England *Higher Education* 10(2) 199-227

17 Taking Account of Mature Students

Alan Woodley

Of the many who have looked at the relationship between age and performance in universities none has as yet produced a definitive answer to the apparently simple question 'Do mature students do better or worse than younger students?'

Harris (1940) in the United States found evidence to suggest that younger students tended to obtain better degree results. Similar findings have been made in Britain by Malleson (1959), Forster (1959), Howell (1962), Barnett and Lewis (1963), McCracken (1969) and Kapur (1972), in Australia by Flecker (1959) and Sanders (1961), in Canada by Fleming (1959), and in New Zealand by Small (1966). However, most of these studies were based on samples of students who were generally aged between seventeen and twenty-one and the correlation techniques employed meant that the relationship between age and performance really only concerned this narrow age band. As such, the results probably suggest that bright children admitted early to higher education fare better than those whose entry is delayed while they gain the necessary qualifications. This view is supported by Harris (1940) who discovered that the relationship between age and performance disappeared when he controlled for intelligence. Other studies have shown that those who gain the necessary qualifications and then delay entry for a year or two are more successful than those who enter directly from school (Thomas, Beeby and Oram 1939; Derbyshire Education Committee 1966; Orr 1974).

Where studies have involved samples containing large numbers of older students the results have indicated that the relationship between age and performance is not a linear one. Philips and Cullen (1955), for instance, found that those aged twenty-four and over tended to do better than the eighteen and nineteen-year-old age group. Sanders (1961) showed that the university success rate fell until the age of twenty or twenty-one, then from about twenty-two onwards the success rate began to rise again. The problem with these two studies is that many of the older students were returning servicemen. They were often 'normal' entrants whose entry to university had been delayed by war and many had undergone some training in science or mathematics while in the armed forces. Also, while Eaton (1980) cites nine American studies which confirm the academic superiority of veterans, there is some contradictory British evidence. Mountford (1957) found that ex-service students who entered Liverpool University between 1947 and 1949 were more likely to have to spend an extra year or more on their courses and more likely to fail to complete their course.

Some studies have shown that whether mature students fare better or worse than younger students depends upon the subject being studied. Sanders (1963) has indicated that the maturity associated with increasing age and experience seems to be a positive predictor of success for some arts and social science courses. The general finding that older students do better in arts and social science and worse in science and maths is supported by Barnett, Holder and Lewis (1968), Fagin (1971), Sharon (1971) and Flecker (1959).

Walker's (1975) study of mature students at Warwick University represents the best British attempt to unravel the relationship between age and performance. He took 240 mature undergraduates who were admitted to the university between 1965 and 1971 and compared their progress with that of all undergraduates. This gave him a reasonably large sample to work with and the timing meant that the results were not distorted by any 'returning servicemen factor'. His methodology showed certain other refinements. First, he excluded overseas students. Such students tend to be older than average and also to fare worse academically (Woodley 1979), thus influencing any age/performance relationship. Secondly, he used two measures of performance; the proportion leaving without obtaining a degree and the degree results of those taking final examinations. Finally he weighted the degree class obtained according to its rarity value in each faculty.

The following findings achieved statistical significance:
  i In total, mature students obtained better degrees than non-mature students.
 ii In the arts faculty mature students obtained better degrees than non-mature students.
iii Mature students who did not satisfy the general entrance require-ment obtained better degrees than all other students.
 iv The degree results of mature students aged twenty-six to thirty were better than those of all other mature students.
Several other differences were noted but they did not achieve statistical significance due to the small numbers involved. The mature student sample only contained thirty-three women, twenty-six science students

and thirty-seven aged over thirty. The aim of the present study was to extend Walker's work to all British universities so that these and other relationships could be tested out on a much larger sample of mature students.

Methodology

The Universities Statistical Record provided data on the 1972, 1973 and 1974 intakes of all United Kingdom universities. To be included in the sample, students had to be:
  − Full-time or sandwich undergraduates aiming for a first degree.
  − New entrants.
  − Enrolled on a course of three or more years' duration.
  − Home fee-paying status, ie not overseas students.
The resulting sample comprised 165,400 students aged under twenty-one and 18,343 mature students aged twenty-one and over. It was possible to follow their progress up until the end of the 1978-1979 academic year, by which time only 3 per cent were still studying, the remainder having successfully graduated or permanently withdrawn. Performance was measured in two ways:
  a Overall progress:
     'Successful' − Graduate or still studying
     'Failed' − Academic failure during the course or in final examinations
     'Withdrew' − Withdrawal for non-academic reasons, eg ill health
  b Degree performance:
     Graduates were divided into those who gained a First or Upper Second and those who gained some other class of degree.
When one is dealing with such large sample numbers, differences of less than 1 per cent can be shown to be statistically significant. In this paper we have therefore chosen to comment on differences and trends that appear to be meaningful rather than merely statistically significant. This approach has its dangers but we have tried to avoid major pit-falls by only calculating percentages when a group contained fifty or more students.

The Characteristics of Mature Students

Before proceeding to the analysis of performance it is worthwhile considering just who the mature students were. For instance, Table 17.1 shows that they were predominantly aged twenty-one to twenty-five and very few were over the age of forty.

The majority of mature students were men and the sex-bias was greater than among younger students (Table 17.2). However, a more

Table 17.1   Age Distribution of Mature Students

	n = 18,343
	%
21-25	66
26-30	19
31-40	12
41-50	3
51 and over	1

detailed age breakdown shows wide variations. Women almost attained parity in the thirty-one to forty age group and actually formed the majority of those aged forty-one to fifty.

Table 17.2   Sex Distribution of Undergraduates: by Age

	Under 21	21 and over	21-25	26-30	31-40	41-50	51 and over
n =	165,400	18,343	12,046	3,502	2,123	498	174
	%	%	%	%	%	%	%
Male	64	71	75	71	53	44	58
Female	36	29	25	29	47	56	42

Mature students were less likely to be taking science subjects and more likely to be studying social science (Table 17.3). The subject breakdown for those aged twenty-one to twenty-five was very similar to that for younger students but as students got older they were more likely to take arts subjects and less likely to take science. Interest in the social sciences peaked among the thirty-one to forty age group.

Table 17.3   Subject Studied: by Age

	Under 21	21 and over	21-25	26-30	31-40	41-50	51 and over
n =	165,400	18,343	12,046	3,502	2,123	498	174
	%	%	%	%	%	%	%
Arts	24	26	23	29	34	47	59
Social Science	27	35	30	40	47	43	30
Science	49	39	47	31	18	10	11

Mature students were more likely to be entering university with non-standard qualifications such as ONCs, HNDs and foreign qualifications (Table 17.4). One in five entered with 'other UK qualifications' which could range from none at all to a three-year teaching certificate, but unfortunately no more detailed breakdown is available. The older the students the more likely they were to have 'other UK qualifications' and the less likely to enter on the basis of ONCs, HNCs, etc.

Table 17.4   Entry Qualifications: by Age

	Under 21	21 and over	21-25	26-30	31-40	41-50	51 and over
n =	165,400	18,343	12,046	3,502	2,123	498	174
	%	%	%	%	%	%	%
GCE	83	52	57	48	35	34	29
SCE	13	10	9	11	15	17	18
ONC/D, HNC/D	1	15	18	14	8	4	5
Other UK qualifications	2	19	14	23	35	40	43
Foreign qualifications	*	3	2	5	6	5	5

* less than 0.5%

The Performance of Mature Students

All Students

Mature students were slightly less likely to successfully complete their courses. 83 per cent of them graduated compared with 87 per cent of the younger students, the difference being largely attributable to a greater rate of withdrawal for non-academic reasons (Table 17.5). Mature students who graduated were just as likely as younger students to gain good degrees. Approximately one in three of each group gained a First or Upper Second.

When we look at the detailed age breakdown we see that those aged eighteen and nineteen were most likely to graduate and those aged under eighteen and over forty were the least successful. However, in overall terms there was relatively little variation between the age groups. Variation was much more marked in the case of degree performance. Generally speaking the pattern found for overall progress was repeated, with a peak in performance among the eighteen and nineteen-year-olds and a falling off with increasing age. However, the twenty-six to thirty-year-olds represented a major deviation from this pattern and, in line with Walker's findings, emerged as the group most likely to gain a good degree. The relatively poor performance of those who entered university aged under eighteen also deserves comment. The great majority of these were Scottish students and in Scottish universities it is common practice to leave after three years with an Ordinary degree rather than study for a fourth year to obtain an Honours degree. The figures should therefore not be taken to indicate that the very young do not fare well at university.

Table 17.5   Performance: by Age

	Under 21	21 and over	Under 18	18	19	20	21-25	26-30	31-40	41-50	51 and over
n =	165,400	18,343	5,898	85,431	60,491	13,580	12,046	3,502	2,123	498	174
OVERALL PROGRESS	%	%	%	%	%	%	%	%	%	%	%
Successful	87	83	82	87	87	84	83	84	84	82	80
Failed	6	7	7	6	6	8	8	5	6	6	5
Withdrew	7	10	11	7	7	8	10	11	10	12	15
n =	137,686	14,555	4,596	71,350	50,783	10,957	9,508	2,823	1,736	400	88
DEGREE PERFORMANCE	%	%	%	%	%	%	%	%	%	%	%
First or Upper Second	33	32	25	34	34	31	31	37	32	28	22
Other degrees	67	68	75	66	66	69	69	63	68	72	78

Analysis by Sex

Male and female mature students were slightly less likely to gain a degree than their younger counterparts. However, within each individual age group women were more likely to graduate than men and less likely to fail on academic grounds (Table 17.6).

Male mature students were somewhat less likely to gain a good degree but in the case of women the reverse was true. Men aged twenty-six to thirty performed as well as the eighteen and nineteen-year-olds but other mature students fared less well, particularly in the higher age groups. Female mature students on the other hand performed well across the whole age range, and those aged twenty-six to thirty were extremely successful, with 44 per cent gaining a good degree.

Analysis by Subject Studied

Within each of the three subject areas mature students were slightly less likely successfully to complete the course than were younger students (Table 17.7). In arts and social science this was because a higher

Table 17.6   Performance: by Age and Sex

		MEN										
		Under 21	21 and over	Under 18	18	19	20	21-25	26-30	31-40	41-50	51 and over
	n =	105,634	12,978	3,313	52,266	40,131	9,924	9,052	2,469	1,135	221	101
OVERALL PROGRESS		%	%	%	%	%	%	%	%	%	%	%
Successful		85	82	80	85	86	83	82	83	81	79	74
Failed		8	9	8	7	7	9	10	7	10	11	9
Withdrew		7	9	12	8	7	8	9	10	9	10	17
	n =	85,944	10,126	2,488	42,513	33,056	7,887	7,068	1,962	882	171	43
DEGREE PERFORMANCE		%	%	%	%	%	%	%	%	%	%	n
First or Upper Second		33	30	29	34	33	30	29	34	26	24	(6)
Other degrees		67	70	71	66	67	70	71	66	74	76	(37)
		WOMEN										
	n =	59,766	5,365	2,585	33,163	20,360	3,656	2,994	1,033	988	277	73
OVERALL PROGRESS		%	%	%	%	%	%	%	%	%	%	%
Successful		90	86	85	90	90	83	85	86	87	84	88
Failed		3	3	4	3	2	3	4	2	2	3	1
Withdrew		8	11	11	7	7	9	11	12	10	12	11
	n =	51,742	4,429	2,108	28,837	17,727	3,070	2,440	861	854	299	45
DEGREE PERFORMANCE		%	%	%	%	%	%	%	%	%	%	n
First or Upper Second		33	38	21	33	35	33	36	44	38	32	(13)
Other degrees		67	62	79	67	65	67	64	56	62	68	(32)

proportion of mature students withdrew for non-academic reasons but in science they experienced a higher failure rate. When we consider the detailed age breakdown it seems to be the case in science that the older the students are, the less likely they are to graduate. No such pattern emerged for arts and social science.

Mature students taking arts and social science gained better degrees than their younger counterparts but the reverse was true for science subjects. In arts, performance increased steadily with age, peaked among the twenty-six to thirty age group, and then declined. The same general pattern was found for social science, apart from the relatively poor performance of the twenty-year-olds. In science the eighteen and nineteen-year-olds were the most successful groups, followed by those aged twenty and under eighteen. Among the mature students those aged twenty-six to thirty again fared best but the proportions gaining good degrees did not vary a great deal.

Table 17.7   Performance: by Age and Subject Studied

		Under 21	21 and over	Under 18	18	19	20	21-25	26-30	31-40	41-50	51 and over
ARTS												
	n =	38,269	4,602	1,252	19,297	14,596	3,124	2,620	970	710	229	73
OVERALL PROGRESS		%	%	%	%	%	%	%	%	%	%	%
Successful		88	83	83	88	89	86	82	84	86	83	75
Failed		3	4	3	3	3	4	5	4	3	6	5
Withdrew		9	13	14	9	8	10	13	13	11	11	19
	n =	33,618	3,818	1,034	16,922	12,980	2,682	2,154	810	608	191	55
DEGREE PERFORMANCE		%	%	%	%	%	%	%	%	%	%	%
First or Upper Second		36	42	22	35	38	40	43	46	39	31	24
Other degrees		64	58	78	65	62	60	57	54	61	69	76
SOCIAL SCIENCE												
	n =	42,418	6,117	1,426	21,232	16,050	3,710	3,524	1,366	980	210	37
OVERALL PROGRESS		%	%	%	%	%	%	%	%	%	%	n
Successful		89	85	84	89	89	87	84	86	87	85	(26)
Failed		5	5	7	4	4	5	6	4	5	5	(3)
Withdrew		7	10	9	6	6	8	10	10	8	10	(8)
	n =	37,687	5,206	1,192	18,949	14,319	3,227	2,973	1,179	850	178	26
DEGREE PERFORMANCE		%	%	%	%	%	%	%	%	%	%	n
First or Upper Second		32	35	25	33	33	30	35	39	30	26	(5)
Other degrees		68	65	75	67	67	70	65	61	70	74	(21)
SCIENCE												
	n =	79,039	6,988	2,967	42,050	27,766	6,256	5,479	1,063	382	51	13
OVERALL PROGRESS		%	%	%	%	%	%	%	%	%	%	n
Successful		84	79	80	84	85	81	80	78	73	61	(7)
Failed		8	12	9	8	8	12	12	11	15	20	(3)
Withdrew		8	9	11	8	7	8	8	11	12	20	(3)
	n =	66,362	5,530	2,368	35,468	23,480	5,046	4,380	834	278	31	7
DEGREE PERFORMANCE		%	%	%	%	%	%	%	%	%	n	n
First or Upper Second		32	23	27	33	32	27	23	25	22	(8)	(1)
Other degrees		68	77	73	67	68	73	77	75	78	(23)	(6)

Analysis by Entry Qualifications

The analysis is presented in Table 17.8.

The figures shed more light on the performance of those aged under eighteen. It can be seen that within the GCE and SCE categories these students perform just as well as eighteen-year-olds. Their poor performance noted in Table 17.5 would therefore seem to be due to the different circumstances obtaining in Scotland.

Among the mature students, those entering with GCE qualifications were the most likely to graduate, closely followed by those with 'other UK qualifications'. Those with ONCs, HNCs, etc. and SCE qualifications fared somewhat worse, and those with foreign qualifications were the least successful. However, those with foreign qualifications were most likely to gain a good degree. Those with GCE qualifications did almost as well but those with ONCs, HNCs etc and 'other UK qualifications' came some way behind. Those with SCE qualifications were least likely to gain a good degree but this is part of the Scottish phenomenon noted above.

Unfortunately it was not possible to test out Walker's finding that mature students not possessing the general entrance requirement tend to gain better degrees. The majority of such students probably fall in the 'other UK qualifications' category but this also contains highly qualified students. Others, to judge from Walker's examples, will fall in the GCE category despite having had some of the entry requirements waived such as a GCE pass in a mathematics or science subject.

As this is such a complex table each qualification group is commented on in detail in turn.

Mature students entering university on the basis of GCE qualifications were slightly less likely to graduate than younger students but equally likely to gain a good degree. Students aged forty-one to fifty were the most likely to graduate but the least likely to gain a First or Upper Second. Those aged twenty-six to thirty showed the best degree performance.

Mature students entering with Scottish Certificate of Education qualifications were slightly more likely to graduate than their younger counterparts and just as likely to gain a good degree. Once again those aged twenty-six to thirty displayed the best degree performance but the proportions gaining good degrees were relatively low among the higher age groups.

Mature students entering with Ordinary National Certificate/Diploma or Higher National Certificate/Diploma (ONC/D, HNC/D) were more likely successfully to complete the course than younger students with similar qualifications but were no more likely to gain a good degree. The best degrees were obtained by those aged eighteen on entry and there was no peak among those aged twenty-six to thirty.

Mature students with other UK qualifications were as likely to graduate but somewhat less likely to gain a good degree. Among the younger students degree performance increased with age and those aged twenty were the most successful group. Among the mature students degree performance was uniformly high for those aged twenty-six to fifty but the overall figure was depressed by the relatively poor performance of those aged twenty-one to twenty-five.

Mature students with foreign qualifications were slightly less likely successfully to complete the course but if they did so they were much more likely to gain a good degree. The detailed age breakdown shows

Table 17.8   Performance: by Age and Entry Qualifications

				GCE							
	Under 21	21 and over	Under 18	18	19	20	21-25	26-30	31-40	41-50	51 and over
n =	138,046	9,560	1,786	69,077	55,703	11,480	6,922	1,667	752	168	51
OVERALL PROGRESS	%	%	%	%	%	%	%	%	%	%	%
Successful	88	85	89	89	88	86	84	86	87	91	88
Failed	5	6	5	5	5	7	7	4	5	3	2
Withdrew	6	9	6	6	7	7	9	9	8	6	10
n =	117,235	7,725	1,498	59,090	47,241	9,406	5,519	1,381	644	151	30
DEGREE PERFORMANCE	%	%	%	%	%	%	%	%	%	%	n
First or Upper Second	35	36	37	36	34	32	34	42	36	30	(13)
Other degrees	65	64	63	64	66	68	66	58	64	70	(17)
				SCE							
n =	21,977	1,893	3,944	14,870	2,634	529	1,057	399	319	86	32
OVERALL PROGRESS	%	%	%	%	%	%	%	%	%	%	%
Successful	77	79	79	78	75	74	77	80	85	76	(29)
Failed	9	8	7	9	12	11	10	6	4	8	(1)
Withdrew	13	13	14	13	14	16	14	14	11	16	(2)
n =	16,373	1,449	2,974	11,131	1,891	377	788	316	267	64	14
DEGREE PERFORMANCE	%	%	%	%	%	%	%	%	%	%	n
First or Upper Second	19	18	19	19	17	13	19	26	10	8	(1)
Other degrees	81	82	81	81	83	87	81	74	90	92	(13)
				ONC/D, HNC/D							
n =	2,142	2,791	4	474	847	817	2,110	482	169	22	8
OVERALL PROGRESS	%	%	n	%	%	%	%	%	%	n	n
Successful	74	80	(2)	74	73	75	80	82	82	(15)	(7)
Failed	15	11	(–)	14	15	16	12	9	10	(4)	(1)
Withdrew	11	9	(2)	12	12	9	8	9	8	(3)	(–)
n =	1,553	2,176	2	352	611	588	1,640	389	127	15	5
DEGREE PERFORMANCE	%	%	n	%	%	%	%	%	%	n	n
First or Upper Second	30	29	(1)	34	29	27	29	30	30	(4)	(–)
Other degrees	70	71	(1)	66	71	73	71	70	70	(11)	(5)

Cont. overleaf

Table 17.8 *(cont.)*

					Other UK qualifications					
n =	2,931	3,497	141	906	1,195	689	1,683	793	748	199	74
OVERALL PROGRESS	%	%	%	%	%	%	%	%	%	%	%
Successful	82	83	77	82	84	81	84	82	82	79	69
Failed	7	7	7	6	8	8	8	6	7	8	9
Withdrew	11	10	16	13	8	11	8	12	11	13	22
n =	2,305	2,763	106	702	961	536	1,369	618	590	153	33
DEGREE PERFORMANCE	%	%	%	%	%	%	%	%	%	%	n
First or Upper Second	33	30	26	27	34	39	24	36	37	36	(4)
Other degrees	67	70	74	73	66	61	76	64	63	64	(29)

					Foreign qualifications					
n =	311	604	24	110	112	65	274	163	135	23	9
OVERALL PROGRESS	%	%	n	%	%	%	%	%	%	n	n
Successful	77	74	(23)	75	76	77	74	73	76	(17)	(7)
Failed	7	10	(1)	9	7	5	9	10	11	(2)	(−)
Withdrew	15	16	–	15	17	18	10	17	13	(4)	(2)
n =	220	432	16	75	79	50	192	119	98	17	6
DEGREE PERFORMANCE	%	%	n	%	%	%	%	%	%	n	n
First or Upper Second	25	38	(8)	25	24	18	39	36	41	(5)	(1)
Other degrees	75	62	(8)	75	76	82	61	64	59	(12)	(5)

that degree performance was high across the twenty-one to forty range and much lower between the ages of eighteen and twenty.

Summary and Discussion

We began with the question 'Do mature students do better or worse than younger students?' The present analysis suggests that in general mature students are slightly more likely to leave university without a degree but that those who graduate are just as likely to gain a First or Upper Second. However, the overall figures conceal important variations.

    a 'Mature students are slightly more likely to leave university without a degree'

         – This was found to be true for men and women, for those studying arts, social science and science, and for those entering on the basis of GCE qualifications. Mature students entering with other types of qualifications fared no worse, and in some cases better than younger students with similar qualifications.

    b 'Mature students are just as likely to gain a First or Upper Second'

         – Mature women students tended to gain better degrees than

younger women but mature men were slightly less successful than younger men.

- In arts and social science mature students gained better degrees than younger students but in science the reverse was true.
- Mature students with foreign entry qualifications were more successful than younger students with similar qualifications. Those with 'other UK qualifications' fared slightly worse than their younger counterparts. In the other qualification groups the degree performance of mature students closely matched that of younger students.

The distinction between mature and younger students is a crude one. By breaking the sample down into finer age groups it was possible to explore the general relationship between age and university perform-ance. The results suggest that the two basic findings should be expanded as follows:

i 'Students aged eighteen and nineteen are the most likely to graduate. Those aged between twenty and forty are slightly less successful and those aged under eighteen and over forty are the least likely to graduate. However, the differences are never great and they are caused by variations in the proportions leaving for non-academic reasons rather than academic failure.'

ii 'Students aged twenty-six to thirty are the most likely to gain a First or Upper Second and beyond this point performance declines with age. In the lower age range those aged eighteen and nineteen gain better degrees that those aged twenty to twenty-five. Those aged under eighteen are relatively unsuccessful but this arises from different practices in Scottish universities.'

The relationship between age and performance is clearly not a simple linear one. Furthermore, the detailed findings presented here show that the relationship varies with sex, subject studied and entry qualifications and any explanations must take these variations into account. In Figures 17.1, 17.2 and 17.3 we show the relationship between age and degree performance, controlling for these other variables, and offer some observations below.

In arts and social science degree performance increases with age, peaks in the twenty-six to thirty age group then declines thereafter. It appears that in these subject areas extra life experience can be translated into greater academic success. However, beyond the age of thirty, although more experience has been gained, this seems to be cancelled out by increased learning difficulties. Older students are likely to have had a considerable break from full-time education and to have lost some study skills. Their capacity for learning may also have decreased both in terms of memory and of the mental flexibility required to adapt to new perspectives. In science, although we are handicapped by lack of

Figure 17.1   Degree Performance: by Age and Subject Studied

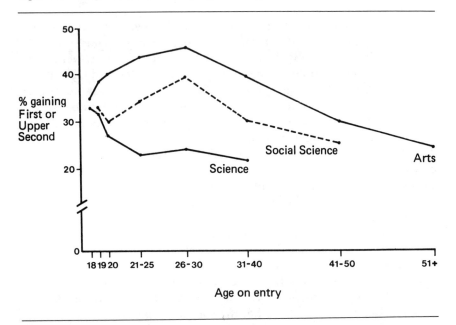

Figure 17.2   Degree Performance: by Age and Sex

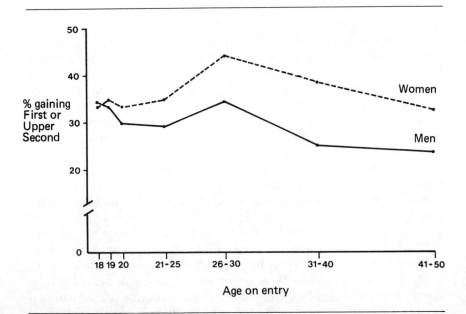

Figure 17.3   Degree Performance: by Age and Entry Qualifications

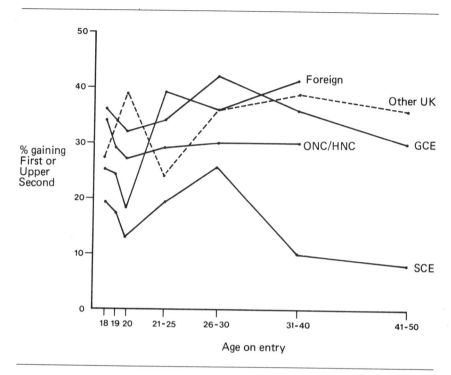

numbers in the higher age groups, there appears to be a general decline in degree performance with age. It appears that increased life experience does not compensate for the decline in mathematical and scientific skills resulting from a break in study which was noted by Sanders (1963).

Women students gain better degrees than men in all age groups except the eighteen-year-olds. One possible explanation might be that women returning to study are of a higher academic calibre than men. Boys are nearly twice as likely to enter university on leaving schooling and therefore there must be proportionately more highly intelligent girls who are excluded at this stage.

When we look at entry qualifications the relationship between age and degree performance is much more varied and complex. In the case of GCE and SCE qualifications those students aged twenty-six to thirty again do best and performance declines among the older groups. However, there is also a decline in performance between the ages of eighteen and twenty which suggests that those who, having spent a year or two since leaving school acquiring the necessary 'school-type' qualifications, then gain entry to university are less likely to gain a good degree. The decline in performance between the ages of eighteen and twenty is also present among those entering with ONCs, HNCs, etc., but there is little variation among the twenty-one to forty age group. The majority of these students probably take science courses at university and this would go some way to explain the shape of the curve and the fact that they tend to perform less well than those with GCE qualifications. The lower performance figures for those with SCE qualifications almost certainly reflects the different degree structure found in Scottish universities.

The categories of foreign and 'other UK' qualifications tell us nothing about level. Within each there will be students with very high and very low qualifications and this may explain why the curves are so different and so erratic. In the case of foreign qualifications there is again a fall in performance between the ages of eighteen and twenty, possibly for the same reason as that suggested for those entering with British school-type qualifications, but then there is a dramatic improvement among those aged twenty-one to twenty-five which is sustained in the higher age groups. It is possible that many of these students have already gained degrees or similar high level qualifications in other countries. In the case of 'other UK' qualifications, degree performance actually improves between the ages of eighteen and twenty, suggesting that those who have done more substantial courses since leaving school are at an advantage. Degree performance between the ages of twenty-six and fifty is high and fairly constant but the most noticeable feature is the relatively poor performance of the twenty-one to twenty-five age group. During the time period in question many of the latter group would be students embarking on a degree course immediately after a three-year teaching certificate course and it may be that they found the higher level of study particularly difficult to cope with.

The relationship between age and performance is clearly a complex one and further analysis is necessary. In part more detail is required. For instance, we would like to break down age, subject studied and entry qualifications into finer groups. This could be done for age and subject studied, if the sample size were increased sufficiently to justify it, but with entry qualifications we are restrained by lack of detailed information held on the record. Further analysis is also required to explore the inter-relationships between sex, subject studied and entry qualifications and how they affect the relationship between age and performance. For example, do women mature students do better than men in all subject areas? Do mature students fare less well in science subjects because they hold lower qualifications?

In terms of policy-making the present findings would suggest that universities should have few qualms about increasing their mature student intakes. As a group they perform as well as younger students and women and those aged twenty-six to thirty are particularly successful.

The only problem area would seem to be in science subjects where mature students are more likely to fail and less likely to gain a good degree.

Acknowledgements

The author would like to thank Cynthia Holme of the Universities Statistical Record for providing numerous computer print-outs and Fran Woodley for wading through the same.

References

Barnett, V.D., Holder, R.L. and Lewis, T. (1968) Some new results on the association between students' ages and their degree results *Journal of the Royal Statistical Society* A (131)

Barnett, V.D. and Lewis, T. (1963) A study of the relation between GCE and degree results *Journal of the Royal Statistical Society* A (126) 187-226

Derbyshire Education Committee (1966) Awards to students (mimeo)

Eaton, E.G. (1980) The academic performance of mature age students : a review of the general literature. In Hore, T. and West, L.H.T. (Editors) *Mature Age Students in Australian Higher Education* Higher Education Advisory and Research Unit, Monash University, Australia

Fagin, M.C. (1971) *Life Experience has Academic Value* ERIC Document Reproduction Service, ED047219

Flecker, R. (1959) Characteristics of passing and failing students in first year university of mathematics *The Educand* 3 (3)

Fleming, W.G. (1959) *Personal and Academic Factors as Predictors of First Year Success in Ontario Universities* Atkinson Study Report Number 5, University of Toronto, Department of Educational Research

Forster, M. (1959) *An Audit of Academic Performance*

Harris, D. (1940) Factors affecting college grades : a review of the literature *Psychology Bulletin* 37

Howell, D.A. (1962) *A Study of the 1955 Entry to British Universities* Evidence to the Robbins Committee on Higher Education, University of London (mimeo)

Kapur, K.L. (1972) Student wastage at Edinburgh University. I. Factors related to failure and drop-out *Universities Quarterly* Summer

Malleson, N.B. (1959) University Student, 1953. I-Profile *Universities Quarterly* 13, 287-298

McCracken, D. (1969) *University Student Performance* Report of the Student Health Department, University of Leeds

Mountford, Sir. J. (1957) *How They Fared – A Survey of a Three-Year Student Entry* Liverpool University Press

Philips, H. and Cullen, A. (1955) Age and academic success *Forum of Education* 14

Sanders, C. (1961) *Psychological and Educational Bases of Academic Performance* Brisbane : Australian Council for Educational Research

Sanders, C. (1963) Australian universities and their educational problems *The Australian University* 1,2

Sharon, A.T. (1971) Adult academic achievement in relation to formal education and age *Adult Education Journal* 21

Small, J.J. (1966) *Achievement and Adjustment in the First Year at University* Wellington : New Zealand Council for Educational Research

Thomas, W., Beeby, C.E. and Oram, M.H. (1939) *Entrance to the University* Wellington : New Zealand Council for Educational Research

Walker, P. (1975) The university performance of mature students *Research in Education* 14, 1-13

Woodley, A. (1979) *The Prediction of Degree Performance among Undergraduates in the Commerce and Social Science Faculty* University of Birmingham, unpublished

18 Articulating Art and Design

Stroud Cornock

Art and design studies together represent a distinct element within Britain's provision of higher education. During the academic year 1980-81 a total of 13,421 art and design students enrolled on 203 undergraduate courses, only seven of them in the university sector, giving the Council for National Academic Awards (CNAA) what it calls a 'near monopoly' in this field. Post-school study in art and design has normally been four years to first-degree level, the first of these being a general 'foundation course', and in character the study is unusual in being both practical and holistic. There are remarkably few recognized textbooks associated with these courses, and their examinations concentrate to an unusual extent on a global assessment of non-written work. So, because this part of the higher education system differs significantly from mainstream provision, it can be viewed as a valuable 'experiment' with potential lessons for non art and design disciplines.

The relationship between art and design has not been clear. The fine arts have traditionally been accorded the status of 'pure' subjects, which should therefore contribute to the study of design subjects, the applied arts. But artists have experienced difficulty in specifying the knowledge that can be applied. In general neither art nor design is studied as a theoretical subject, yet both strongly resist the notion that they are made up of manual and technical skills. The emphasis has been on practicality: on attention to the student's ability to set up and manage complex projects. These may involve: first, problem formulation; second, bringing to bear conceptual and physical tools; and, third, the presentation and evaluation of results. Thus each student is likely to be working on a unique project.

The learning experience in art and design is measurably different from that of an engineering student. It is not simply that the former have horny hands; it is that practical, and especially visuo-spatial concerns develop aspects of mental performance which together give graduates a distinct character, and one which persists (Cornock 1982). Its basis lies in a non-verbal form of consciousness. 'Tacit consciousness' (Cornock 1984b) may receive greater attention if Britain moves away from an atomistic, specialized and theoretical approach to higher education and considers ways of encouraging capabilities, setting more realistic problems and establishing a profile of the individual student's capabilities (cf Ramsden and Entwistle 1981).

Art and design share a unity of concern for the quality of the visual environment and have common roots in tacit knowledge, which gives them an epistemological unit. Thus we should be justified in viewing the art and design subjects as having a great deal in common, and standing somewhat apart from much of the rest of higher education. In what follows the aim will be to do three things: outline the development of art and design within the educational system; indicate the level and type of relevant research effort; and point to a gathering debate on change stimulated in part by the fifth SRHE Leverhulme seminar and reflected in a number of conference discussions.

Art and Design in Education

The first academy of painting and sculpture opened its gates in 1490 (Pevsner 1940). This was motivated by a desire on the part of painters and sculptors to raise their tradesman status to that we would think of as the educated professional. The strategy was to show the scientific principles underlying these practices so that they could be made the subject of intellectual dispute. Within two hundred years they had succeeded in gaining acceptance as courtiers at Versailles, the *Academie Royale de Peinture et de Sculpture* had been established, and those practices were assimilated within a metaphysical concept of 'art' (Karel 1974).

In the early nineteenth century Britain encouraged the decorative arts through an expanding network of schools based on South Kensington whose core subject was drawing (Ashwin 1975). These British schools were distinguished by two tendencies: first, a drift of attention from the applied to the 'fine' arts; and, second, preoccupation with practice rather than theory. The municipal art school infrastructure taught a hierarchy of practices with the fine arts at its apex and became invested with a lofty sense of carrying forward a European cultural tradition.

At the end of the 1950s a major review culminated in the Coldstream Report (HMSO 1960) and changes followed. A new National Council for Diplomas in Art and Design (NCDAD):

 i   placed responsibility for curriculum and assessment in the hands of art schools approved by panels of practitioners;
 ii swept away classroom teaching (eg of life drawing, studio pottery, lettering, anatomy) and reoriented art schools towards contemporary developments; and

iii grafted a twenty per cent component of theoretical and written
work on to the courses.

The art schools thus put the old associations with craft training firmly
behind them and emphasized their role as engines of high culture.

At the level of higher education the art schools' three-year programmes of study have been significantly shaped by individual students under
tutorial guidance. What has been achieved is stylistic contemporaneity in
the artefacts produced in the schools, and a capacity for independent
development on the part of graduates.

Two further changes threw the arts schools into contrast with the rest
of the higher education system. The proud and fiercely autonomous art
schools were first pressed into amalgamation with relatively undisting-
uished technical schools and, in the early 1970s, the NCDAD was
incorporated into the CNAA in such a way as to preserve its special
character (Cornock 1984a).

It is also important to note that the system has reacted to rather than
initiated debate on change. Few who work within the colleges and
faculties of art and design think of themselves as members of an
academic community because they are appointed and encouraged as
practitioners. Courses have tended to acquire legitimacy by association,
relying upon a prestige which derives from the fact that society
celebrates its cultural values by displaying products considered to be
'fine'. There has been a good deal of anti-intellectualism in the art
schools, which have often relied upon defensive arguments and
extra-mural achievements in frustrated efforts to forestall change; for
example, in 1971 a distinguished artist's claim that the art schools were
being 'murdered' by the polytechnics sparked off a controversy culmi-
nating in the mass resignation of the Fine Art Panel of the NCDAD.

Relevant Research

Practice in art and design occupies the position taken by research in
scientific and other fields. It is the index of lecturing ability, a parallel
with the publication of results, and a means of staff development (cf
CNAA 1983). The terms 'research', 'experiment' and 'inquiry' are widely
used with a conviction born of the belief that the processes giving rise to
art and design match in seriousness those which produce scientific
achievement. A statement of the case for practice as research is given by
Jones (1980), and current moves to institutionalize this approach include
a decision by the Royal College of Art of introduce the degree of 'Doctor
of Art' and the policy statement on research published by the CNAA
(1983). An earlier discussion paper forming a part of the council's review
and revision of the 1974 Rochester Report argued that, because most
lecturers in art and design are practitioners, it follows that they should

both study for and supervise essentially practical 'research' degrees for examination by members of the art and design world. The policy statement recognizes art and design activities 'which equate with research' as artefactual and encourages theses supported by practical work, noting that this may not go far enough to meet fine art, where 'an entirely new award' may be necessary.

Because of this emphasis on practice there has been relatively little formal research in these fields. Semi-formal work has been reported by the journal *Leonardo*, and in recent years there has appeared *Design Studies* and the *Journal of Art and Design Education*. In fact art education and art history make up the largest bodies of relevant (or at least adjacent) research.

Aims

A number of sharply different aims can be served by inquiry in the art schools. For example:
  i   to provide useful and reliable facts (eg concerning graduate career profiles);
  ii to help to establish the social and educational value of work in the field (ie policy research);
  iii to facilitate educational evaluation and development (ie increasing effectiveness of courses); and
  iv to further art and design through commissioned projects, staff development or individual creative work.

It will be apparent from the account already given that there has been little effort on the part of the art schools to arm themselves with facts (i), to initiate change (ii), or to question traditional approaches (iii), so that most effort has gone into the fourth of the classes of aims listed above. Three direct contributions have been made to this debate. The first was prepared for the Council for Higher Education in Art and Design (CHEAD) in 1974 by Robin Plummer (1974); it argues the need for disciplined research necessitating the challenging of previously unquestioned assumptions so as to strengthen art and design courses within the mainstream of higher education provision, and even to influence other disciplines. The second contribution arose out of SRHE Leverhulme seminar 5 whose various sections point to the need to identify more clearly what Plummer had called:

   ...the whole area of visual/tactile/performance/kinaesthetic and design disciplines which has no convenient word, such as numeracy or literacy, by which it may be identified.

– and to place this whole area within an educational context (Robinson 1982). But the third and most recent contribution, the revised Rochester Report (CNAA 1983), sets a limit to the link between teaching and research (para. II, 2.3), and where Plummer and SRHE Leverhulme 5 seek to give priority to academic considerations, the art and design lobby as it has influenced the revised Rochester Report has re-emphasized a concern with practice.

Art and Design

The CNAA awarded its first PhD in the art and design field in 1973 and has to date awarded a total of fifteen PhDs and twenty-three MPhils. The premier institution in art and design at postgraduate level is the Royal College of Art (RCA), whose Department of General Studies has awarded seventy-nine Masters degrees by thesis since 1970, and eight PhDs, the first in 1979. An important policy change behind these figures lies in the fact that in 1979 the department began to accept a number of people in mid-career who were seconded to studies directly relevant to art and design in the further and higher education sector. (This providing an opportunity for staff development which can lead to a critical evaluation of institutional aims and teaching.)

The two indexes of educational research are a cumulative *Index of British Studies in Art and Design Education* (Allison 1983), and a *Register of Current Research in the UK 1983* (Institute of Education 1983): they indicate that some 800 Masters and Doctoral studies have been completed and some sixty studies are current, of which at least thirty-four are registered for a higher degree.

Fine Art

Semi-formal projects involving experiments in art and technology were formulated in Britain in the late 1960s, of which the best examples were the electro-mechanical structures designed and built by the sculptor Edward Ihnatowicz; but the absence of funding limited projects in scale and number and those involved tended to move on to other interests, although at least one project of this kind was registered for a PhD and two were externally funded.

Of studies directed at the work of the art schools perhaps the best-known is Madge and Weinberger (1973), which examined some extreme staff and student attitudes. Other attitudinal studies have followed, and continue. Some sixteen fine art studies are on record, of which at least seven were of a kind that could contribute to educational development.

Design

Because architecture is organized as a separate profession it is not included within faculties of art and design whose design courses usually include graphic design, industrial design (which includes interiors, products, furniture, jewellery and ceramics), and fashion and textiles. The Leicester *Index* (Allison 1983) includes six studies, three current, which have apparent reference to design studies in higher education. Nine current registrations of this kind are listed by the CNAA and three current studies are outlined in the *Register*, whilst the Department of Design Research at the Royal College of Art has mounted some seventy-seven projects over twenty years, of which twenty-five are currently registered, ten at PhD level. Of these design studies eight appear to be relevant to educational development but the majority are technical studies.

Research Method

High-level art and design studies call for an ability to initiate projects and to present their outcome; the student identifies a set of concerns and working practices which, even within a single course, can differ widely as individuals elect to work with a range of technical processes. Reductionist research into these studies is therefore even less likely to bear fruit than in other subjects since we are unlikely to be guided by the attempt to define causal relationships between the elements of art and design studies in terms of statistical correlates (Elton and Laurillard 1979).

The problem is to capture aspects of these learning milieux not manifest in textbooks, examination papers or syllabuses so that there is scope for illuminative evaluation of work in this field (Parlett and Dearden 1981) for: 'What we do not have...are vivid protrayals of educational life as it is experienced by teachers and students' (Eisner 1977, p.19). Two benefits could accrue: it is now widely acknowledged that it would help in the legitimation of courses to have rich descriptions of the processes involved; and a progressive focusing on to more specific research topics will allow scrutiny of practices commonly attacked (and defended) as being inaccessible because subjective. An example of a qualitative study in this field is described by Cornock (1983a, 1984c).

Practical Problems

There *is* no research council for the arts. There is an Arts Council with substantial funds, but it does not exist to support research or study in higher education. The way forward is perhaps shown by the Design Council which has moved to stimulate curriculum research by attracting research from government departments (Design Council 1983). Also, in the absence of an equivalent for University Grants Committee funding, public sector institutions have few departments equipped and staffed to initiate and sustain a research effort. This is particularly true in faculties of art and design, which further reduces their scope for attracting external funding by shaping (or distorting) proposals so as to attract funding from other fields (cf CNAA 1983, section II, para.7; Robinson 1982, p.104). Hence there is no widespread community of art and design researchers with their own tradition, literature and funding body. A small community which has succeeded in attracting external fundings for sixty-four projects is the Department of Design Research at the RCA.

One answer to this problem of funding was put forward by SRHE Leverhulme seminar 5 in the form of a recommendation that a number of bodies discuss the establishment of a research council for the arts (SRHE 1983, pp.16 and 59).

A second limitation is the absence of qualified supervisors and examiners in the field, to which one response has been to suggest that practice be treated as research. The review and revision of the Rochester Report (CNAA 1983) leaves the way open to a policy and to regulations which could result in the diversion of already meagre research funds into the subsidy of art and design practice; obstruction of the development of much needed knowledge within the field; and, by flattering those concerned that they are exempt from requirements placed on others, such changes could precipitate a further decline in the level of attention paid to and respect for the work of art and design colleges. This is not to encourage pseudo-scientific work in art and design but to counter the danger of pseudo-research. Only by achieving rigour will art and design research earn respect and attention within the wider intellectual community, yet it is only by evolving their own research traditions that researchers can expect to influence policy and provision in the field of art and design. Nevertheless, some encouragement is needed and there have been calls for an easing of the conditions limiting the appointment of readers in art schools (Plummer 1974; CNAA 1983).

The Current Debate

The arts were brought within the scope of the SRHE Leverhulme programme at the instigation of the director of the Gulbenkian Foundation, which also funded SRHE Leverhulme seminar 5 in April 1982. The report (Robinson 1982) reached the Brighton follow-up conference participants just before it convened in November 1982. The majority of participants at Brighton were drawn from fine art and foundation courses, and they were shocked by what they took to be the recommendations and implications of the Leverhulme art and design group (*ibid* pp. 143-55):

  a that the foundation courses should be abolished;

  b that the boundaries separating art and design lead to premature specialization and impede curriculum development;

  c that a pervading 'fine art ethos' should be replaced by a hierarchy of explicit aims and objectives for art and design;

d that craft and design provision should be expanded by sacrificing fine art courses to release resources; and

e that postgraduate course provision is insufficient and is over-concentrated in the metropolis.

In addition to strong complaints about the unrepresentativeness of the art and design group at the seminar (eg CHEAD 1983; Bally *et al.* 1983) it has been widely acknowledged in recent conferences that the lack of a record of research and constructive debate during the Coldstream era obliged the SRHE Leverhulme group to rely on personal experience, unrepresentative statistical information, and opinion.

The principal conclusion drawn by the art and design section of the Brighton follow-up conference was therefore that there was an urgent need to initiate a long-term programme of research, debate and development in the field (Beech 1983). This conclusion was strongly echoed by a national Seminar on Fine Art Studies in Higher Education held at Leicester Polytechnic in September 1983 (Cornock 1983b) and by a subsequent seminar held at the Institute of Contemporary Arts (Cornock 1984a). A CHEAD paper (1983) calls for '... an authoritative, comprehensive and accurate survey of the present situation and the future needs of Art and Design in Higher Education.' As if answering this call, at least one art school has produced an institutional response to SRHE Leverhulme 5, challenging with factual information the assertion that provision has grown in proportion to the post-Robbins expansion (Canterbury 1983), and the Leicester seminar recorded agreement on similar aims, identifying means to mount fact-finding studies and to communicate results (Cornock 1983b).

The follow-up conferences and seminars do not offer a readily summarized set of endorsements of or counter-proposals to the recommendations of SRHE Leverhulme 5. What they do appear to show is that it has stimulated debate and has contributed to a changing attitude to inquiry. Some broad issues have emerged from recent discussions:

1 Developments within the secondary curriculum which have serious implications for art and design in further and higher education and demand active attention (eg Yeomans and others in Cornock 1983b).

2 The equivocal status of foundation studies

3 The tension between 'personal development' and a structured curriculum (in other words, a reopening of the debate on the second of the Coldstream changes mentioned earlier)

4 The relationship between art and design (which is to be examined by the annual conference of the National Society for Art Education in 1984)

5 The aims of the theoretical component of courses and the need to make them relevant to art and design practice (the need for

articulateness was discussed in a Scottish art school seminar (Ryan 1982) and the question of relevance was discussed by Pearson 1980).

6 The specification of defensible and achievable objectives for existing courses and for those which are needed.

We stand at a turning point and may proceed with an equal degree of probability in one of two directions. The most obvious course is further towards the institutionalization of art and design practice as research. In the other direction lies education itself, and here the priority is to provide an educational experience through the study and practice of art and design itself. Recent discussion has included consideration of the educational alternative, which would require of the art and design community that it acquire some of the tools of thought needed for educational research and development. Those tools of thought must be adapted for application in this special field, and the results of inquiry have, in part, to be addressed to the wider intellectual community.

In short, the main issue is whether further to institutionalize the isolation of the art schools and their defensive reliance upon implicit assumptions, or to subject those assumptions and the practices based on them to sustained rational inquiry. The balance lies in favour of the former, but recent discussion indicates the possibility of change.

The lack of debate and communication during the Coldstream era once caused lost opportunities but now invites attrition. In attempting to conserve essentially non-verbal traditions, the art schools, now fully incorporated into Britain's system of higher education, must take up the tools rather than the rhetoric of educational research in the confidence that rational inquiry will in fact strengthen their non-verbal tradition.

References

Allison, B. (Editor) (1983) *Index of British Studies in Art and Design Education* Leicester Polytechnic: Centre for Postgraduate Studies in Education

Ashwin, C. (Editor) (1975) *Art Education : Documents and Policies 1768-1975* Guildford : Society for Research into Higher Education

Bally, N. *et al.* (1983) Letter *Journal of Art and Design Education* 2 (1) 124

Beech, B. (Editor)(1983) Unpublished report on Brighton Polytechnic follow-up conference held on 27 November 1982

Canterbury School of Art (1983) Unpublished response to Robinson (1982) qv

CHEAD (1983) Unpublished report of a Working Party concerning Robinson (1982) qv

CNAA (1983) *Draft Policy Statement on Research and Related Activities* London: Council for National Academic Awards

Cornock, S. (1982) *Forms of Knowing in the Study of the Fine Arts* Leicester

Polytechnic Monograph
Cornock, S. (1983a) Towards a methodology for students of fine art *Journal of Art and Design Education 2 (1) 81-99*
Cornock, S. (Editor) (1983b) Fine art studies in higher education *Bulletin of Leicester Polytechnic*
Cornock, S. (1984a) The art schools shape up *Artscribe* 45, 66ff
Cornock, S. (1984b) Implications of lateralization of brain function for art education: a critical review *Educational Psychology* 4 (2) 139-153
Cornock, S. (1984c) Learning strategies in the study of fine art *Journal of Art and Design Education* In press
Design Council (1983) *Industrial Design Requirements of Industry* A report of the DES in association with the Design Council, Chris Hayes Associates and Keller Dorsey Associates
Eisner, E. (1977) Thoughts on an agenda for research and development in arts education *Journal of Aesthetic Education* 11 (2) 17-30
Elton, L.R.B. and Laurillard, D.M. (1979) Trends in research on student learning *Studies in Higher Education* 4 (1) 87-102
HMSO (1960) *First Report of the National Advisory Council on Art Education* London : HMSO
Institute of Education (1983) *Register of Current Research in the UK 1983* University of London : Institute of Education
Jones, T. (1980) A discussion paper on research in the visual fine arts *Leonardo* 13, 89-93
Karel, D.G. (1974) *The Teaching of Drawing at the French Royal Academy of Painting and Sculpture from 1790 to 1793* Thesis, University of Chicago
Madge, C and Weinberger, B. (1973) *Art Students Observed* London : Faber
Parlett, M. and Dearden, G. (Editors) (1981) *Introduction to Illuminative Evaluation* Guildford : Society for Research into Higher Education
Pearson, N.M. (1980) *Art Colleges, Art History and the Training of Artists* Unpublished paper commissioned by Welsh Arts Council
Pevsner, N. (1940) *Academies of Art: Past and Present* Cambridge : University Press
Plummer, R. (1974) *Postgraduate Study in Art and Design* (Report) Corsham : National Society for Art Education
Ramsden, P. and Entwistle, N. (1981) Effects of academic departments on students' approaches to studying *British Journal of Educational Psychology* 51, 368-383
Robinson, K. (Editor) (1982) *The Arts and Higher Education* Guildford : Society for Research into Higher Education
Ryan, D. (1982) *Articulate Artists* (Conference report) Glasgow : Queens College
SRHE (1983) *Excellence in Diversity* Guildford : Society for Research into Higher Education

Part 5
Strategy and Technology

19 The Research Factor

John Maddox

What I want to say is based on three assumptions. The first is that it is ridiculous that the government should be seeking to reduce the numbers of people in full-time higher education, that it would be foolish of the universities and of academics in general to assume that because the government has expressed this as its intention it will actually come to pass, and that it would be neglectful and indeed irresponsible of people like us to accept that a reduction in the numbers of people in higher education is in any way consistent with the national need or the interests of young people in this country. That is an assumption that is going to run through everything I say, and I take it to be possible, politically and otherwise, to bring about a state of affairs very different from the one now in prospect. I want to say no more about that topic.

   The second point I would like to make has a more direct bearing on my subject and nevertheless is also an assumption that I should make explicit. I think that what this country needs is not more universities or fewer universities, or better links between universities and polytechnics, or bigger gulfs between universities and polytechnics, or larger universities or smaller universities. What this country needs is a greater diversity in the pattern of higher education, and a diversity that is not represented merely by differences of quality or of style between different institutions, but is also made possible by a kind of inner dynamic. I think that one of the curious things about British higher education (which seems in this respect to compare very badly with the American or German pattern) is that it is harder in this country for a university to strike out on its own and, if it does so, to feel that if it succeeds it will indeed be a highly respected and successful institution. It's not so long ago since the University of Texas, one of the largest universities in the United States, was widely scorned by people like us (and indeed in the 1950s and even the 1960s, the University of Texas had, justly, an exceedingly bad reputation). But I think that all of us would now agree that the

University of Texas, by spending money, by hiring good people, by pushing its weight about, within the American pattern of higher education, has become a university of which any state might be proud. I think that we lack that kind of opportunity in this country, and indeed the incentive for higher education institutions to differ from each other.

The third assumption I want to make (and this is a kind of non-Leverhulme assumption, it might even be said to be an anti-Leverhulme assumption, so I apologize all round) is that the question should be asked whether three years, the standard pattern for an undergraduate degree, is long enough. Even though it can be argued that for many people's vocational purposes two years is enough time to pick up the kind of skill that they may need, my own belief is that the degree of personal and intellectual maturity acquired in such a time is really not sufficient to allow somebody to take his place in the adult world confidently and with a sense of being independent. For that sort of reason, quite apart from what can be put into the curriculum in two years, quite apart from the economic advantages of shorter university courses as far as the government is concerned, it does seem to me that we ought really to be considering whether longer courses for most people should not be the norm, perhaps with a bit at the end which is frankly vocational. And if anyone should say, 'But that would cost the government and us all a great deal more money', my reply is not the perhaps valid but debating reply, 'If it's wise, we can't afford *not* to afford it', but rather that, if this is indeed what education needs, and if we are at the same time constrained by this whole business of overspecialization both in universities and in schools, then for goodness sake let us do away with 'A' level, and if need be with the sixth form.

That's by way of a preliminary. It seemed only fair to let you know where I stand. What is research in higher education for? We all of course have the answers at the tips of our tongues. Some people say (and indeed it is a widely held view) that even though undergraduates do not necessarily have to become acquainted with research in the true sense during their undergraduate careers, it is nevertheless some kind of intellectual crime to ask teachers to teach undergraduates if the teachers themselves are not engaged in research, and indeed engaged in research that's exciting and innovative. This is a common assumption which I believe to be untrue. We all know, I suspect, of people in university departments who are valued for their capacity and their willingness to teach undergraduates, and who are not themselves deeply engaged in research, indeed, may not be engaged in research at all in the sense in which the Science and Engineering Research Council would understand that term, and nonetheless are valuable members of university departments. I think that for that and more general reasons it is possible to argue that research is not an indispensable part of undergraduate education. What research does for those researchers who acknowledge that they have the time to engage in this humdrum task of teaching undergraduates is to stimulate them, to make them stimulating people. But they can acquire that capacity in other ways; and if they do, we all recognize them to be, if not researchers in the strict sense, at least to be valuable teachers, scholars in some broader sense than is intended by 'researchers'.

All right, you may say that's a debating point. I think it's a very relevant point to the argument I want to put to you, because, if it is indeed true that many good teachers of science subjects in universities are not necessarily researchers of the first water, then does it not follow that some higher education institutions and some departments could be institutions and departments whose claim on public attention is not that they are churning out a few FRSs every year and a Nobel prizewinner every now and again, but rather that they are very, very good indeed at teaching undergraduates? In other words, I would like to put it to you, for the reasons I have given, that in practice it is not essential that universities should be up with the front runners in research, in this strict sense in which 'research' is defined by success in getting grants from the research councils. And that, it seems to me, is an important conclusion, because it does mean, if you accept my argument, that such an institution is nevertheless entirely respectable. It does mean that we could think it entirely permissible within the United Kingdom for some of our universities, some of our institutions of higher education, to be places whose chief social contribution is undergraduate teaching, and whose contribution to research is negligible.

Some of you may say that that sounds just like a liberal arts college, and of course we all know how much scorn there is, particularly in this country, for the liberal arts education as practised in the United States and also in many countries in mainland Europe. And yet if places like Swarthmore and Reed College in the United States have earned the kind of reputation they justly deserve by being very, very good at teaching undergraduates in the whole field of their academic interest, there's no reason why we should fear the arrival of such institutions in this country. Indeed, I would put it to you that it's not a question of fearing a prospect that may arise, it is already the case that we have a great many liberal arts colleges financed by the University Grants Committee in this country, and there's nothing wrong with them. I think that they would be happier and we would find our problems less difficult if in fact we recognized that.

So I want diversity, and I want it to be possible for some institutions not to consider that to be successful in research qualifies them to be universities. And of course the reason I want that is because the other contributions of the research enterprise to the health and welfare of higher education are important and can only be safeguarded by a concentration of resources in some places. I think that in present circumstances we undervalue the contribution of research, by which I mean the process of discovery, collation, analysis, in science and all other fields and what passes in engineering for research, which tends much more often to be the use of projects as ways of solving problems which are educative for postgraduate students, enlivening for the staff and of great social and national value. I think that all these activities are essential to the education of graduate students and to the liveliness and stimulation of the people involved in teaching. These are points, I suspect, with which nobody will disagree, but it seems to me that if one accepts them, one quickly comes to some conclusions about the way in which it should be supported.

For the past ten years, but increasingly in the past five years or so, everyone has been under great pressure to be useful. The old word 'relevance' is rarely used, but the idea that universities have not in the past contributed sufficiently to the national economy and should bend their energies and their wills to doing just that is one of the constant messages from government, from people who think they know about industry (and who are quite often industrialists), and, I am sorry to say, often from academics, academics' organizations and the like. The argument is that research costs a lot of money, that much research leads nowhere and is indeed of intellectual curiosity value only, does not contribute to national prosperity, nor even to the health of the nation, and that therefore the people engaged in such research should instead get their money from industry and should carry out projects more directly of value to industry.

The question I want to ask is: in what circumstances and to what degree should this siren-song be listened to? Let me emphasize that I've said already that we need a greater diversity of higher education institutions in this country than we have at present, and that we need also to recognize that it might be respectable for an institution not to be engaged in research in the strict sense. I think that it's entirely right and proper that some universities should decide that their future lies in striking out in an industrial direction, working closely with industrial companies, doing research, even undertaking teaching that's directly relevant to the needs and interests of industrial sponsors, and becoming known for being good at it. Loughborough University is an obvious case; the University of Salford is another, which I am glad to see surviving in spite of everything that has happened in the past four years. And there are of course many, many good examples overseas of universities that have followed exactly that course. We all know of Massachusetts Institute of Technology (MIT), we all know of the University of Aachen, where if anything the collaboration between the industries of the Ruhr and the academics of the university is closer than anywhere else. So it's entirely proper that this should be a legitimate course of development for some universities.

But I want to point to some obvious dangers. I don't know how many of you know the tale, which has been written up quite recently, of what happened at MIT in the 1930s. The pursuit of industrial goals, particularly under the umbrella of a contract with the Dow Chemical Company, created such havoc in the chemistry department at MIT that it's not an exaggeration to say that all the good people left and the consequence was that until quite recently the chemistry department at MIT was not really a match for the other departments there. The essence of the warning that I would give is that these industrial links, if they are too close and too absorbing, are dreadfully distracting, and it's not that they consume people's time, it's actually that they consume people's interest, even their being. My own opinion is that the industrial liaison at MIT now has gone too far for the health of the institution: it's an industrial liaison not with large companies, but actually with companies often founded by members of the faculty themselves. And so there are dangers which I know institutions are aware of which have chosen that road in this country, and nevertheless it is a road they will have to tread carefully in the years ahead.

Earlier this year I spent several weeks in Japan (which of course we all wonder about, 'admire' in the strict Latin sense, I suppose). But in practice, as you know, the universities of Japan are exceedingly run-down compared with institutions of that kind in this country. It tends to be that the only departments housed in modern decent buildings are those that happen to have close links with generous industrial companies, and it's only at the graduate level that even those departments reckon to teach seriously. It's a sad business to go and visit the other departments, and to talk to their rather depressed, hang-dog academics, the ones who haven't yet signed themselves up for a deal of the kind that's made their fellows prosperous.

So, there are dangers in the industrial link. There are even more dangers in the repetition of the demand from government and from industry that universities should be more responsive to the needs of industry, because the more the message is repeated and the less conspicuous are the dangers in a full-blooded development of that kind for every institution, the more it becomes accepted that these indeed are the goals of higher education, to make the country prosper. In my opinion, what we need are some institutions that follow the industrial path and some quite different institutions that do in fact remain distinctive and academic. Let us indeed hope that some universities in this country will make their way in the world in the years ahead by doing what the government has for many years hoped higher education would do, contribute to national prosperity. But let's be sure that a great many other institutions, for educational as well as tactical and economic reasons, go off in quite different directions.

I would like then to ask the question, 'Who's going to pay for this?' It is no secret that a part of the government's enthusiasm for industrial collaboration with higher education is the hope that ultimately industry will pick up a large part of the bill. Only time will show how successful that ambition is. But more immediately there are other problems, such as where the money will come from, that need to be looked at very carefully. As you know, we have for the past three years had a whole succession of reports (the Merrison Report, and other documents published under government sponsorship) which have said, 'The dual-support system is breaking down'. It's no longer possible for university academics to be sure that they can get a bright idea supported financially with the help of a grant from one of the research councils and with the basic support for research that is supposedly a large component (40 per cent, some say) of the recurrent grant from the University Grants Committee. Some research councils (the Medical Research Council, for example) have gone so far as to acknowledge this situation, and to say, 'If you don't have the basic equipment, we will pay a kind of overhead', thereby breaking with the traditions of the past. And as the gloom has deepened about the dual-support system, people have begun to ask: would it not make better sense if, when the University Grants Committee hands out its money each year, it earmarked some of it for research, so that university vice-chancellors would not be able to use some of the recurrent grant, that they should be spending on backing up research, on making sure the carpark is resurfaced this year, or making sure perhaps that the problems of paying staff salaries don't become too clamant? This is a question which the Merrison Report answered in the negative. Nevertheless, it remains a controversial question.

I would like to ask, thinking back to the assumptions I tried to make explicit at the beginning, what should one's view be on the mechanism for supporting research? I would like to make a few qualitative statements that really spring from seeing the kind of material that's sent in for publication to *Nature*, from talking to authors, and from general observation here and elsewhere. I think that it's been an immense achievement in the past twenty-five years that the research council system in Britain has become as widely respected as it is. If people apply to a research council for a grant to carry out a particular research project, they can be certain that their application will be judged fairly; broadly speaking nobody suspects that the money has gone to Joe Bloggs and not to oneself because Joe Bloggs is older, or is an FRS, or for some other such reason. The system is fair, widely respected, and indeed immensely valuable.

Nevertheless, it's a committee system, and my impression of the texture of research now going on in the academically-inclined academic departments in this country, is that it is sound and worthy but it's unexciting. In this country, even in the largest universities, one doesn't find the kind of excitement that you get in, shall we say, the physics department at Stanford, not because of the presence of a linear accelerator nearby, but because it just happens to have a crowd, not just a group, a crowd of exceedingly innovative, original and adventurous people. And I think that in spite of the fairness of the research-council half of our dual-support system, because it's a committee system, and because it has to try and make judicious decisions on virtually impossible questions like 'To what extent should Britain be committed to high-energy physics at the expense of, shall we say, nuclear physics?', it tends to create a feeling that the object of research is to get one's grant proposal accepted, rather than to get the results that that should make possible. So I have a prejudice, in this argument about how the dual-support system should be adjusted, that even though the research councils have hitherto been exceedingly valuable, the time has come for their influence to be diminished financially.

Several things follow. Too many research councils have institutes of their own that pretend to do basic research which could just as well be done in universities; let them be parts of universities. It is ridiculous, in my opinion, that the best molecular biology laboratory in the country at Cambridge should not be part of Cambridge University. Lots of anomalies like that abound; it's silly, if we value the research enterprise as we should, that we administer it so haphazardly. I think it follows also that if universities are to be more directly responsible for deciding on which research projects funds should be spent, they will need mechanisms they lack at present, ways of deciding internally which department should perhaps get the largest share of next year's cake, or which people in which departments. The Merrison Report two years ago pleaded that universities should set up effective research committees but alas, with all their other preoccupations, they have been slow to work. But you see this is why I made explicit at the beginning my view about the importance of diversity within the system. I think that we haven't yet gone far enough along the road towards the autonomy of institutions in higher education, be they universities or polytechnics. These institutions like to think of themselves as autonomous, but in their general education they are too much the prisoners of the school educational system, and at the research end they are too dependent (not because there is any malevolence or ill-will in the relationship, but just because dependence is a bad thing for autonomous institutions that wish to do great research) on external bodies like the research councils, which with the best will in the world make decisions that universities themselves should be making.

Reflections on the Logic and Assumptions of Research Funding

Donald Bligh

When I was asked to give my personal reflections upon the 1983 SRHE Annual Conference, my mind went back to the time when I was writing the draft of my first paper for the SRHE Leverhulme programme. Feeling very defensive, I tried to work out my argument in the form of syllogisms, and I then presented the paper as a series of propositions to a group of twenty senior Scottish academics. Not one of them recognized that these propositions built up a logical structure. Consequently, although my conclusions were fairly radical, they considered sections of the paper to be quite banal – and so they were, if the rigour of logic has no merit. On the other hand, passages which contained passionate yet unjustified assumptions and blatant rhetoric were greeted with more favour.

I am not advocating that we should return to the days when every academic enterprise was inhibited by the rigours of logic. Different enterprises need different styles of reasoning and presentation. But I do think that the practice of testing the logic of arguments is underused and ought to be revived. For this reason, I want to look at the reasoning used by some of the keynote speakers at the conference on one particular issue – the funding of research – which was repeatedly mentioned but which was not given close attention. It is an important issue, not only for the finance, staffing, and workloads of universities, but also for the future of the binary line between the university and public sectors of higher education in the United Kingdom and for the nation's economic redevelopment.

The Logic of Research Funding

Peter Brooke addressed the conference in his capacity as the minister with responsibility for higher education in the present government. In his contribution to these Proceedings (Chapter 8), he makes the following remark: 'There appears to be some consensus emerging for an increase in selectivity in the funding of research both within and between universities.' I think this statement is simply not true, and I should not like the Minister to be under such a misapprehension. So, what reasoning should resolve our disagreement?

First, we should note that the disagreement is over a matter of fact, and it can therefore only be resolved by methods which verify facts. It is true that we might also disagree about the value of selectivity in research funding (which is a question of values), and about whether such selectivity ought to be increased (which is a moral question). But there is no disagreement on matters of inference.

We are fairly good at knowing how to verify facts, even though we can't or don't always do it. For example, most of us can soon judge what kind of evidence would justify Peter Brooke's claim that some consensus on the selectivity of research funding is emerging. Indeed, arguments about the validity of the sort of consensus-taking exercise which is currently being carried out by the University Grants Committee could easily become quite sophisticated. We are also quite good at saying, 'It all depends what you mean by ... "consensus".' But how quick are we to notice errors of inference? In the long run, educational policies depend upon inferences because they involve conclusions about the future.

In Clifford Butler's contribution to these Proceedings (Chapter 1), he infers, I suspect correctly, that if there is to be selective funding of research within and between educational institutions, then there will be some departments and some institutions which only teach and do no research. At least as far as universities are concerned, he argues against this, recollecting from his early days that the best researchers in his department were also the best teachers. What I notice when people challenge this kind of reasoning is that they are much more likely to ask:

– What are your criteria of good researchers and good teachers?
– Can you generalize from one department to others?
– Can you generalize from your subject to mine?
– Are the conditions of thirty years ago applicable today?
– Are your subjective recollections valid?
– Do the recollections of vice-chancellors constitute a valid sample?

than they are to ask:

– Does this conclusion follow from the premise?
– Can you generalize from good researchers to all researchers?

In other words, we are much better at challenging the methodology on which our reasoning is based than the inferences which we draw from our findings.

Yet I think that you only have to remove the rhetoric and present the premises and conclusions baldly to see the invalidity of such arguments. I hope I am not misrepresenting what Clifford Butler says, but his basic propositions seem to be:

Good researchers were good teachers.

∴ All teachers ought to be researchers.

The reversal of subject and predicate from the first line to the second line of this argument is one of the most common errors in everyday reasoning. There is also what is called the 'Naturalistic Fallacy' – a shift from an assertion of what is the case to an assertion of what ought to be the case. I suspect that there are two intermediate inferences that 'Some good teachers were good researchers' and hence that 'Some teachers were good researchers'. These inferences seem to me to be valid, but the need to say 'some' rather than 'all' gives away the very point about selectivity that Clifford Butler seeks to defend. Hence the temptation to have a conclusion about 'all' teachers.

John Maddox arrives at an opposite conclusion (Chapter 19). On the case of it, his reasoning appears to be much tighter:

Not all good teachers are good researchers.

∴ Not all good teaching departments are good research departments.

∴ Not all teaching departments ought to be research departments.

Even the Naturalistic Fallacy looks more acceptable here if you imagine a suppressed moral premise to the effect that only good teachers and good researchers ought to be teachers and researchers, respectively. Moreover, the shift from the first statement to the second looks all right if you imagine a department full of good teachers who are not good researchers. But that is a possibility that some people at the SRHE Leverhulme seminar on the research function of higher education sought to question. The view was expressed that, while it is possible to be a good teacher and not be doing research oneself, in higher education it is not possible to be a good teacher for long unless one works in a research environment; that is, an environment where at least some people are testing their putative knowledge against new discoveries, against criticism, and against research methods. The step from individuals to departments is one that has to be scrutinized. If a similar step were taken from departments to institutions, this too would require some scrutiny. (Of course, such a step was taken, almost by default, when the binary line between the universities and the public sector institutions was drawn.) But I don't think that the arguments would be the same.

The Assumptions of Research Funding

Why don't I think the arguments would be the same? Implied within the argument about the research environment is a whole set of assumptions about staff development within a social and working group, commonly an academic department. These are assumptions about a complex set of cause-and-effect relationships.

Next, I suspect (though I may be wrong) that Clifford Butler's premise that 'Good researchers were good teachers' subsumed another, quite different set of assumptions about the cause-and-effect relationships involved in the qualities that make someone a good researcher or a good teacher.

A third set of assumptions about good researchers is being made by the University Grants Committee in pursuing its policy of instituting 'new blood' lectureships and in its expressed disappointment in the 'quality' of the people subsequently appointed. There is more than a suggestion that young people have the best research ideas and that potentially good researchers can be judged from the class of their degree and similar written qualifications. Statistically, these generalizations may be true, but surely they are over-simple. Good research ideas could well be produced more cheaply and with less long-term commitment if the Leverhulme recommendations to increase staff mobility were put into effect.

A fourth assumption influencing research policy is that research is essentially a postgraduate activity. Perhaps it is, but this assumption seems to operate in a negative way as if there were a premise to the effect that 'No undergraduates are good researchers'. I believe, though I cannot prove it, that in most academic subjects the benefits of research attempted by undergraduates (even if they are not good researchers) outweigh its possible harm and may exceed the benefits of much else that they do. This may be less true in subjects like mathematics and chemistry that build upon themselves in a rigid structure, but much more research could be done at an undergraduate level and even at school level in the arts and social sciences than is currently attempted.

Conclusions

I don't think that these four assumptions or sets of assumptions are incompatible. Indeed, when they are combined, their drift is towards teaching in a research atmosphere, towards the same people doing teaching and research, and towards a greater involvement of people at all levels in research activity. Yet this may seem like the opposite drift from that of the first half of my paper, where John Maddox's argument for selectivity of research funding seemed to survive better than Clifford Butler's argument against it.

However, this short contribution cannot resolve the question of selectivity of research funding. There are many other issues involved. For example, while John Maddox believes that independent research units in medicine and the social sciences are too expensive, Guy Neave points out that such units appear to work well on the continent (Chapter 4). In another presentation to the conference, Hans Daalder talked

192 Strategy and Technology

about other methods of funding such as conditional budgets. These issues draw attention to a limitation of logical analysis: while it may assist in showing the limits of what is possible, it does not create new ideas, and in the long run policies depend on that creativity.

20 The Demands of the Labour Market

Richard Pearson

Higher education has multiple objectives, educational, social and economic, the relative priorities of which have been debated over the years. The Robbins principle has been the predominant feature of the last two decades, allowing the size, but not the particular balance between institutions and subjects, to be shaped by student demand. Recent proposals for a 'broad steer' for higher education have been rejected and the role of student demand and market forces re-affirmed (Education, Science and Arts Committee 1980). One argument commonly used against economic/manpower criteria when planning higher education provision has been the apparent 'failure' of manpower forecasting (Fulton, Gordon and Williams 1982). Thus the debate has been set in terms of simple choices, for example manpower or social needs, without allowing the multiple objectives. In this time of financial stringency and anticipated falling student demand, a major reappraisal of the role of higher education is underway. The Leverhulme programme has initiated a conceptual debate, while financial cuts have forced the pace regarding the initial parameters of change. The University Grants Committee (UGC) is now publicly discussing the long-term future of the universities while the National Advisory Body's (NAB) planning exercises are reshaping the public sector. However, as yet there is no clear set of explicit national priorities for higher education. The purpose here is to argue that part of higher education provision should and can be determined by manpower needs criteria. Drawing on current research[1] and using the 'new technologies' as an illustration, it will be shown that 'market forces' coupled with local initiatives are inadequate in meeting the future manpower demands of a successful economy, and that higher education needs a strategic framework which incorporates an employment dimension in its planning priorities. Such a policy need not, however, exclude or override all other objectives for higher education, be they social demand, academic excellence or educational opportunity.

The New Technologies and Higher Education

In the last two years an increasing emphasis has been placed on the 'economic' role of higher education, with priorities directed towards science and technology, although the desired effect has not always been achieved, viz the declining output in key engineering disciplines (Pearson 1983c). The new technologies, micro-electronics, information technology (IT), and biotechnology are currently regarded as critical ingredients for economic success and are attracting a considerable degree of government financial support. It is an area where higher education provision might be expected to have highly specialized degree courses, closely related to meeting the needs of industry. In practice this is not always the case, yet a small shift in national priorities could dramatically improve the supply of suitable skilled manpower and minimize manpower constraints. Although these technologies are called 'new', a closer examination shows that they are not so much new, as extensions of existing technology, although often involving radical technological and scientific advances. These, however, tend to be incremental, and their role and contribution to society is driven as much by their application as by technological breakthroughs.

Employers' recruitment needs also focus largely around extensions of existing disciplines, with a heavy dependence on higher education for its supply of skilled manpower. Thus the electronics industry relies almost exclusively on its annual graduate intake to meet its future intake into professional jobs, with the traditional entry routes to professional level jobs, of promotion from craft or technician ranks, and of part-time study having virtually disappeared (Pearson, Hutt and Walsh 1980). In terms of specific disciplines most employers are seeking graduates with broad-based electronics or related skills at a first-degree level, and have little specific demand for, or interest in, highly specialized first degrees in, say, fibre optics or microprocessors, or indeed postgraduates at Masters or PhD level. Even in the case of the most highly specialized areas of electronics, semi-conductor (chip) design and production, the reliance and preference is still for the majority of recruits to have come from good quality first-degree programmes, rather than highly special-ized first or postgraduate degree courses (Pearson and Gordon 1983). Indeed the key role of higher education for this industry is in the provision of electronics graduates; it has only limited involvement through research or in the provision of specialist training or short courses.

The picture that emerges for IT (including computing) is similar. There is a high dependence on higher education, although a large proportion of the intake to computing functions is fulfilled by graduates regardless of discipline, together with significant numbers of broadly-based electronics and computing science graduates. Again, there is only a limited demand for highly specialist or postgraduate level entrants (Anderson and Hersleb 1979). Turning to robotics, the demand is for graduates who can link mechanical, electronic and software skills: again an application of existing knowledge and experience, and not a demand for fundamental science and a highly specialized type of degree. Of all the new technologies it is in biotechnology, which is only likely to employ a relatively small number of professional staff, a few thousand at most, that postgraduate qualifications are most relevant, but again the disciplines sought are not novel, but built around existing programmes. Here the industry is much more closely linked to basic science and the qualification profiles of research teams are correspondingly high, with few professional staff in biotechnology having less than a PhD and, say, three further years' research experience. There is also an easier interchange of experienced staff between industry and higher education (Parsons and Pearson 1983).

Thus, while the new technologies are almost exclusively dependent on higher education for the supply of skilled manpower, few of the skills initially sought are highly specific or dedicated to one type of narrow technology/process/employer. Rather, they allow for some flexibility in terms of course content and indeed a degree of substitution, for example between physics and electronics. These demands are also not numerically large, with electronics and IT each taking several thousand new graduates each year and biotechnology taking only a few hundred. These are not large figures when compared with an annual graduate output of up to 100,000 per annum.

Of course, other vocational areas also exist which would expand the number, but looking more widely at the nature of employers' demand for graduates it is only in some of the 'specialist' streams that degree subject is likely to be important (Pearson 1976; Gordon 1983), and they account for only a minority of all graduates, perhaps one in three[2]. Thus, when seeking to relate the balance of subjects within higher education to future manpower demands, there is only a need to focus on one minority part of higher education, and then not necessarily always on very narrow specialist disciplines.

Higher Education/Labour Market Links in Practice

Higher education's key role in the new technologies is in the supply of new graduates. The main linkage to date has been through market forces, interacting with student demand. However, one of the consequences of 'market forces' is that student actions and market demands can be (and usually are) out of sequence. The field of electrical/electronic engineering is an example of the 'cycle of mismatch' that can develop between supply and demand for skills.

The early 1970s saw a cyclical recession; demand for newly-graduating engineers fell dramatically. Some employers were accused of withdrawing job offers and industry was seen as undesirable and unreliable. Market signals 'worked' and the level of application for engineering places fell dramatically (Figure 20.1). Increasingly places in engineering were filled by overseas students and many remained unfilled. By 1976 engineers were back in demand, the 'Great Debate' had been initiated, the Finniston inquiry was in preparation, and differential starting salaries for graduates were being offered, with premiums of up to £500 or more being paid for good engineers. Market signals 'worked' again and applications began rising. However, the consequences of the earlier fall were only then beginning to be felt, with a significant decline in the

Figure 20.1

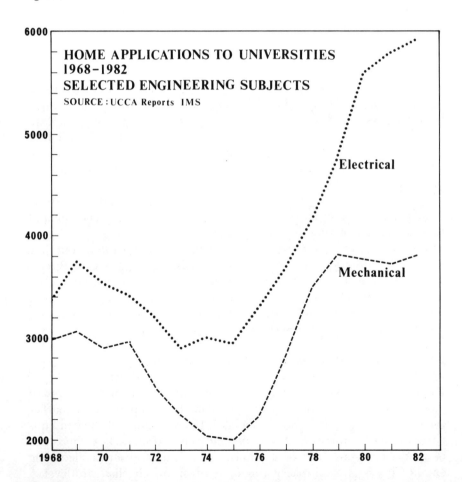

HOME APPLICATIONS TO UNIVERSITIES
1968–1982
SELECTED ENGINEERING SUBJECTS
SOURCE : UCCA Reports IMS

Electrical

Mechanical

Figure 20.2

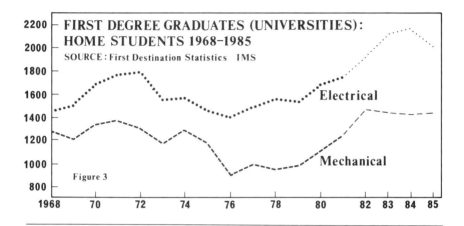

FIRST DEGREE GRADUATES (UNIVERSITIES):
HOME STUDENTS 1968–1985
SOURCE: First Destination Statistics   IMS

Electrical

Mechanical

Figure 3

numbers of students qualifying in electrical engineering (Figure 20.2). The years of 1978 and 1979 saw severe 'shortages' of electronics and other engineers which coincided with the low point in the supply cycle. Student numbers had, however, started rising again and the output from universities in 1982 had finally recovered to the level of ten years earlier. Although demand has slackened since 1980, there are still significant shortages of engineers with three to six years' experience, essentially those who would have applied to colleges in 1973-76 and graduated between 1977 and 1980. This is a classic 'cobweb' cycle of supply responding to market signals but being four years out of phase, with the negative signals being transmitted particularly quickly (Pearson 1983a).

At the micro level there have always been specific schemes aimed at linking higher education to industry, and the range and number of these has been expanding. Perhaps the longest-standing has been the sandwich course, which aims to give practical experience to undergraduates. However, the proportion of students taking such courses is falling (Pearson 1983b) and the current problems in finding sufficient industrial placements do not augur well for the future. Industrial sponsorship is a related phenomenon and one that is at present being driven by concerns about shortages. Thus the majority of companies sponsoring do so 'to ensure a supply of well-trained engineers' and 25 per cent of final-year engineering students are now sponsored (Gordon, Hutt and Pearson 1983). One particular manifestation of industry's desire to influence the content of degree courses is the course at Bath University, devised in conjunction with GEC-Marconi, which only takes sponsored students. Where there is employer involvement in courses the aim is rarely to increase the extent of specialization, for example to meet the needs of specific technologies, but more to ensure the broad balance is in line with industrial needs (Wassell and Friston 1983). At a postgraduate level the Science and Engineering Research Council, through its CASE awards and the Teaching Company Scheme, is encouraging many more 'individual' collaborative schemes. It has also established specialist Masters degrees courses geared to the needs of particular industries, such as in integrated circuit design for the 'chip' industry, although evidence suggests that industry is not always seeking many recruits from such highly specialized courses (Pearson and Gordon 1983). All of these schemes, however, involve only small numbers of students, with individual courses enrolling, say, twenty to thirty students per annum at the most, but sometimes as few as six. In contrast, in the last year, acting on concerns about possible manpower constraints in the new technologies and a need to respond to the university 'cuts', the government has set up the IT and biotechnology initiatives. The former has included the rapid provision of one-year postgraduate 'conversion' courses for 1000 or more graduates from non-technical disciplines, including the arts and social sciences, to be taught the basics of information technology. Their impact is currently being evaluated[1].

Conclusions

Higher education policy needs to recognize the crucial role higher education has in meeting labour market demands in many sectors, not just in the new technologies, and that this dependency will continue in the future. There are, however, shortcomings in the existing system where a series of ad hoc 'micro' initiatives are not big enough to meet labour market demands, as witnessed by the existence of some current shortages at the low point in the economic cycle. Higher education should have a priority that ensures a base level throughput of graduates in relevant disciplines. There is also a need to ensure that not only are the places made available, but suitable incentives exist for students to fill them, through employers offering more consistent manpower policies and better career prospects, sponsorship, improved careers advice (in schools, and higher education), and perhaps the provision of differential grants. Given the long lead times involved there will always be some imbalances, so there is also a need to increase flexibility in the system, as was bought out in the SRHE Leverhulme conclusions (*Excellence in Diversity* 1983). There is also a need to experiment more with new types and methods of training for converting and updating skills in the light of changing needs, and a continuing requirement to monitor and update priorities.

Better information and further research is needed to identify those areas where the link between higher education and employment is critical; these are only likely to account for perhaps one third of student output. The evidence suggests that even in the new technologies, the disciplines required are still fairly broad-based, with the key need being to impart basic principles and practices. This allows a degree of flexibility and substitution in relation to planning courses and in recruitment policies. There is, however, a need to understand better employment utilization and flows, and the critical factors such as economic, technological and organizational change likely to bring about significant variations in future specialist manpower needs.

Higher education is embarking on a period of rapid change. Many valuable and exciting initiatives are being undertaken to improve, within the resources available, the interrelationships (it is a two-way process) between higher education and employment. These must be encouraged, but must also be supplemented by a clear set of priorities within higher education, one of which should be for part of its provision to relate to manpower needs. This requirement does not need to dominate higher education; the majority of places can still be allocated according to other social and educational criteria. However, a failure to meet future manpower demands can only undermine the longer-term ability to fund higher education.

Notes

1 The author is currently involved with a series of studies relating to the manpower needs of the new technologies. The research relates to employment and training in biotechnology, micro-electronics and IT in the UK and Europe, and also embraces such issues as higher education policy and industrial sponsorship of undergraduates.
2 This figure has been estimated from data collected by the Central Services Unit which acts as a clearing house for advertising in graduate vacancies in the UK.

References

Anderson, A. and Hersleb, A. (1979) *Computer Manpower in the 1980s* London: HMSO

Education, Science and Arts Committee (1980) *The Funding and Organisation of Courses in Higher Education* London: HMSO

Excellence in Diversity (1983) Guildford: Society for Research into Higher Education

Fulton, O., Gordon, A. and Williams, G. (1982) *Higher Education and Manpower Policy* Geneva: ILO

Gordon, A. (1983) Attitudes of employers to the recruitment of graduates *Educational Studies* 9 (1) 45-64

Gordon, A., Hutt, R. and Pearson, R. (1983) *Undergraduate Sponsorship: Implications for the Labour Market* Brighton: Institute of Manpower Studies

Parsons, D. and Pearson, R. (1984 forthcoming) *Enabling Manpower for Biotechnology in the UK* Brighton: Institute of Manpower Studies

Pearson, R. (1976) *Qualified Manpower in Employment* Brighton: Institute of Manpower Studies

Pearson, R. (1983a) Planned education or shortages of skills? *Nature* 305, 82

Pearson, R. (1983b) The training dimension *Industry and Higher Education: Future Collaboration* Brighton: Institute of Manpower Studies

Pearson, R. (1983c) Output after the cuts *The Times Higher Education Supplement* No.542, 25 March

Pearson, R. and Gordon, A. (1983) *Key Skills and the UK Semi-Conductor Industry* Brighton: Institute of Manpower Studies

Pearson, R., Hutt, R. and Walsh, K. (1980) *Electronic Engineers in Industry* Brighton: Institute of Manpower Studies

Wassell, H. and Friston, A. (1983) Collaboration over courses - the case of the integrated degree *Industry and Higher Education: Future Collaboration* Brighton: Institute of Manpower Studies

21 Learning at a Distance

Peter J. Murphy and Margaret L. Haughey

The Province of British Columbia is undoubtedly one of the most beautiful regions of the world. The snow-capped mountains, dense forests and rushing rivers make it a photographer's paradise. But this terrain has served as a barrier to effective communication among communities for decades. Modern highway and railway systems network the province; yet severe weather conditions and great distances between communities restrict travel. Thus professional people from rural areas, until very recently, were offered few continuing professional education experiences in their local communities. The doctors, nurses and teachers who worked in the small towns of British Columbia had to travel hundreds of miles, often at their own expense, to maintain a reasonable level of professional competence.

During the early seventies, rural people began to realize that the quality of social services available to them in their communities was dependent, to a significant extent, upon the experience, commitment and qualifications of the professional people offering those services. Professional associations were similarly becoming concerned that their members working in small rural communities were not aware of many recent advances in their fields of expertise. The provincial government was lobbied by these political pressure groups to ensure that British Columbians, irrespective of their places of residence, should all have a similar quality of social services.

This demand for social equality, concerns about the migration of rural people to urban centres and the economic implications of natural resource development in isolated areas of the province resulted in the provincial government forming a Distance Education Planning Group, under the direction of Carney (1978), to examine alternative distance education systems. After completing a comprehensive survey of distance education systems in Canada, the United Kingdom and the United States, a report was submitted to the Minister of Education which contained an institutional model for the delivery of distance education programmes in the province.

The planning group made the following recommendations:

1 That a new educational institute or agency be designated as the provincial agency responsible for the development of distance education delivery systems.

2 That planning proceed toward the acquisition of educational channels on provincial cable systems, and that the exploration of other delivery models, such as telephone networks, be continued.

3 That planning proceed toward the provinces' participation in the proposed ANIK-B satellite experiments. This participation would provide opportunities for satellite delivery of instructional programming lasting for periods of up to two years, which would provide the opportunity to thoroughly evaluate this mode of programme delivery.

4 That adequate funding be provided to carry out further planning in the distance education field, and to initiate pilot programmes in order to evaluate alternative delivery modes.

5 That educational delivery services be co-ordinated and operated where appropriate. (Carney 1978, p.3)

These recommendations served as the guidelines for establishing a distance education system in British Columbia which accommodated the physical geography of the region, the distribution of the population, the unique learning needs of the people and the bureaucratic structures of provincial post-secondary institutions.

The Evolution of a System

Initially, provincial universities provided people in rural and isolated areas of British Columbia with a limited number of courses and programmes. These distance learning experiences were mainly print based and founded on the traditional correspondence course model. At regular intervals the students received course material by mail which was prepared and evaluated by faculty members at the universities' main campuses. Students were able to communicate directly with on-site tutors and by telephone with their campus instructors. The absence of face-to-face communication between student and teacher creates a number of difficulties. However, this mode of delivery, as Ruggles (1982) points out, does have certain compensating advantages, namely: 'Geographic distance can be overcome and widely dispersed individuals can be reached. Since little capital expense is required for school buildings, economy is achieved and more students can be served' (p. 2). Correspondence courses in specific subjects continue to be offered every year by provincial universities with great success. Without these courses many people in isolated communities would have access to very few post-secondary learning experiences.

In June 1978 the Open Learning Institute, a new university modelled on the British Open University, was established to provide individuals in all regions of the Province of British Columbia with courses in adult basic education, vocational subjects and university undergraduate studies in the arts. Satellite campuses were established in several large communities, which served as important regional centres, so students had access to guidance, counselling, remedial and tutorial services.

The Knowledge Network of the West Communications Authority was formed in May 1980 to offer post-secondary institutions a telecommunication system for delivering courses by cable television and satellite transmission. The purposes of the Knowledge Network are:

1 To assist and collaborate with universities, colleges, provincial institutes, school districts, ministries and agencies of the Province in the development, co-ordination and delivery of educational programmes and materials.
2 To establish, maintain and operate a telecommunication network including cable, microwave, satellite and broadcasting elements.
3 To operate one or more broadcasting undertakings primarily devoted to the field of educational broadcasting.
4 To foster, stimulate and participate in the development and production of high quality educational programmes and materials. (Ruggles 1982, p.27)

Since it was established the Knowledge Network has enabled post-secondary institutions to broadcast programmes which can be received by over eighty-nine per cent of British Columbians. The rapid expansion of the system was achieved with minimal difficulty because the province is heavily cabled and the cable companies are required to offer an educational channel (Zuckernick and Haughey 1983). Consequently, people throughout the province were able to receive educational courses on their home televisions. Students were easily able to converse with their instructors on air by merely dialling a long distance number. A special 'Information Line' accessed students to the library facilities of the provincial universities.

Eighteen months previously, British Columbia universities had been invited to participate in an experimental project with the ANIK-B satellite. The University of Victoria took advantage of this offer and transmitted three credit courses in education, two in public administration and one in professional development in nursing by satellite over a two-year period to a selected number of 'receive' sites. The interactive capacity of the satellite provided the university with a two-way audio, one-way video network which enabled students and instructors to communicate in a manner close to a facsimile of face-to-face interaction

(Haughey 1983a). The development of the Knowledge Network now provided a province-wide distribution system for satellite signals.

Initially, all courses were broadcast from the studio of the Knowledge Network at the University of British Columbia in Vancouver. By September 1982 broadcasting facilities had been decentralized, which enabled the University of Victoria to originate broadcasts from its own campus studio. The signal was then 'carried via microwave to the Knowledge Network master switching centre where it was uplinked to the satellite, currently ANIK-C' (Zuckernick and Haughey 1983, p.149). This decentralization enabled the university to offer a greater variety of courses, better to utilize faculty members' time, and reduce travel costs associated with the production of satellite courses. Commenting on this development, Zuckernick and Haughey (1983) reported that there was a continued commitment to:

> Making the system as learner-focused and therefore as interactive as possible so that instructors can utilize instrumental strategies such as group discussions, role plays and problem-solving in their teaching and so that the learners feel that ease of access to the instructors is a standard feature of the interactive system. (p.150)

While there is no doubt that the development of the new technologies had a strong impact on the delivery of courses at the University of Victoria, it would be inaccurate to consider these developments as driven by technological innovations alone. Rather, the university has a widely exercised mandate to provide higher education to British Columbians and has offered hundreds of undergraduate and graduate courses at sites throughout the province in the last five years. The strengths of operating on an integrated programme model rather than by provision of random course offerings meant that the university was mounting two- and three-year programmes 'in situ', each of whose total enrolment was less than thirty students. The concurrent pressures of economic restraint, mounting costs, and the faculty's increasing resistance to travel culminated in a search for alternative delivery methods. Once the university was satisfied that it was both possible and feasible to offer courses via distance education technologies the subsequent development of courses was a natural outcome.

The model used for the development of distance education courses was based on a team approach. Each course (project) had a project director whose major responsibilities were overall administration and budget, a course specialist who was usually the subsequent instructor of the course and who was responsible for the development of the course content, and a distance education consultant who worked with the academic on the instructional design aspects of course and had major responsibility for the production of the various components, regardless of media. This group formed the core team and others joined depending on the task in hand.

Besides emphasizing a team approach, the model was also dependent on a view of extension activities as an integral part of university affairs. At the University of Victoria, all extension activities beyond the regular on-campus academic offerings are co-ordinated through a Division of University Extension which administers credit and non-credit programming both for the local community and at any site off-campus. Each faculty has an extension co-ordinator who plans and administers the extension offerings for that faculty. This organizational model reinforces the idea that extension activities originate from within the faculty and are sponsored by it. Furthermore, it is the faculty extension co-ordinator who becomes the project manager, thereby bringing expertise both in the general content area and in terms of student needs and characteristics.

While our enrolment in distance education courses continues to climb and we are beginning to recycle some of the courses, we are in no position to compete with the 'factory' production of large-scale universities. We produce all our own video and audio materials through the AudioVisual and Television Services department at the university. We have purchased some pre-packaged materials but in some cases have found it more cost efficient and instructionally effective to produce our own.

We have gathered data on all the courses we have offered from four sources: the learners, the instructor, the course team, and documents including budget sheets and student grades. In retrospect, we have observed several trends in our research and evaluation activities. Originally we started out with the premise that the broadcast television sessions of a course were equivalent to face-to-face on-campus sessions and therefore they were planned to include similar instructional strategies: eg lecture, discussion, question and answer, role plays. Questions asked students in those first courses reflected this viewpoint: ie 'Do you talk to the instructor as frequently as you do in face-to-face classes?' or 'Do you have a similar opportunity to speak ...?' This paradigm began to fall apart however when our programmes became fully public and students no longer gathered in groups at specific 'receive' sites but participated from their homes.

As the numbers grew from a reasonable class group of thirty to over one hundred and fifty, learners took a different perspective on the television sessions. They commented that they did not want to hear colleagues whom they did not know ask questions, nor did they want to ask questions themselves. Reasons given included the pressure of scarce time which might best be used listening to the instructor, the lack of confidence in asking a question before such a public group, or the topic under discussion. Given such reactions, we began to examine the contexts for interaction and found some differences. Situations where the learner had to give one piece of information or response were more successful than either general requests for comments on a presentation or a question of a general nature. If a learner called in once, they often called during subsequent broadcasts. The subsequent reaction of the instructor to a question or response also seemed to be a key factor in determining future responses. We are now re-examining the importance of 'interaction' as part of broadcast television programmes. Specifically we are asking, 'what does "interaction" mean, both cognitively and emotionally, both to the instructor and to the learner and how can we best facilitate it?'

Similarly we have been gathering data on the use of instructional strategies by instructors, and the importance of video inserts and graphics in explaining, elucidating and enlarging a session's content within the broadcast television sessions, and the use of graphics and questions in the course package.

In a recent course which used print, audio conferencing and site facilitators at selected sites, preliminary data suggest that students with only direct telephone access to the instructor were more satisfied than those with audio conferencing, site facilitators, and telephone access.

Over the past two years we have been gathering budget data to determine actual costs. While a detailed analysis remains to be done, general figures suggest that a thirty-nine-hour undergraduate course (usually offered on-campus over thirteen weeks) delivered via print and ten one-hour television sessions cost in the magnitude of $20,000-$25,000 direct costs, or $60,000-$70,000 with indirect costs included, for development. University policy requires that we recover all delivery costs.

Data on student grades and instructors' comments on the quality of student work have served to reinforce what twenty years of research elsewhere had already made evident, that in terms of grades, distance education learners do as well or better than their on-campus counterparts.

In the face of increased governmental spending cuts, it is expected that distance education will continue to provide a healthy alternative for the university. The importance of continuing professional education is growing and the opportunity to take university courses while remaining in your home community has been welcomed. According to Haughey (1983b):

> The next five years will see an emphasis on the development of greater sophistication in audio-conferencing, print and computer. Perhaps, we will also expand our repertoire to include radio, a second satellite channel and independent learning programs. (p.9)

Given the present demands for courses, the increase in the numbers of part-time learners and the economic constraints on all professional groups, it is likely that we will also see the development of further courses and programmes, each of which uses the delivery vehicles most appropriate for its subject matter and clientele. As an example, Murphy originally (1980) proposed the offering of a Master's degree programme in educational administration to school leaders in rural and remote areas throughout the province, using distance education technologies. This was rejected because there were on-campus, summer-only programmes at the three universities. A recent proposal (Orion II) has instead identified administrators in a variety of similar service professions as a better potential client group. The proposed programme would be delivered partly through on-campus offerings, and partly through distance education courses. Increased emphasis in planning for continuing professional education has been on programmes of an interdisciplinary nature which offer a credential and have a strong experiential component. More frequently, planning for such programmes is being shared with the major professional association. In the end, the use of distance education methods has become an integral part of most programme proposals.

Conclusion

At the beginning of this decade Toffler (1980) suggested that in the very near future we would be living in an 'electronic cottage'. Recent advances in communication technology and computer science may bring this perception into reality much sooner than we expect. During his presentation, at the Second World Conference on Cooperative Education, Axworthy (1981), the Canadian Minister of Employment and Immigration, stated that:

> I come to you not as an expert in education, but as someone who will be making some hard policy choices in the next year or two. Existing educational systems will not make them, or cannot make them, so we will find institutions that will. We will go to employers and to the private sector and insist that they develop their own institutes and centres which we will help to fund because we have got to make things happen. (p.219)

It is imperative that universities, technical institutes and community colleges consider seriously the potential applications of modern communication technology in higher education, otherwise the decision to direct such changes may be taken out of their hands in the future.

References

Axworthy, L. (1981) Directions for the future. In Neinemann, H.N. and Dube, P.E. (Eds) *A Strategy for the Development of Human and Economic Resources* Boston: Northeastern University

Bandy, H. (1983) *An Evaluation Report on Professional Development Programmes Delivered by Distance Education Methods by Education Extension* Unpublished (Available from Mrs. H. Bandy, University Extension, University of Victoria, British Columbia, Canada)

Carney, P. (1977) *Report of the Distance Education Planning Group on a Delivery System for Distance Education in British Columbia* Victoria: Ministry of Education, Province of British Columbia

Daniel, J.S., Stroud, M.A. and Thompson, J.R. *Learning at a Distance: A World Perspective* Edmonton: International Council for Correspondence Education Association University

Haughey, N. and Murphy, P.J. (1983a) *The Continuing Professional Education Interactive Satellite Interface* Paper presented at the 1983 Joint Conference of the Commission on ABE of AEA/USA, North West Adult Education Association and Alaska Adult Education Association, Anchorage, Alaska

Haughey, M. and Murphy, P.J. (1983b) *Continuing Professional Education: Meeting New Demands for Modern Telecommunication Systems* Studies in educational administration. Armidale: Commonwealth Council for Educational Administration

Haughey, M. (1983a) *Teaching and Learning via Interactive Satellite: A Janus View* SPESA 6th Biennial Forum: Toowomba, Australia

Haughey, M. (1983b) *Distance Education at the University of Victoria: The First Five Years* Unpublished (Available from Dr. M. Haughey, University of Victoria, British Columbia, Canada)

Hohmann, L. (1980) The professional association. In Frandwon, P.E. (Ed.) *Power and Conflict in Continuing Education* Belmont: Wadsworth

Johnson, T.D. and Ollila, L.O. (1980) *Long Distance Education via Interactive Television Satellite* Unpublished (Available from Dr. L. Ollila, Faculty of Education, University of Victoria, British Columbia, Canada)

Martin, Y.M. (1980) Analysis of an experimental university course via satellite: Implications for interactive teacher-learning systems. In Parker, L.A. and Olgren, C. (Eds) *Teleconferencing and Interactive Media* Madison: Extension Centre for Interactive Programs, University of Wisconsin

Martin, Y.M. *Analysis of an Experimental University Course via Satellite: Some Findings and Implications* Paper presented at the Seventh Annual SIETAR Conference, Vancouver, British Columbia

Murphy, P.J. (1980) *Orion I: A Distance Education Programme for Practising and Potential Public School Administrators* A working paper. Victoria: Faculty of Education, University of Victoria, British Columbia

Muzzin, L.J. (1982) *Technology in Higher Education - Does it Really Improve Accessibility and Quality and Cost Tests in the Long Run?* Paper presented at the Learned Societies Conference, Halifax, Nova Scotia

Potter, G. (1982) Comparative models of distance education: Institutional design and management. In Danile, J.S., Strond, M.A. and Thompson, J.R. (Eds) *Learning at a Distance: A World Perspective* Edmonton: International Council for Correspondence Education

Toffler, A. (1982) *The Third Wave* New York: William Morrow and Company, Inc.

Ruggles, R.H. (1982) *Learning at a Distance and the New Technology* Vancouver: Educational Research Institute of British Columbia

Worthington, W. and Murphy, P.J. *Student Teaching Supervision: A New Application of Teleconferencing* Unpublished research proposal (Available from Mrs. W. Worthington, Faculty of Education, University of Victoria, British Columbia, Canada

Zuckernick, A. and Haughey, M. (1983) Using an audio-teleconference bridge to enhance live satellite-based instruction in British Columbia. In Parker, L.A. and Olgren, C.H. *Teleconferencing and Electronic Communications II: Applications, Technologies and Human Factors* Madison: Centre for Interactive Programs, University of Wisconsin-Extension

22 The Impact of New Educational Technologies

Robert M. Pike

As in Britain, although on a less punishing scale, the post-secondary sectors of Canada's ten provinces are going through difficult times as a result of the redistribution of government funds among other spheres of public activity. In the light of my topic, I am struck, therefore, by the statement in the SRHE Leverhulme Report that British post-secondary institutions 'must be capable of responding to academic developments and to fresh demands from society. They must be in the forefront of technology, both initiating and evaluating it' (SRHE 1983, p.1). This admonitory statement is, however, followed by the warning that 'little additional capacity will be created. New developments must come from adaptation, not expansion' (*ibid*). Precisely! Transferred to the Canadian scene, this statement implies that our universities and colleges, like those in Britain, will only be able to consider heavy investment in new educational technologies if they are prepared to plan for the re-allocation of finite resources from other institutional spheres. In the present urgent debate amongst members of the Canadian academic community about the use of these technologies in teaching and learning, I have yet to see more than a sliver of evidence that this point is understood: that, as Geoffrey Sims noted in his contribution to the SRHE Leverhulme seminars, coherent academic planning (including the measure of priority given to the technologies) is required for efficient university resource management (Sims 1982, p.166).

In the context of these observations, one purpose of this paper is to review briefly some recent developments in the applications of the new technologies in Canadian higher learning. My main point here will be that considerations of cost and appropriate software creation are now giving post-secondary institutions some reason to move beyond short-term strategies in planning for these technologies: the sliver of evidence to which I have referred. Secondly, and more in tune with my sociological bent, I will link some macro-theories of socio-historical change in the communications field to a couple of areas in which the new technologies could have major impact on Canadian universities and colleges by, say, the year 1990. I stress here the importance of considering information as a commodity which groups and organizations may control, or be excluded from access to. This way of looking at the impact of the new technologies is one which might have been given some consideration in the Leverhulme documents and most notably in the report on access to higher education (Fulton 1981).

A few words on matters of definition. My definition of the new educational technologies (hereafter called NET) can be taken to cover those aspects of computer systems and other communication technologies, including computer assisted instruction (CAI), videotex, videodiscs and satellite television, which seem particularly relevant to higher learning at the present time. Also, the focus of my attention will be primarily on the role of NET in teaching and learning, although I am well aware that the new technologies are now having a major impact in many other spheres of university and college activity.

Recent Developments and their Limitations

Recently I wrote a brief piece for *The International Newsletter* of the Society for Research into Higher Education in which, as a response to a request for information on Canadian national policy for the introduction of computer-based programmes into post-secondary teaching and learning, I stated that jurisdiction over education by each of the ten provincial governments makes national planning in any educational sphere virtually impossible. The relevant role in NET of the federal government, excluded as it is from direct intervention in educational planning, has lain primarily in the funding and development of major communication systems which have important educational applications: notably, satellite TV and the Telidon videotex system. The latter, which is similar to Prestel in Britain, incorporates the most recent interactive developments in computer graphics and telecommunication technologies with the use of the TV set. The system can provide text, graphic animation and images of nearly photographic quality which, so its proponents claim, make it uniquely adaptable to future educational and business needs (Syrett 1982).

Telidon may have a bright future, particularly in the field of distance education (Smith and Stroud 1982). However, two major limitations would appear to be dimming its prospects of speedy adoption as an educational mode. First, whilst the various field trials of Telidon have generally been considered successful, a just completed study by the federal Department of Communications suggests that substantial attention to hardware has not been matched by attention to software development. Quality is seen to be the key to Telidon applications in education and business, but the report notes that 'very limited content development [has led to] rejection after initial enthusiasm' (Chevreau 1983). Secondly, the Telidon system has been vigorously marketed and subsidized by the federal government, but without much reference to those on-going support and maintenance costs which some universities and colleges may find difficult to meet. Thus again, initial enthusiasm is often followed by a quick backing-off when administration and faculty find that Telidon is a cost item which must come out of the institutional or departmental budget (Weston 1982). For example, in gathering information for this paper, I wrote to a senior administrator at Athabasca University, which is a large distance learning institution in the province of Alberta, in order to inquire about their current experiments with Telidon and also with CAI. I was informed in reply that the former, though judged successful, had been stopped for the 1983-84 budget year as a result of financial restraint. As for the latter, 'although the University has a stated commitment to computer-assisted instruction, no projects are currently underway ... that is the state of the nation currently' (Cowper 1983).

This response from Athabasca University should be seen in the context of a country which, because of its large size and widely-dispersed population, has a natural interest in the utilization of the new technologies to serve the educational needs of adults in remote communities. However, both the response and, more generally, the cost, software limitations and squeezed institutional budgets which are limiting the adoption of the Telidon system, strike me as being rather typical of the problems associated with the adoption of sophisticated NET modes in Canadian higher learning at the present time. Thus, I spoke above of CAI, by which I mean the application of computers to teaching non-computing types of subject matter rather than initiatives which may, formally or informally, teach students and instructors about computers and computer skills. On this latter score, as is presumably the case in Britain, many Canadian students acquire a fair measure of familiarity with the use of the computer, and some universities – notably the University of Waterloo, an institution of about twenty thousand students in southwestern Ontario – have established a solid reputation for innovation in the field of information technology (Knapper and Wills in press). As for CAI, however, my own limited review of developments in this area suggests that most significant initiatives have occurred, not as a part of any co-ordinated provincial or institutional plan (though some institutional funding may be involved), but rather because individual scholars or teaching units have been interested in using the computers within their particular disciplines. Thus, such initiatives are relatively rare, experimental and sometimes ephemeral. Amongst the many reasons for this state of affairs, and incidentally I do not think that inherent faculty resistance to new technology is one of them, must be included a heavy cost/time commitment in the production of sophisticated CAI packages (see also Knapper 1982a, 1982b). As with the Telidon experiments, institutions and faculty tend to balk at devoting an estimated three hundred hours of preparation in order to provide one hour of a full-blown CAI tutorial which includes, say, integrated audio, visuals and graphics. The result may be exciting, but the initial outlay in resources is daunting too.

I do not believe that the present hard times are going to bring NET experimentation in Canadian higher learning to a grinding halt. Rather, it may be a case of *reculer pour mieux sauter*: a time to take stock of costs, assess resources, make those realistic development plans to which I referred earlier. Indeed, there is some evidence that this is beginning to occur: witness, for example, the creation of university-wide CAI planning committees (the University of Calgary is a case in point), and the recognition in British Columbia that satellite delivered education requires inter-institutional co-operation to cover its heavy costs (Robertson 1981). Most interesting, however, from a sociological as well as an economic perspective, is the response to the new technologies in Atlantic Canada which comprises the provinces of Newfoundland, New Brunswick, Nova Scotia and Prince Edward Island. Atlantic Canada has traditionally been an economically-dependent area of low income and high unemployment (the type of region with which you are quite familiar here). Its post-secondary institutions are large in number but generally small in size and divided between four provincial jurisdictions which have, up to now, shown little enthusiasm for substantial investment in the new technologies. As a result, the fear that the region and its educational institutions will become dramatically disadvantaged in access to future technological developments, and subject to exploitation by powerful commercial interests, has been voiced by a number of groups, most notably a committee of The Atlantic Provinces Association for Continuing University Education (1981). The committee calls for the creation of a 'Technology and Education Forum' by the combined universities of the Atlantic region in order to co-ordinate and plan future work in the new technologies. Such a Forum might, in the committee's view, forestall the traditional Atlantic fate of 'the bitter legacy of lost opportunity' (*op. cit.*, p.2).

Power, Inequality and Future Use

You can assess the parallel relevance, if any, of these Canadian patterns of regional economic and institutional disparity for British higher learning. For a sociologist, they point to issues of power over, and inequality in, access to the new technologies: issues which are well understood by Canadians who have relied, far more than most peoples, upon their transportation and communication systems to overcome the economic and political strains of regionalism. Indeed, our most distinguished economic historian, the late Harold Innis, was a pioneer researcher on the role played by communications in the process of social and economic change. In two books (1951, 1972), Innis propounded his view that changes in the main medium of communication are causally linked to major changes in social structure and especially the loci of power in society. For example, the widespread use of the medium of paper, when combined with the technology of printing in the fifteenth and sixteenth centuries, could be associated, in Innis' view, with the spread of Bibles and Bible-reading in the vernacular languages and ultimately with the declining power of the medieval Catholic church, which had hitherto been the guardian of the fund of accumulated knowledge. Also, as historian Elizabeth Eisenstein has more recently indicated, printing led to radical transformations in the way the European intellectual élite of the period came to perceive their past and present: in short, it created a revolution in symbolic perception (Eisenstein 1979). Jumping the centuries, one can link these historical observations to the comment of Anthony Smith, the Director of the British Film Institute, that the contemporary transformation to the 'Information Society' is 'a transformation of perception as much as reality, for society has, of course, always been based on information. But until the coming of modern electronics, we did not think of class relations, government, economics and diplomacy as if they were mere functions of information transfer' (1980, p.112). Like the impact of printing on the Renaissance, modern electronics can be seen as changing the ways in which we think about and conceptualize our world.

I will draw out two relevant points from this socio-historical excursion. One is, in line with Innis, that future scenarios for the possible impact of NET upon the universities and colleges should, at least in Canada and the United States, consider the likelihood of shifts in power over information from the educational sector to private enterprise. The other, linked to Smith's comment, is that the perception of future class relations in terms of possible inequalities in information access is pertinent to post-secondary education in all industrial societies. Let me expand upon this latter point first, because it is most relevant to the recommendations of the SRHE Leverhulme programme. In a nutshell, there is a distinct possibility that social inequalities in opportunity of access to the new technologies may, like differential access to (as well as interest in) books in past times, become a new form of educational inequality and, as such, have a major impact upon social selection for higher learning. The apprehension of this new form of inequality is implicit in the report of the Atlantic provinces committee to which I have already referred. It is explicit in a recent report of the Social Impacts Sub-Committee of the Canadian Videotex Consultation Committee, an advisory group connected with the federal Department of Communications, which notes its concern with 'the issue of equity. Lack of access to videotex systems could create a new form of poverty' (1983, p.2). Of course, the new technologies are often held to offer new and bright horizons for educationally disadvantaged groups in society, as indeed they already are in the case of some physically and perceptually handicapped people. However, as a sociologist, I have learned to be wary of sweeping claims for the equalizing benefits of technology in the context of societies which, like Britain and Canada, show major regional and group variations in economic circumstances and in basic preparedness for learning. Usually, educational innovations which yield social advantages are exploited for the benefit of those who are already socially advantaged, rather than those who have the greatest need.

The Leverhulme recommendations on access to higher learning express a desire to diagnose and remedy the causes of low post-secondary participation amongst women, particular social classes and some ethnic minority groups. However, this aspect of educational equity was not, to my knowledge, touched upon directly in one or other of the reports. Apple Canada profiles its typical home microcomputer user as a family with annual income in excess of $45,000 (£24,000). Undoubtedly, as the cost of microcomputers drops, so will the average income profile of their users: but, as the marketers are well aware, middle-class parents in industrial nations are still going to be the ones who, anxious to provide maximum educational advantages for their children, will buy the sophisticated educational packages, and the access to data banks, which will supplement whatever CAI takes place in the schools. Thus, whilst all children are likely to acquire some measure of familiarity with NET at school (though not necessarily the same measure of familiarity at schools in prosperous and poor neighbourhoods alike) the relative gaps in access to sophisticated information flow may become much more glaring than the current gaps in access to printed material. Sadly too, since motivation to use the new technologies will probably be just as relevant as physical access to these technologies, the current limited North American evidence that girls are less likely than boys to seek familiarity with their more sophisticated aspects does not augur well for womens' future educational opportunities and employment options. In such circumstances, those students who enter higher learning in Canada – and Britain – in 1990 will probably be highly sophisticated creators and users of information; but they may also be those with substantial advantages derived from social background and early sex-role socialization.

The other concern – that is, potential shifts in the loci of power as the result of technological advance – must perforce be dealt with very briefly. In a recent article, George Bonham, who is Executive Director of the US Council of Learning, has suggested that, as the result of 'the stampede' (his words) of American universities and colleges into new computer technologies, for the first time in the history of American education a significant new force is almost exclusively controlled by profit-making corporations. The result, as he sees it, is 'that much of the future shape of computer education is being determined by computer manufacturers and major textbook publishers' (Bonham 1983). Bonham is worried because, in his view, profit margins and sales goods rarely coincide with educational effectiveness. Canadian universities and colleges have perhaps more cause to be worried than their US counterparts because, as our past experience has shown, the major textbook publishers are multi-national organizations usually with an American head office. Thus, one possible future scenario is a major increase in the marketing by US corporations in Canada of complete course packages which will include videodisc material, CAI and computer network accessing. Should this occur, and should the packages in, say, introductory political or social studies be bought by some Canadian universities, there is a danger that their entire thrust of regional and national studies as well as the traditional autonomy of the individual faculty member within his or her classroom could well be compromised.

In the light of these potential developments, it is not surprising that a recent report from my university stresses the importance of encouraging Canadian educational and public media organizations to involve themselves in various aspects of educational software development, not so much perhaps because these organizations are public, as because they are Canadian (Queen's University 1982, p.17). However, the commercialization of higher education, irrespective of the national origins of the commercial interest, is also an ominous prospect which Canadian post-secondary institutions should not ignore. For example, what happens to the traditional universities as 'controllers' of accredited knowledge if, as is now occurring in some American states, private corporations offer high quality educational programmes which receive accreditation recognition from state governments (see Holmes 1981)? Does their control go the way of the control of the Catholic church when printing was introduced in late medieval Europe?

Acknowledgement

The author acknowledges the financial assistance of the School of Graduate Studies and Research, Queen's University, in the presentation of this project.

References

Bonham, J. (1983) Computer mania: academe's inadequate response to the implications of the new technology *Chronicle of Higher Education* March 20:12

Chevreau, J. (1983) Revised goals recommended by Telidon *Globe and Mail* Toronto: October 14:B1

Cowper, D. (1983) Manager of Academic Systems, Athabasca University, personal correspondence

Eisenstein, E. (1979) *The Printing Press as an Agent of Change: Communications and Cultural Transformation in Early Modern Europe* New York: Cambridge University Press

Fulton, O. (Editor) (1981) *Access to Higher Education* Guildford: Society for Research into Higher Education

Holmes, J. (1981) Ph.D. (corporate university) – what is the future of corporate education in Canada? In MacDonald, J.J. (Editor) *Telematics and Higher Education: Report of a Colloquium* Halifax: Maritime Provinces Higher Education Commission

Information Technology: A Call for a National Dialogue on the Emerging Information Society (1983) Ottawa: position paper of the Social Impacts Sub-Committee of the Canadian Videotex Consultation Committee

Innis, H. (1951) *The Bias of Communication* Toronto: University of Toronto Press

Innis, H. (1972) *Empire and Communications* Toronto: University of Toronto Press

Knapper, C. (1982a) Technology and teaching: future prospects. In Knapper, C. (Editor) *New Directions for Teaching and Learning: Expanding Learning through New Communications*, No. 9, San Francisco: Jossey-Bass

Knapper, C. (1982b) Information technology and instruction. In Sheehan, B. (Editor) *New Directions for Institutional Research: Information Technology – Innovations and Applications*, No. 35, San Francisco: Jossey-Bass

Knapper, C. and Wills, B. (in press) Teaching computing across the curriculum: a Canadian viewpoint. In Lovis, F. and Tagg, E. (Editors) *Informatics, Education for all Students at University Level* Amsterdam: North Holland Publishing

Report of the Dean's Committee on New Information Technology (1982) Kingston: Queen's University

Robertson, W. (1981) Satellite delivered instruction – implications for higher education in the 80's. In MacDonald, J.J. (Editor) *Telematics and Higher Education: Report of a Colloquium* Halifax: Maritime Provinces Higher Education Commission

Sims, G. (1982) Resource allocation within universities. In Morris, A. and Sizer, J. (Editors) *Resources and Higher Education* Guildford: Society for Research into Higher Education

Smith, A. (1980) *The Geopolitics of Information* New York: Oxford University Press

Smith. W. and Stroud, M. (1982) Distance education and new communication technologies. In Knapper, C. (Editor) *New Directions for Teaching and Learning: Expanding Learning through New Communications*, No. 9, San Francisco: Jossey-Bass

Society for Research in to Higher Education (SRHE) (1983) *Excellence in Diversity: Towards a New Strategy for Higher Education* Guildford: Society for Research into Higher Education

Syrett, J. (1982) Videotex: the implications for education. In Knapper, C. (Editor) *New Directions for Teaching and Learning: Expanding Learning through New Communications*, No. 9, San Francisco: Jossey-Bass

Universities and the Public Interest: The Challenge of Communications, Technology and Education in Atlantic Canada (1981) Halifax: interim report and recommendations of the Committee on Communications, Technology and Education of the Atlantic Province Association of Continuing University Education

Weston, J. (1982) Telidon: a fantastic teaching package or not *University Affairs* June-July 1982:2-3

Epilogue

Colin Flood Page

Some 600 years ago, William Langland fell asleep on the Malvern Hills and saw a vision of 'a fair field full of folk' which he enshrined in the poem of Piers Plowman, wherein the characters of Do Well, Do Better, and Do Best figure prominently. As I now live within sight of the Malverns perhaps I am well placed to survey the fair field full of folk lore which we call higher education, and to consider the ways in which we could do better in our research into it. In the course of the SRHE 1983 Annual Conference, participants had the opportunity to discuss, both formally and informally, the shape of research to come. In the final pages of this book I am going to look briefly at some of the ideas that were broached, and to add a few of my own. There was no shortage of concerned and urgent thinking, and the discussion groups often produced that stimulating intellectual fizz which is one of the great pleasures of education. To reproduce in detail the plethora of sugges-tions that were put forward would make for confusion in this small compass; but I hope that the following paragraphs will give a reasonable sketch of the scene.

The problem of access to higher education frequently came to the fore, expressed not in terms of attracting more of the traditional type of student, but in terms of research into *ways and means of increasing the population of mature students, of unemployed people, of those isolated by geography, of women, and of other groups who are under-represented*. In the same cluster of thought and feeling came calls for inquiry into *the possibility of much greater use of people's life experience as credit towards qualifications*, and the *development of flexible academic credit transfer systems, to allow individual students greater choice of time and place in their studies*. One can certainly applaud the general desire to break down barriers and promote a free flow of knowledge and skills towards all those who would like to have them; but there seem to me some prior values and assumptions hovering over such proposals which were not (so far as I am aware) questioned by any of the discussion groups, and which are linked to some of the questions I shall be asking later. Higher education has just growed – is it time for a little root surgery?

Partly connected with easier access is a range of questions about the use of modern technology in all its numerous, sophisticated, and rapidly developing forms, and about the difference this might make to the way we organize education and the way it could be adapted to its clientele. One group put forward such questions as : *Are teachers being made obsolete? What planning is being done within institutions for the new developments? What is the cost effectiveness of new open learning methods? What use is actually being made of new technology?* The history of attempts to use new hardware in higher education does not hold out much hope of any profound revolution : to the vast majority of us education is, and has always been, essentially a matter of person to person, with machines only used grudgingly in the teaching process. Perhaps this time it will be different? Perhaps aficionados of keyboards, switches, screens and automatic feedback are about to take a 'megabyte' out of the educational cake? It is certainly a matter of major importance worthy of close investigation. *To what extent and in what circumstances people are prepared to be instructed by machines* could be a question of profound and far-reaching significance in the coming age of cable communications.

Another major theme mulled over by several groups was the paucity of *rigorous comparisons between institutions and between countries*. It was felt that much benefit could come from *a series of international and inter-institutional studies*. Most educational planning and many pronouncements have a sadly parochial air about them, are based too much on hunches, wishes, and a few haphazard figures. The studies proposed might enable us to see more clearly what are the underlying strong structures of good education and what merely the froth of local habits and fashion. There might be some surprises there.

The administrative side of higher education is probably a bit more rational than the academic; but even here it was felt that there was plenty of room for research. Most people saw this theme as *'the management of innovation'*, but I'm not sure that that term best expresses the major crux of the business. The economic and social climate in many countries is putting more and more pressure on administrators to cut out the fat, as others see it; and it is always better to forestall a hatchet job from outside by an efficient inquiry inside. Education has a long history of reacting after the event instead of sensibly planning in advance, and studies of how this tradition could be altered might be of particular value.

Other voices were raised in support of *weighing up the two-year degree; examining the function of buffer organizations like the University Grants Committee and the National Advisory Body; probing the relationship of teaching and research; and exploring the prospect of separate teaching and research establishments.* As John Sizer remarked from the chair in the conference's closing session, there is unquestionably a rich agenda for research; but, as he also pointed out, there is a major snag.

Looming low over all the wealth of ideas is the deep shadow of finance. To start with there is the problem that research into higher education has long tended to be under-funded. Perhaps because it promises no quick and easy returns, offers no spectacular and publicly gripping results, grant-giving bodies tend to pass it by. The bigger problem is the financing of higher education itself in all its manifestations. One group called for a *wide-ranging inquiry into all elements that might be involved in the process, including such apparently minor matters as the effects of travel grants.* After the fleshy euphoria of the sixties and seventies the grisly skeleton of economics sits at the table whenever academics are gathered together to make almost any decisions whatever : should this be the first target of any research effort?

Certainly there is no shortage of causes for concern and dissection; but at this stage I should like to add a few of my own. I think I can detect a number of gaps in the list above. I won't try to be exhaustive, any more than the discussion groups were; but here are a small group of trains of thought to start down the line. As you will see, they link in at some junctions with ideas already put forward in the conference. First : there still lurks in many of the denser groves of academe a vague but strong feeling that we're good chaps and gals who should be left to get on in peace without any disturbing look at the foundations of our occupation. But is this good enough? We're all for probing everything else in the universe around us as deeply as possible. Isn't it time we focused a spotlight (laser?) on the fundamentals of our own existence? Many years of experience have taught me that my colleagues mostly shy violently away from any rigorous talk about the rightful place of higher education in society. They prefer the folklore and the chummy feelings. A lot of our habits have no sanctions other than custom and age. Some are literally mediaeval, and lack a modern justification. Large-scale higher education systems are a recent growth. What was expected of them, and have they fulfilled expectations? There is another vast agenda for research on these lines. And what about staff? Do we pick the right kind of people in the right ways and train them appropriately for the difficult and important job they have to do?

Let me spell out in more detail some of the queries these general thoughts give rise to. There is much talk of two-year degrees, and passionate defence of three years; but why three, why two, why not one or four or five? What is sacrosanct about three years? Who first fixed it? What is a degree anyhow? How comparable with a degree in nursing is one in English literature? What are the right lengths for terms or semesters? Why not a continuous process of variable length dependent on the person and the subject? Why do we have to fit everyone into the Procrustean beds of courses? Would it be a good idea to have a system built round the fact of students' extremely varied needs as the health service is built round patients? Is it better to have large heterogeneous institutions catering for umpteen different subjects with extremely diverse requirements, or smaller ones catering for a restricted range with closely allied needs? What about the notion of vertical institutions teaching the same subjects at all levels, rather than the present horizontal hurdle races? Is the idea of a university obsolete? Should we equalize resources for all establishments of higher education to prevent damaging competition for status and prestige? Is competition for status and prestige damaging? Would the money spent on higher education be better used in other ways to make a better society? What is a better society, and how should education fit into it? Why do so many staff avoid rational consideration of the job they are supposed to be doing? Why has research such high status? How do you change staff attitudes?

I do not pretend that these questions are new, but they have not usually been tackled in any large-scale and rigorous fashion. Some would need a lot of time and money to answer thoroughly; but even so might well pay good dividends. Others could be begun straightaway with minimum outlay. Adumbrations of answers and samples of the right kind of data already exist in scattered form, but they need marshalling more publicly and more powerfully to force changes in the climate of opinion and decisions, to bring higher education more rationally into the twenty-first century, to enable it to function more in consonance with its own best principles. Let us hope.

Appendix A
Paths for Future Research

Participants at the SRHE 1983 Annual Conference were allocated to small discussion groups for one of the timetabled sessions, and were asked to consider the various issues raised by the guest speakers. Specifically, they were: to identify a few issues for detailed consideration; to translate these into concrete research programmes; to formulate these programmes as research proposals; to evaluate their proposals; and to commend a single proposal for future research. Six of the groups subsequently submitted a report to the conference organizers.

Group A Chaired by David Billing

Concerning a system of unit accreditation which might be coupled with distance and non-traditional modes of learning it was hypothesized that:
  a Access to higher education would be significantly increased for the socially disadvantaged, for lower socio-economic groups, for people living in remote areas, for women, and for minority ethnic groups.
  b Significant cost benefits would be achieved by intensifying the use of resources and by making economies of scale (for instance, by the use of consortia).
  c The quality would be maintained both of academic standards and of student experience.
Among questions and doubts that were raised were the following: that the educational experience might be fragmented; that there might be some limit to the range of subject areas and approaches to study to which the structure could usefully be applied; that the value of such learning experience might be attenuated as students broke into and out of the credit system; that there might be strong resistance to such a system from the professional bodies; and that difficulty might be experienced in arranging to expose students to covert but vital learning experiences.

The methodology for such a research programme would consist of five stages: the collection of evidence concerning existing credit and distance learning structures in the United Kingdom; the comparison of this evidence with overseas experiences; an approach by the Society of Research into Higher Education to the Open University and the Open Tech with a proposal for joint study; the collection of data from consumers of current examples of credit and distance learning structures in the United Kingdom, in order to test the first and third of the group's hypotheses; and the design and implementation of a system linking these ideas on a medium scale.

Group B Chaired by David Jaques

Two main areas were explored:
    a The acceptability of a two-year degree to students and the labour market.
    b The interchangeability of modules and ease of student transfer between institutions.
There is a certain amount of complementarity between the two in the sense that the acceptability of such a course might well be connected with its transferability.

Acceptability of a two-year degree

The main object of this proposal was to put political arguments on one side and to determine in respect of a two-year degree:
    a what alternative forms it might take;
    b whether it could place responsibility on employers to do more of their own selection and training;
    c what kinds of access could be countenanced: eg adult part-timers;
    d to what extent it would fulfil the needs of students and employers, particularly in respect of the much-revered 'all-round liberal education'.
The group was aware of the deeply-seated views of many on the inviolability of the three-year degree course and the consequent lower status of the old two-year General degree and two-year Diplomas.

Interchangeable Modules

The aim of this proposal was to determine to what extent institutions would and could co-operate to provide more ready movement of students between courses. It would in particular:
    a explore the provision of a wider range of study especially for adult part-timers whether on a first or a refresher/retraining course;

b study the DipHE experience and the overseas experience, especially in North American Community Colleges;

c examine the alternatives of voluntary association between institutions as opposed to more formal connections;

d consider the possibility of institutions providing choice and scope at the level of both the system and the individual student.

The project would take the form of action research with change and development occurring symbiotically with seminars and publications.

The group also touched on, but did not develop, two other research questions:

– What are the processes whereby institutions fail to achieve or maintain their good intentions, especially with radical schemes?

– How could a clearing house be provided for the exchange of institutional research and development round the UK?

Group C Chaired by Haydn Mathias

Questions, issues, implications, and ideas relating to the notion of a two-year degree were considered. In general, they were concerned with the implications of such a notion for funding, flexibility, structure, responsibility in learning, diversity of provision, and access to higher education. Existing data might be obtained from the Scottish system (especially in relation to the generalist/specialist distinction), the University of Buckingham, courses in the United States, and the BTEC Diploma.

Questions and issues raised included the following. What might be the length of a two-year course in teaching weeks? What are the implications for the funding of higher education: should this be centralized or diverse, and should there be a two-year mandatory grant, with funding from other sources for additional years of study? What would be the cost-benefit implications: should these be achieved by teaching more in less time, or by making access to higher education more flexible? What would be the effect of such a course on subsequent course structures, such as Honours degrees, Masters degrees, and other postgraduate and professional qualifications? What would be the nature of a two-year degree: should it be described as a Diploma, a Pass degree, or an Honours degree, and how is it supposed to affect the current three-year degree? How might a two-year degree course be implemented: is the control of funding arrangements the key to this? What would be the effects of this on different disciplines in higher education? How successful would such a degree be in attracting markets other than the usual 18 to 21-year-old? What are the implications of a two-year degree for course content, curriculum, and teaching methods? And what would be the relationship between a two-year degree and current, superficially similar schemes?

Group D Chaired by Graeme Moodie

The problem area identified was described in the following terms. Higher education will have to enrol more mature students if places are to be filled in the 1990s and thereafter. At present, to judge by the marked differences in the numbers of mature students actually enrolled in different institutions and countries, there exists an untapped supply of mature students who are either unable to gain access or are deterred by existing provision. Why do more mature students not enrol, and what could institutions do to attract them?

The group's research proposal involved a comparison of different institutions and national systems of higher education in search of the differentiating factors that might account for different rates of participation among different categories of mature students. This type of broad institutional and aggregate inquiry might be supplemented by more intense investigations (by means of interviews and surveys of attitudes and opinions) of institutions and groups with distinctive features. For instance, redundant steel workers in South Wales and Corby seemed to have turned to higher education in the 1970s in unusual numbers.

Group E Chaired by Graham Stodd

No detailed research proposals were developed, but the following main areas of investigation were identified. First, an intensive study of students ten years after graduation to establish their perceptions as well as those of their employers of the strengths and weaknesses of their courses. Second, a number of investigations into the notion of a two-year degree course including: an investigation into the use that current students make of vacations; a consideration of students' perception and experience of current extended-year courses such as those at the University of Buckingham; and a study of the likely acceptance of the two-year degree by employers and students.

Group F Chaired by Joanna Tait

Six areas for future research were identified. The first was the study of the effectiveness of 'new technology' teaching and learning methods. The group considered that, while there was much innovation at present, little or no research was being carried out into the cost effectiveness or learning effectiveness of such methods in comparison with previous traditional methods. A number of specific questions needed answering: What is currently happening? What is the cost effectiveness of new open learning methods? Are teachers being made obsolescent? What planning is being carried out within institutions for these new developments?

The second area was that of research into the management of innovation. Here the questions raised were: What savings are being made? What links are being set up between institutions? What uses are there for particular courses across the market as a whole? How is innovation affecting management structures and processes? To what extent is management concentrating too much on short-term solutions?

The third area was that of research into improving access to higher education. In particular, market research was needed into the mid-career market. Pressures from specific professional areas should be investigated, and it determined under what circumstances the geographical proximity of a local college might be important. The fourth area was that of international research, for instance into the experiences across the European Community of different educational programmes, and into the rewards offered to students in different systems of higher education.

A fifth area where research was needed was into the organizations which act as a buffer between institutions of higher education and national government. For instance, in the United Kingdom the University Grants Committee and the National Advisory Body occupy this role. It was felt that significant decisions are made, and will have to be made at these interfaces between government and institutions. Research was needed into the role, the tasks, the organizational structures and staffing of these bodies, as well as the matter of secrecy and openness in decision-making, and the relationship between these buffer organizations and long-term planning.

The final area identified for future research was that of the role of women in higher education.

Appendix B
UGC Circular Letter 16/83
Development of a Strategy for
Higher Education into the 1990s

Introduction

1. You will probably have seen already the recent exchange of correspondence between the Secretary of State for Education and Science and my predecessor: however, for ease of reference, I attach a copy at Annex A. The Secretary of State asks for a debate on the issues that face higher education over the next ten years; and he asks that this debate should be conducted in as open and wide-ranging a manner as possible. This letter is the Committee's first step towards encouraging such a debate.

2. The Committee will be giving the Secretary of State its advice not later than October 1984 and wishes to take full account of the contributions of universities and other interested parties. We could simply have invited comments on the Secretary of State's letter; but we believe it will be more helpful if we try to list the questions which we consider the Committee should cover in its advice and which participants in the debate should think about, whether or not they feel it reasonable for them to answer them at this stage.

3. With two exceptions, we do not ask your university *as such* to answer these questions, because there is likely to be a great diversity of views within each university and nothing will be gained by disguising this fact. The two exceptions are Questions 1 and 2, which are addressed to institutions and not to groups within them. We would be grateful to receive replies to these two questions by 31 March 1984.

4. It is, of course, open to your university, if it wishes, to comment on any of the remaining questions: indeed we hope that it would at least be able to answer Questions 8 and 13. We would also ask you to encourage general debate on these issues within your university and we would welcome comments from groups and individuals, whether in the form of answers to particular questions or otherwise. Some of the questions – 4,

for example – are ones on which we would particularly value the answers of those officers who have been concerned with the relevant problems. In particular, we hope that you yourself will be able to comment on some of the issues as an individual. On Questions 28 and 29, for example, the experience of Vice-Chancellors must give their views especial authority. Again we would ask for replies by 31 March 1984 but where it is possible we would appreciate earlier replies to spread the load.

5.   The Secretary of State has asked the National Advisory Body for Local Authority Higher Education (NAB) to encourage the same kind of debate in respect of the public sector institutions for which it is responsible. NAB's first step has been to produce a consultation paper 'Towards a Strategy for Local Authority Higher Education in the Late 1980s and Beyond', and a copy of this is attached at Annex B. It is clear that there will have to be an eventual reconciliation between the replies of NAB and UGC to the Secretary of State.

6.   Parts of this letter refer primarily to the situation in England and Wales. We would ask readers concerned with the different systems in Scotland and Northern Ireland to make the appropriate adjustments.

Resources and Student Numbers

7.   We see no possibility of the resource per student (ie, home fees plus recurrent grant) being increased in real terms, except, we would hope, to take account of a shift in the balance of students from cheaper to more expensive subjects. Indeed the Secretary of State suggests that we should consider the possibility of a cut in the resource per student of up to 2 per cent in real terms in each of the next five years and of up to 1 per cent in each of the following five years. At the same time he hopes that universities will move towards raising a greater proportion of their income from private sources, thus reducing their dependence on public funds.

8.   The DES has revised its earlier calculations of the demand for higher education and has also produced forecasts of total numbers in higher education which are based on a high and a low projection of the proportion of qualified demand being met. These projections are given in Annex C.

9.   On the DES' high demand projection, numbers remain at or above the 1983/84 level until 1988/89. Between then and 1996/97 they drop by almost 20 per cent, after which there is a small recovery until the end of the century. On the low demand projection, numbers do not fall below the 1983/84 projected level until 1987/88, after which they drop by 5 per cent by 1989/90 and a further 20 per cent between 1989/90 and 1996/97, with a small recovery during the rest of the century. It must be emphasized that these projections assume that the present distribution

of lengths of courses will remain unchanged; and any major changes in the pattern of higher education (for example, those discussed in paras. 29 and 30) are likely to affect the figures for total numbers of students.

10. It would be unrealistic to expect the drop in the number of qualified school-leavers to be compensated by an increase in the average length of course. However there is the possibility of a growth in some of the various forms of continuing education. The Committee has a working party on this topic, which sent you a substantial questionnaire some months ago and which is expected to report early next year. In this letter, therefore, we are not asking the range of questions on continuing education which would otherwise have been appropriate, but it does come up in Question 17. I would only say that, provided a number of problems can be solved (for example, in the area of student support), there is the potential for substantial development of continuing education, though it cannot be assumed that this will make good the loss of initial students resulting from the demographic trends.

11.   It will be clear from para. 9 that the demand projections for the next five years and for the five that follow pose quite different problems. For the next five years the obvious questions are the following:

Q.1.   On the assumption of a) constant numbers of home and EC students and b) constant resource per student in real terms from 1983/84 to 1989/90 inclusive, what changes will your institution want to make and how do you plan to achieve them?

Q.2.   How would the answer to the previous question be affected if student numbers in this period were to remain constant but the resource per student in real terms were to drop at a steady rate of:

(a) 1 per cent per annum?

(b) 2 per cent per annum?

12.   In a number of subjects, notably medicine, dentistry, veterinary science and education, the number of students depends on the Government's policies on manpower requirements. This external factor creates obvious constraints and pressures on resources but for the purpose of answering Questions 1 and 2 you should assume that the current policies continue at least until 1989/90.

13.   For the five years that follow (ie from 1990/91 – 1994/95), and indeed to the turn of the century, it is difficult to consider the university system in isolation, because we do not know how any reduction in higher education numbers resulting from the drop in the number of qualified school-leavers will be distributed between the universities and the public sector. But any shift of balance will only diminish the problems of one side by exacerbating those of the other. Some further reduction in the resource per student in real terms must be accepted as a possibility – the

Secretary of State has suggested that we should consider a figure of 5 per cent over the years 1990/91 to 1994/95 – but its effect can only be small in comparison with the effect of falling numbers.

Q.3. On the assumption of constant resource per student in real terms from 1990/91 to the end of the century, how should the higher education system as a whole cope with student numbers dropping by 15-20 per cent between 1989/90 and 1994/95 and remaining constant thereafter? What scope is there for reorganization? Do you see mergers or other forms of association between universities and public sector institutions as desirable and practicable? What scope is there for greater collaboration? Should a significant number of institutions be closed during the five years 1990/91 to 1994/95? If so, what criteria and what machinery should be used to decide which institutions to close?

Capital

14. The Secretary of State did not refer in his letter to the provision of funds for capital building but it is likely that resources will be extremely limited.

Q.4. How might any necessary reorganization be financed from recurrent grant and proceeds of sale? Are the conditions which apply at present to the use of proceeds of sale or any other rules relating to the use for capital purposes of resources from public funds unduly restrictive? If so, what changes would be helpful?

Balance of Subjects

15. The Secretary of State is anxious to see a shift towards technological, scientific and engineering courses and towards other vocationally relevant forms of study, and has asked how, and how fast, this can be achieved. Universities can of course shift the balance of their admissions, so far as their accommodation permits; but this could merely mean admitting more marginal candidates in the sciences and fewer in the arts. The Secretary of State also wishes to see a shift of balance among the first-class candidates. This would require changes in the schools or the provision of conversion courses.

Q.5. Does your experience suggest that there would be a demand for conversion courses? If so, how and in what kind of institution might it be appropriate to provide them? Can you see any other way of meeting the Secretary of State's wishes?

16. Even without deliberate pressure, changes in student choice are likely to change the balance of student numbers. This ought to be reflected in a similar change in the balance of staff numbers which will not be easy in a period in which there will be very little flexibility; indeed it can only exacerbate the difficulties noted in the next few paragraphs.

Q.6. Which subjects do you expect to become more popular, and which less popular, over the next decade?

Q.7. Are there other reasons why you would wish to favour some subjects at the expense of others?

Research

17. In the natural sciences (in the widest sense) there is a reasonably clear distinction between scholarship and research. Scholarship means keeping abreast of the current state of one's own subject, and may include writing books and papers which expound and systematize what is known: research means advancing what is known. It is harder to draw this distinction in the social sciences, and harder still in the arts. It is axiomatic that scholarship is part of the duty of every teacher in higher education (regardless of sector) and that higher education institutions must make adequate provision for scholarship – which includes provision for libraries and for travel. But research in some subjects requires facilities additional to those needed for scholarship; and in some subjects these facilities are expensive. In all subjects the largest component of university research is the thinking time of staff, which it is extremely difficult to quantify.

18. It is widely believed that the cuts of the last few years have fallen more heavily on research (and in particular on scientific research) than on teaching. This appears not to be what the Government would have wished, as is shown by, for example, the degree of protection that has been given to the Science Budget.

Q.8. Do you think that this has happened in your institution? Have you any quantitative evidence that bears on this question? If it has happened in your institution, are you taking, or do you intend to take, any counter-measures?

Q.9. Do you think that the dual support system can survive and would you wish it to do so?

Q.10. Would you favour earmarking, or indicating, the research component of the UGC grant? If so, what items of expenditure would be covered by this earmarking or indicating?

Q.11. The Secretary of State has suggested that greater selectivity of research funding may be needed, both within institutions and between institutions. What are your views on this?

Q.12. What priorities, if any, would you suggest for special research investment (beyond those already identified, such as microelectronics, information technology and biotechnology)?

Dependence on Public Funds

19. As I said in para. 7, the Secretary of State believes that universities ought to reduce their dependence on public funds – which include student fees reimbursed by local education authorities. He has already held discussions about ways in which this might be achieved with a number of Vice-Chancellors, at which my predecessor was present. These discussions have not yet led to a clear or agreed solution, but it is apparent that any solution involves giving individual universities greater freedom from the control of the DES and the UGC; and this is a policy to which the Secretary of State is attracted for other reasons also.

Q.13. Are there respects in which you would wish your university to have greater freedom from the control of DES and UGC? What do you see as the financial advantages of this? And the non-financial advantages? What scope do you see for raising additional income, whether tied to specific purposes or not? Could the prospects be improved by a change in the tax laws? If so, what?

The Nature of Universities

20. The binary line, and more generally the differences between universities and major public sector institutions, are currently a topic for debate. There are three headings under which these differences can be considered – the interface with Government to which I revert in paras. 31 and 32, the constitutional differences one of which is touched on in para. 21, and the differences of function.

Q.14. Is there an essential difference in function between universities and other institutions of higher education, or should they be regarded as a continuous spectrum of institutions?

Q.15. If there is an essential difference in their teaching function, what is it, and how, in measurable terms, can one distinguish between those school-leavers who would benefit most from university-type education and those who would benefit most from other types of higher education?

Q.16. Should there be more variety among universities in respect, for example, of disciplinary specialization, type of student (mature, overseas etc), teaching style and involvement in research?

Q.17. Do you have views on a desirable balance in the university system, between provision for:
  i.   undergraduates, taught postgraduates and research postgraduates?
  ii. initial and post-experience provision?
  iii. full-time, sandwich and part-time provision?
  In what ways does your view of the desirable balance for your own institution differ from your view of the desirable balance for the system as a whole?

Validation

21.   Almost all public sector courses are validated by external bodies – mainly by CNAA and BTEC. Some university courses are accredited in varying degrees by professional bodies – in law, medicine or engineering, for example – and all university courses have external examiners who play a certain moderating role.

Q.18. What is your experience of the process of accreditation by professional bodies in those subjects in which they operate? What are your views on any other possible system of accreditation or validation of university courses?

Tenure and Premature Retirement

22.   Universities largely coped with the 1981 cuts by means of early retirements. This has left a very unbalanced age distribution of academic staff: detailed figures, broken down by subject, are given in Annex D. The Annex also shows how the overall age distribution will vary up to the end of the century, on the assumption that all posts falling vacant will be filled. This is essentially the assumption of constant level of support per student and constant student numbers. For comments on these assumptions see paras. 7 and 9. Even on these assumptions the rate of new appointments in most subjects during the next decade will be between 1 per cent and 1½ per cent per annum in the system as a whole; and in many universities it will be well below that. For comparison, in its proposal last year for 'new blood' posts the ABRC argued, and the DES accepted, that a replacement rate of 1¼ per cent was the least that could keep a subject in good health. (The argument was concerned with research rather than teaching, and it was put forward only for the sciences; but this estimate remains the only one available).

23.   For the next five years, therefore, the replacement rate will be slightly below the acceptable minimum even on the most favourable hypothesis (ie, that the level of support per student will be constant in real terms) and a *nil* replacement rate is not unlikely. The continuation

of the 'new blood' scheme must be a possibility, even though it could involve the Government giving new money with one hand while taking away existing money with the other. But if this happened it would almost certainly be operated in a highly selective way.

Q.19. Would you favour the continuation of the 'new blood' scheme? What do you see as its disadvantages and to what extent can they be overcome?

Q.20. What other realistic ways do you see of overcoming the problems of the next five years outlined in paras. 22-23?

24. For the five years 1990/91 – 1994/95, the position is far more serious. If student numbers fall as projected and the balance between the university and the public sector is maintained, the size of the university sector will drop by 15-20 per cent. At most, half of the necessary reduction in staff can be obtained from normal retirements; and the Secretary of State has made it clear that the Government is not prepared to find extra money to pay for premature retirements after the end of the current academic year.

Q.21. Would you favour reducing the retiring age to 60, with the possibility of extending some academic staff beyond 60 on a non-tenured basis? (It is accepted that this would require legislation.)

25. One of the main reasons why contraction presents far greater difficulties for universities than for most other enterprises is the existence of tenure, so that appointments cannot be terminated before normal retirement age other than for 'good cause'. In some universities the tenure provision is strong, in others it is weak, and in yet others the combined effect of statutes and conditions of appointment is so obscure that it could only be determined in the courts.

Q.23. Should the tenure provisions be the same in all universities? If so, what should they be? If not, would there be any long-term consequences?

The Leverhulme Proposals

26. The most recent programme of study of higher education is the series of conferences and reports organized by the Society for Research into Higher Education and financed by the Leverhulme Trust. Some of the proposals in the final volume 'Excellence in Diversity' have already been covered in this letter, but there are two important ones which have not. These are:

(a) the reduction of specialization both in the sixth form and in the earlier parts of higher education; and

(b) the reorganization of higher education into a sequence of two-year modules.

27. Neither of these changes could come about quickly, if only because of the preparatory work that would be involved. Thus if they are to be set in a particular context, that context should be the declining number of 18-year-olds between 1989/90 and 1994/95, or the constant but lower numbers in the following five years.

28. One of the major acknowledged disadvantages of the present degree of specialization in the sixth form is that decisions taken by school-children at the age of 15 or 16 often restrict their choice of degree courses two or three years later. The amount of specialization in the sixth form is, of course, greatly influenced by the demands of universities. There is a considerable body of opinion among school heads in favour of a broader sixth form curriculum, but they say that they cannot themselves implement such a policy because it would put their pupils at a disadvantage in the competition for university places.

> Q.24. Would you favour the universal replacement of the present system of 'A' levels by a broader sixth form education and, if so, on what pattern? What would this imply for the quality and skills of your graduates?

> Q.25. Alternatively, would you favour making a broader sixth form education available to those who preferred it? If so, would you be willing to see your university's admission criteria altered so that students with a broader sixth form education were not at a disadvantage in applying for admission to your university?

29. An initial two-year non-vocational module within higher education already exists, in the form of the Diploma of Higher Education; but it has not gained much support because it is generally seen as inferior to a three-year degree. (The two-year course at Buckingham is not wholly relevant, because the academic year there is substantially longer.) Moreover there would be serious problems in transfers between a university based on two-year modules and a university with the present structure of courses, whereas now students have no problems in taking a first degree in one university and then going on to postgraduate work in another. So if a change to a sequence of two-year modules is to happen at all, it needs to happen simultaneously in as many universities as possible.

> Q.26. Would you favour such a change?

30. There have also been suggestions (though not in the Leverhulme Report) that the structure of university courses in England and Wales should be modified somewhat along the lines of the present structure in Scotland, where there is a choice between a general and an Honours degree. In such a scheme there would be choice between a two-year general degree and a three-year Honours degree: whether the choice would be made at entry or after one year at university is an open question.

Q.27. Would you favour such a change, or indeed, any other change in degree format (including a longer academic year)?

The Role of the UGC

31.   The role of the UGC has changed very considerably since it was set up in 1919, and it may change further in the next few years.

Q.28.   Have you any comments on the nature and role of the UGC, or on the way in which it should carry out that role?

32.   There have been suggestions that a single body should be set up to take over some or all of the work of the UGC and, for example, NAB and the Wales Advisory Body, either replacing them or standing between them and Government.

Q.29   Do you favour such a proposal, and if so in what form? More generally, do you see centralized co-ordination of both sections as either desirable or feasible?

Editors' Note

There are twenty-eight questions in all – number twenty-two does not exist.

The questions and accompanying commentary were published in *The Times Higher Education Supplement* 11 November 1983.

The Editors are grateful to Sir Peter Swinnerton-Dyer for permission to reproduce the questions here.

Appendix C
The SRHE Leverhulme Series

1   *Higher Education and the Labour Market* Edited by Robert Lindley (1981) 0 900868 83 X
2   *Access to Higher Education* Edited by Oliver Fulton (1981) 0 900868 84 8
3   *Agenda for Institutional Change in Higher Education* Edited by Leslie Wagner (1982) 0 900868 85 6
4   *The Future of Research* Edited by Geoffrey Oldham (1982) 0 900868 86 4
5   *The Arts and Higher Education* Edited by Ken Robinson (1982) 0 900868 89 9
6   *Professionalism and Flexibility for Learning* Edited by Donald Bligh (1982) 0 900868 87 2
7   *Accountability or Freedom for Teachers?* Edited by Donald Bligh (1982) 0 900868 88 0
8   *Resources and Higher Education* Edited by Alfred Morris and John Sizer (1983) 0 900868 90 2
9   *The Structure and Governance of Higher Education* Edited by Michael Shattock (1983) 0 900868 91 0
10 *Response to Adversity. Higher Education in a Harsh Climate* By Gareth Williams and Tessa Blackstone (1983) 0 900868 92 9
    Excellence in Diversity. Towards a New Strategy for Higher Education. The SRHE Leverhulme Report (1983) 0 900868 99 6

All published by the Society for Research into Higher Education and available from SRHE & NFER-NELSON, Darville House, 2 Oxford Road East, Windsor, Berks SL4 1DF